THE NEGRO AND APPRENTICESHIP

THE NEGRO AND APPRENTICESHIP

by

F. Ray Marshall

and

Vernon M. Briggs, Jr.

The Johns Hopkins Press   Baltimore

This book is based on a report prepared under a contract with the Office of Manpower Policy, Evaluation and Research, U.S. Department of Labor, under the authority of Title I of the Manpower Development and Training Act of 1962, as amended. Researchers undertaking such projects under Government sponsorship are encouraged to express freely their professional judgment. Therefore, points of view or opinions stated in this document do not necessarily represent the official position or policy of the Department of Labor. Reproduction in whole or in part is permitted for any purpose of the United States Government.

ACKNOWLEDGMENTS

It is impossible for us to acknowledge the contributions of the hundreds of people who helped us with this study. We would, however, like to express our gratitude to our principal collaborators, I. Lamond Godwin and Eugene Solon, whose dedication and resourcefulness as interview co-ordinators contributed greatly to the completion of our field interviews. We also received valuable assistance on a part-time basis from Lee Balliet and Emory Via. Judith Schluter, our very efficient project secretary, made a major contribution to the study by maintaining orderly records and handling our correspondence. We also are grateful to Florence Mishnun, Howard Rosen, and Joseph Epstein, of the Office of Manpower Policy, Evaluation and Research, for their logistic support of the project. Florence Mishnun was "responsible" for our project within the Office of Manpower Policy, Evaluation and Research and made many valuable suggestions for improving the first draft of the manuscript. Others who made special contributions to this study will be acknowledged in the following pages. Of course, we alone are responsible for the accuracy of our information as well as for the conclusions drawn from it.

F. Ray Marshall
Vernon M. Briggs, Jr.

Austin, Texas
December, 1966

TABLE OF CONTENTS

List of Tables viii

I. Introduction 3

II. The Nature of Apprenticeship Training in
the United States 11

III. Negro Participation in Apprenticeship Training 27

IV. New York 47

V. Philadelphia 83

VI. Cleveland 99

VII. Pittsburgh 113

VIII. Cincinnati 121

IX. Detroit 137

X. Washington, D.C. 151

XI. San Francisco-Oakland 159

XII. Houston and Atlanta 175

XIII. Policies To Increase the Number of Negro Apprentices. . 191

XIV. Recommendations 229

Appendix. The Interviews 247

Index 279

LIST OF TABLES

1-1 Cumulative Breakdown of All Interviews Conducted with Officials Concerned with Negro Participation in Apprenticeship Programs 8

1-2 Interviews of Negro Apprentices and Applicants by Craft 9

2-1 Active Apprentices, New Registrations, Completions, and Suspensions, Registered Programs, by State, 1964 ... 20

2-2 Apprentices in Selected Construction Trades Registered with State Apprenticeship Agencies or the Bureau of Apprenticeship and Training for the Calendar Year 1964 .. 22

3-1 Negro Apprentices, by Occupation, 1950 and 1960 28

3-2 Negro and White Construction Apprentice Selections in Specified Construction Trades for Selected Southern Cities, 1964 30

3-3 Negro and White Construction Apprentice Selections in Specified Construction Trades for Selected Non-Southern Areas, 1964 32

4-1 Employment in Selected Occupations by Race, 1960— New York Metropolitan Area 48

4-2 Nonwhite Participation in Apprenticeship Programs in Selected Building Trades Unions since March, 1963 52

4-3 Nonwhite Journeymen Admitted to Selected Building Trades Unions between March, 1963, and March, 1966 .. 53

4-4 Referrals Made by the Rodgers Committee to Specific Building Trades, 1963 56

4-5 Specific Placements of Initial Referrals by the Rodgers Committee 57

4-6 Sources of Application to Workers Defense League for Plumbers Local 1 Examination, Summer, 1966 77

5-1 Employment in Selected Occupations by Race, 1960— Philadelphia Metropolitan Area 85

5-2 Progress Report on Nonwhite Participation in Six "Discriminatory" Unions, April, 1965—Philadelphia 86

5-3 Status of Negro Participation in Construction Trades (Other Than Those Held To Be Discriminatory), April, 1965—Philadelphia 86

5-4 Nonwhite Members of Printing Trades Unions in Philadelphia, June, 1965 87

6-1 Employment in Selected Occupations by Race, 1960—Cleveland Metropolitan Area 100

6-2 Negro Apprentices in Selected Unions in Cleveland, Fall, 1966 101

6-3 Results of Efforts by the Cleveland Community Relations Board To Place Negro Youths in Seven Apprenticeship Programs, June, 1963, to October 1965 105

6-4 Reasons Given by Negroes Who Were Recruited, Who Applied, but Who Failed To Show Up for the Test at the Appointed Time—Cleveland 106

7-1 Employment in Selected Occupations by Race, 1960—Pittsburgh Metropolitan Area 114

7-2 Nonwhite Participation in Selected Building Trades Unions, July 8, 1963, to December 31, 1964—Pittsburgh 115

8-1 Employment in Selected Occupations by Race, 1960—Cincinnati Metropolitan Area 122

8-2 Negro Participation in Apprenticeship Programs in Selected Building Trades Unions in Cincinnati, Fall, 1965 123

8-3 Summary of Data as of May 1, 1964, Concerning Racial Membership of Building Trades in Cincinnati, as Reported to the Human Relations Commission 127

9-1 Employment in Selected Occupations by Race, 1960—Detroit Metropolitan Area 138

9-2 Negro Participation in Selected Building Trades Apprenticeship Programs, February, 1966 140

10-1 Employment in Selected Occupations by Race, 1960—Washington, D.C., Metropolitan Area 152

10-2 Negro Apprentices in Apprenticeship Programs in Selected Trade Unions in Washington, D.C., 1963, 1964, 1965 154

10-3 Placements into Apprenticeship Classes in the Building Trades by the Washington AIC, June, 1963, to January, 1966 156

11-1 Employment in Selected Occupations by Race, 1960—San Francisco-Oakland Bay Area 160

11-2 Negro Participation in Apprenticeship Programs in California, December, 1964 170

11-3 Enrollment in Apprenticeship Classes in Oakland, April, 1964 171

12-1 Employment in Selected Occupations by Race, 1960—Houston Metropolitan Area 177

12-2 Minority Participation in Building Trades Apprenticeship Programs in Houston, April, 1966 178

12-3 Employment in Selected Occupations by Race, 1960—Atlanta Metropolitan Area 183

12-4 Negro Apprenticeship Applications and Selections in Five Atlanta Building Trades, 1964 184

12-5 Negro Participation in Apprenticeship Classes in Selected Building Trades in Atlanta, 1965 184

13-1 Placement Experience of Apprenticeship Information Centers, 1964 to 1965 214

13-2 Approved MDTA (Institutional) Projects in Building Trades in Selected Cities, July, 1966 221

Appendix

A-1 Source of Initial Information on Apprenticeship in General 248

A-2 Source of Specific Information on the Apprenticeship Program Applied to by Negro Interviewees 250

A-3 Written Tests and Oral Test Experience of Negro Applicants Who Were Accepted into Apprenticeship Programs 253

A-4 Educational Background of Negro Interviewees by Classification 254

A-5 Reasons for Negro Applicants' Being Rejected by Apprenticeship Programs to Which They Had Applied 255

A-6 Reasons for Failing To Complete Application Requirements to Apprenticeship Programs 256

A-7 Reasons for Dropping Out of an Apprenticeship Class after Having Been Admitted 256

THE NEGRO AND APPRENTICESHIP

CHAPTER I

INTRODUCTION

A number of developments during the 1950's and 1960's focused attention on the problem of equal apprenticeship opportunities. The clashes between increasingly militant civil rights organizations and discriminatory unions during the 1950's drew attention to the absence of Negroes from many unions and apprenticeship programs.[1] While the unions' motives for exclusion were not based entirely on racial considerations, the vigor with which they defended their restrictive policies, and the fact that there were few if any Negroes in their unions, made it difficult to avoid the racist conclusion. These contests gave the apprenticeship issue a symbolic significance which often obscured the quantitative importance to Negroes of the jobs they were likely to get through apprenticeship training. As presently constituted, apprenticeship programs are not quantitatively very important.

The apprenticeship question also attracted attention as a solution to some of the economic problems facing young Negro males during the 1950's and 1960's. Declining employment opportunities in jobs traditionally open to them, together with population shifts which increased the number of young Negro males, caused these groups to experience declining relative labor force participation rates, rising unemployment rates, and declining relative incomes during these years.[2]

[1] For a discussion of these see Ray Marshall, *The Negro and Organized Labor* (New York: John Wiley & Sons, 1965).

[2] The relative income position of Negro males declined in every region during the 1950's, in spite of improvements one would ordinarily expect as Negroes moved increasingly from low-income agricultural activities to urban jobs. (Alan B. Batchelder, "Decline in the Relative Income of Negro Men," *Quarterly Journal of Economics*, August, 1964, pp. 539–47.) After having been consistently *less* than double the white rates before 1957, nonwhite unemployment rates were consistently *more* than double those of whites after 1957. In 1948, teen-age male unemployment rates were 7.6 per cent for nonwhites and 8.3 per cent for whites; in 1965, these relative positions were reversed and the teen-age male unemployment rates were 22.6 per cent for nonwhites and 11.8 per cent for whites. It is also significant that in 1964 the rate at which unemployed Negroes

3

The urgency of the need to get more Negroes into the skilled trades is indicated by the U.S. Department of Labor's projections of nonwhite employment and unemployment patterns. Between 1965 and 1980, the nonwhite labor force is expected to increase by 41 per cent as compared with an increase of 28 per cent for whites. These projections are based on the high population increases expected among nonwhite youths. Nearly half of the projected increase in the labor force between 1965 and 1970 (3.5 million of 7.6 million) will be among workers 14 to 24 years old; nonwhites in this age group are expected to increase by nearly 30 per cent compared with 20 per cent for whites. As a consequence of these projections, by 1980 nonwhites in the 14 to 24 age bracket are expected to constitute 14 per cent of the total labor force as compared with 12.3 per cent in 1960.[3] Coming at a time of declining opportunities in the unskilled and semiskilled jobs, these projected increases make it obvious that unemployment rates among Negro youths will continue to increase ominously unless something is done to produce significant shifts in traditional racial employment patterns.

Although as presently constituted apprenticeship programs are not important enough quantitatively to have much impact on this problem, the fact that these programs provide skilled job opportunities primarily for male youths obviously makes apprenticeship opportunities *qualitatively* very important to Negroes.

Efforts to get more Negroes into apprenticeship programs increased tensions between the civil rights movement and the ap-

---

had involuntarily lost their jobs was at least two and a half times that of unemployed whites. (Curtis L. Smith, Jr., "The Unemployed: Why They Started Looking for Work," *Monthly Labor Review*, October, 1965, p. 1199.)

Unemployment rates do not, however, tell the whole story, because there also has been a worsening of the extent to which nonwhite males have participated in the labor force. In 1948, the civilian labor force participation rates for both nonwhite males and females were higher (84.8 per cent and 44.4 per cent) than the rates for whites (84.2 per cent and 30.6 per cent). In 1965, the participation rate for nonwhite females (46.0 per cent) remained much higher than the rate for white females (36.9 percent), but the rate for nonwhite males (75.2 per cent) was now *lower* than the rate for white males (77.6 per cent).

The participation of nonwhite males in rapidly expanding white-collar and service jobs also has been less than any other group. Employed nonwhite men constituted 9.2 per cent of the employed male labor force in 1955, but only 3.0 per cent of white-collar workers; their proportions in 1965 were 9.7 per cent of the labor force and 4.2 per cent of white-collar workers. Nonwhite females constituted 12.4 per cent of the employed female labor force in 1955 and 12.6 per cent in 1965, but their proportions of white-collar workers increased from 3.4 per cent to 5.3 per cent. (Joe L. Russell, "Changing Patterns in Employment in Nonwhite Workers," *Monthly Labor Review*, May, 1966, pp. 503–9).

[3] Sophia Cooper and Denis F. Johnston, "Labor Force Projections, by Color, 1970–1980," *Monthly Labor Review*, September, 1966, pp. 965–7.

prenticeship establishment (unions, employers, and specialized government agencies). During the early 1960's civil rights pickets sought to halt work at some construction sites, and civil rights leaders threatened unions with legal proceedings designed to get more Negroes into apprenticeship programs. Various levels and branches or government responded to these developments by adopting measures designed to cool tensions and increase the number of Negroes in the skilled trades.

It became very clear during these disputes that there was much mutual misunderstanding between the apprenticeship establishment and the civil rights movement. There was therefore an obvious need to clarify the issues, to evaluate the measures being taken to promote equal apprenticeship opportunity, and to make recommendations for further remedial action.

The present study is designed to accomplish these objectives. The remainder of this chapter will discuss the reason for the attention given this problem and the research procedures which produced our findings. Chapter II presents a brief general discussion of the nature of the apprenticeship system in the United States. Chapter III discusses the extent of Negro participation in apprenticeship programs. Chapters IV to XII present our findings with respect to Negro participation in apprenticeship programs in various cities. Chapter XIII analyzes various remedial measures which have been adopted to increase Negro participation in these programs. Our recommendations for increasing the number of Negro apprentices are presented in the final chapter. The Appendix contains a brief summary of some of our interviews.

THE PROJECT

Staff

In the summer of 1965, the Department of Economics of The University of Texas entered into a contract with the Office of Manpower, Automation and Training (OMAT, now known as the Office of Manpower Policy, Evaluation and Research) to undertake a study of Negro participation in apprenticeship programs. The project's principal staff members were F. Ray Marshall (Professor of Economics at The University of Texas), Director, and Vernon M. Briggs, Jr. (Assistant Professor of Economics at The University of Texas), Associate Director.

Although the director, the associate director, and two interview co-ordinators conducted most of the interviews in the ten cities selected for study, twenty-one special interviewers also were utilized. These special interviewers, selected mainly on the basis of their interviewing experience, came from a variety of occupational backgrounds: graduate students, human relations commission staff members, university instructors, high school teachers, social workers, and staff members of civil rights and union organizations.

The main immediate objective of our study was to identify the approaches and methods which had succeeded in increasing Negro participation in selected apprenticeship programs and to determine why other approaches had not been successful. Our main ultimate objective was to recommend policies which would make it possible for Negroes to increase their participation in and successful completion of apprenticeship programs.

Because of our mandate, we took two basic propositions as given (not to be explained): that the apprenticeship system is a good form of training and that to get more Negroes into these programs is a desirable objective. We recognize that these questions need to be examined critically, but they are beyond the scope of our assigned task.

Procedures

We sought primarily to examine the recent dynamic situations involving the participation of Negroes in apprenticeship programs in ten major cities with large Negro populations. The cities were selected in such a way as to illustrate a variety of problems and remedial programs, as well as to be representative geographically. The cities were selected after consultation with civil rights, government, industry, and union spokesmen.

Since we were primarily interested in "trouble spots" where civil rights organizations or government agencies were attacking or about to attack the apprenticeship establishment, we did not attempt to study Negro participation in all apprenticeship programs. We therefore paid less attention to the trowel trades and the carpenters, where Negroes are known to have had little difficulty, and concentrated our efforts on such programs as the electricians, ironworkers, sheet metal workers, the plumbing and pipefitting trades, the printing trades, and some mechanical trades in industrial plants.

We decided that revealing answers to our questions would require an examination of many published and unpublished documents and detailed interviews with two groups of people. One consisted of officials concerned with Negro participation in apprentice programs. Included in this group were representatives of the Bureau of Apprenticeship and Training (BAT), the Bureau of Employment Security (BES), state employment services, state apprenticeship offices, local building and construction trades unions, regional and national AFL-CIO bodies, employer and joint industry associations, employer training groups, joint apprenticeship committees, apprenticeship information centers, city government agencies, local human relations commissions, schools, federal equal employment opportunity agencies, and civil rights organizations. From this group we sought to elicit background information, to gather names of potential Negro interviewees, to seek suggestions for remedial action, and to verify conflicting reports. In most instances, these interviews were conducted by the director and associate director.

The second group of interviewees consisted of Negroes who were currently indentured in apprenticeship programs, awaiting a decision on their applications, rejected when they applied, dropouts from programs after they had been admitted, or those who had failed to complete the application procedures after expressing an initial interest.

In addition to these two broad groups of interviewees, a number of miscellaneous persons were interviewed. Those included in this catch-all category were Negro journeymen (to learn how they entered the trade), white apprentices and white journeymen (to learn how they entered but, more importantly, to gain some insight into their explanation for the paucity of Negroes in their trade), and several Negro and white youths involved in various ways with the subject.

In retrospect—while we gathered many interesting incidents, experiences, and opinions—the interviews with the second group were highly impressionistic and, in many respects, uniform in their conclusions. However, the most informative and instructive interviews were those with the various officials. The officials represented the differing facets of the apprenticeship issue and usually had accumulated a vast amount of knowledge or first-hand experience with the issue. We profited greatly from their accounts. Although we sought to obtain some uniform kinds of information from each interviewee, we did not use a structured questionnaire because we wanted the interviewees to tell their own stories.

Yet, we feel the study gained from tapping both sources. The Negro youths themselves provided specific details about particular happenings; the officials contributed broader, overview comments. Both sources—for different reasons—were valuable to our understanding of the depth and the scope of this complex topic.

Interview Statistics

Table 1-1 shows a breakdown of interviews with 121 different officials. Actually the number of interviews exceeds this total, since in many instances these people were interviewed more than once. We also held group discussions with Negro high school and college teachers and counselors, Negro college students, groups of international union representatives, joint employer-union groups, equal employment opportunity officials, and special seminars, which are not included in these totals. The totals therefore represent only those written interviews which are in our files.

Table 1-1

Cumulative Breakdown of All Interviews Conducted with Officials
Concerned with Negro Participation in Apprenticeship Programs

Organization	No. of Interviews
Civil rights organizations	15
Employer associations or training officials	8
Human Relations Commissions and State Fair Employment Practices Commissions (or equivalents)	12
Public school officials	8
Bureau of Apprenticeship and Training	12
Employment service (state and federal)	12
Other federal agencies involved in equal employment opportunity	15
National union officials	10
Regional union officials	3
Local union officials	19
University experts and specialized consultants	7
Total interviews	121

Table 1-2 presents the distribution of the 127 interviews of the Negroes involved directly in apprenticeship programs. As is indicated, of the 127 interviews, 61 were with currently enrolled Negro apprentices, 11 were with Negroes whose applications were pending at the time of their interview, 25 were with Negroes who were rejected when they applied for admission, 20 were with Negroes who —after expressing initial interest in apprenticeship—failed to complete the application requirements to be considered, and 10 were with Negroes who, after being admitted to an apprentice program, subsequently dropped out of their own volition.

Table 1-2

Interviews of Negro Apprentices and Applicants by Craft

Plumbers	14
Pipe- and steamfitters	4
Ironworkers	5
Electricians	29
Operating engineers	11
Sheet metal workers	21
Lathers	1
Plasterers	1
Cement masons	2
Roofers	1
Carpenters	10
Reinforced concrete workers	2
Painters	5
Other building trades	9
Bookbinders	1
Printing industry	9
Machinists	2
Total interviews	127

If we include 25 miscellaneous interviews, a total of 273 different individuals were interviewed and discussions were conducted with many other individuals and groups.

Problems

No undertaking worth doing can expect completely smooth sailing. Our project was no exception. From the start it became apparent that the topic involved two almost equally controversial matters: Negroes and apprenticeship. When both subjects were combined, the investigating task was compounded many times over. Everywhere we were assured that the issue was a vital one and that our research design—based upon extensive personal interviews— was the proper approach; yet few would initially volunteer precise information. In many interviews, it was clear that those being interviewed were often more interested in finding out what we knew and concealing information from us than in adding to our knowledge. On the other hand, once we gained the confidence of many of these people we received confidential reports, special studies, memoranda, and verbal statements (that could not be quoted) which, frequently, were not even available to people in the highest positions of power in each city. In more than one instance, interviewees wanted to co-operate but did not want their collaboration known.

The most difficult information to collect was the number and names of Negro apprentices or of Negroes who had sought admission to these programs. In few instances in the cities was the information made available from the same source. In each city the rounds had to be made to schools, apprenticeship information centers, union offices, civil rights groups, and human relations commissions to seek leads. Locating interviewees and arranging interview times often proved to be difficult. We found that many young people in their late teens and early twenties changed addresses very often and therefore were difficult to locate. Since most of the interviewees were employed during the day, interviews were held most often at night. Difficulties in transportation and finding addresses in ghetto districts at night added to the problem of the interviewers. In some instances, neighbors would refuse to give any assistance in locating interviewees. In addition, some of the interviewees did not have telephones and interviews had to be arranged through the use of telegrams.

This study was not designed to be comprehensive in a statistical sense. Although we have interviewed a high proportion of Negro youngsters in all of the categories in our cities, the numbers are too small—because there are few Negroes in most programs—and Negroes have gotten in too recently to give a statistically reliable sample about such things as the attitudes of Negro youngsters in general about apprenticeship training, their performance in apprentice programs, and their performance on the job after they complete their training. It would, of course, be useful to compare Negroes and whites on all of these points and to take a large enough sample, with sufficient disaggregation, to give meaningful answers on an industry or craft basis. It also would be useful to know the training sources and employment experiences of Negro journeymen who currently are employed in the skilled trades.

In spite of the foregoing limitations, however, we feel that our understanding of the various facets of this problem is sufficient to make a meaningful diagnosis of its causes and therefore to recommend remedial programs that have a chance of being successful.

CHAPTER II

THE NATURE OF APPRENTICESHIP TRAINING IN THE UNITED STATES

The adoption of effective programs to increase Negro participation in apprenticeship programs requires some understanding of the apprenticeship system. This chapter outlines the apprenticeship system of the United States. Public policy on apprenticeship will be presented first, after which some of the main characteristics of apprenticeship will be discussed.

PUBLIC POLICY

The basic federal law establishing apprenticeship policy is the National Apprenticeship (Fitzgerald) Act of 1937, administered by the Bureau of Apprenticeship and Training (BAT) of the U.S. Department of Labor. The BAT has a field staff and offices in every state, and its main function is to promote apprenticeship programs by giving technical assistance to unions and employers, who determine their own requirements and administer their own programs within the framework of broad standards laid down by the BAT or state apprenticeship agencies. The Bureau also has responsibility for the on-the-job training programs established under the Manpower Development and Training Act (MDTA) of 1962. BAT is assisted by the Federal Committee on Apprenticeship (FCA), which is authorized by the Fitzgerald Act and which comprises five representatives each from labor, management, and the Office of Education.

The administration of apprenticeship is complicated by the fact that thirty states have programs of their own. These state programs are administered by state apprenticeship councils (SACs). The SACs usually confirm by a majority vote the apprenticeship director nominated by the state's commissioner of labor. Although the FCA establishes general apprenticeship standards, the SACs take major responsibility for the registration of apprentices and the administration of apprenticeship programs in SAC states. There is, however, no clear line of jurisdiction between the functions of SACs and BATs state and regional officials in SAC states. Of the cities covered by our survey, San Francisco, Cincinnati, Cleveland, New York,

Philadelphia, and Pittsburgh are in SAC states. In October, 1966, there were 40,437 registered programs in the United States, of which 31,157 were in SAC states.

BAT approves state programs which meet certain minimum standards. To receive federal approval, a state apprenticeship program must be administered by a state's department of labor. Other federal standards for apprenticeship programs include:[1]

1. A starting age of not less than sixteen years.
2. A schedule of work processes in which the apprentice is to receive training and experience on the job.
3. Organized instruction designed to provide the apprentice with knowledge in technical subjects related to his trade. (A minimum of 144 hours a year is normally considered necessary.)
4. A progressively increasing schedule of wages.
5. Proper supervision of on-the-job training with adequate facilities to train apprentices.
6. Periodic evaluation of the apprentice's progress, both in job performance and related instructions, and the maintenance of appropriate records.
7. Employer-employee co-operation.
8. Recognition for successful completion.
9. Selection of men and women for apprenticeship, without regard to race, creed, color, national origin, or physical handicap.

State laws usually provide for specific requirements to which agreements between apprenticeship sponsors and apprentices must conform. If apprenticeship programs meet the standards set up by the FCA and the state apprenticeship agencies, they can be registered by the BAT or the SAC, and those who successfully complete those programs are given certificates of completion either by the state agency or by BAT.

The apprentice normally is required to take related instruction of at least 144 hours a year as well as to undergo training on the job. Although some programs rely on correspondence courses for related instruction (and for keeping journeymen up to date), this training normally is given through the public school system and is financed through state, federal, and local funds. The Smith-Hughes (1917) and George-Barden (1946) Vocational Education Acts provide for partial reimbursement from federal funds for salaries of teachers and vocational administrators to states with approved vocational plans. Some joint apprenticeship programs supplement the salaries of apprentice instructors.

The local supervision of apprenticeship programs registered with

[1] United States Department of Labor, p. 24 (booklet, no date).

the BAT usually is by joint apprenticeship committees representing labor and management. These committees may be national, state, or local in scope, depending upon the trade or industry. There are national joint apprenticeship committees (JACs) in most of the building and the printing trades. Those national committees do not set standards or supervise individual training programs, although their standards usually are followed by the local committees. Local JACs might comprise a group of employers, as they do in the construction industry, a single employer and a union, or an employer without a union. Joint apprenticeship committees sometimes merely advise employee and employer representatives who actually carry out the programs, but in a few states the JACs actually direct the programs. There are approximately 9,000 joint apprenticeship committees.

UNION AND EMPLOYER ATTITUDES TOWARD APPRENTICESHIP

Unions use apprenticeship as a means of job and wage control. By maintaining control of apprenticeship, unions are able to standardize the skill content of their crafts and protect their wage rates. Union craftsmen can maintain their wages only if they have lower unit costs than the alternatives available to an employer. Apprenticeship, by maintaining craft identity, also strengthens the craft union as an institution and makes it possible for the union to supply competent workers to maintain its jurisdiction. If the union acquires many unqualified or incompetent workers, the employer has a strong incentive to mechanize, become nonunion, or look elsewhere for his workers.

Unions also take an interest in apprenticeship programs as a means to prevent the excessive use of low-wage apprentices in competition with their journeyman members, as a means of controlling the supply of labor and as a technique for providing job opportunities to friends and relatives. The unions' interest in apprenticeship is such, according to Felician Foltman, that "although some people feel that apprenticeship is moribund, many in organized labor feel just the opposite and so strongly that if the Federal Government discontinued its modest programs, these unions would continue to develop apprenticeship training as they have over the years."[2]

[2] Felician F. Foltman, "Public Policy in Apprenticeship Training and Skill Development," in Senate Committee on Labor and Public Welfare, *The Role of Apprenticeship in Manpower Development: United States and Western Europe,* Vol. III of *Selected Readings in Manpower* (Washington, D.C.: Government Printing Office, 1964), p. 112.

The employers' views on apprenticeship are not very clear and seem to vary considerably from case to case. Construction and graphic arts employers seem to share their unions' interests in apprenticeship, though they seem often to be willing to leave the administration of these programs to the unions. Employers in industrial plants are interested in apprenticeship training if they require craftsmen in identifiable and recognized classifications. Employers in the larger, high-wage industries seem to be willing to support apprenticeship programs, because they are less likely to lose their skilled workers after they are trained than are lower-wage employers. However, there seems to be considerable ferment among employers over apprenticeship. While many employers who do not already have programs are perhaps not interested in establishing them (because they can pirate skilled labor from other sources), as the skilled manpower shortage grows and wage costs (and therefore apprenticeship costs) rise, employers who already are paying for apprenticeship programs seem to be taking more interest in their administration in order to see that they get more qualified and competent craftsmen.

IMPORTANCE OF REGISTRATION

While they might be paying more attention to the apprenticeship question, many industrial employers do not seem to be interested in registering their apprenticeship programs with the BAT or an SAC. Although registered programs do not have to be jointly administered by unions and employers, some employers consider the federal apprenticeship program to be too closely tied to unions. Others, including some government installations, are not interested in training well-rounded craftsmen with general skills; rather, they seek primarily to train workers for the specialized tasks required in their particular operations. These employers are more interested in flexibility of manpower utilization across several craft lines. Some large employers also have no interest in registering their programs because they wish to avoid additional government regulation and red tape.

Most of the following advantages to be derived from registration of an apprentice program, therefore, seem to be of much more interest to the construction and printing industries than to others for the following reasons:

1. Wage advantages. Although little use apparently is made of these, federal and state minimum-wage regulations often permit registered apprentices to be paid less than the minimum wage.

14

The Davis-Bacon Act of 1931 provides for the establishment of prevailing wages on federal construction projects, and allows apprentices to be paid less than journeymen. The Davis-Bacon Act also requires the maintenance of journeyman–apprentice ratios. If a program loses its registration, apprentices must be paid the journeyman rates.

2. Another advantage to having registered apprentices is the recognition which the certificate of completion bestows on the journeyman. The graduate of a registered apprenticeship program knows that his training is a passport to jobs in geographic areas other than his own because of the minimum standards to which his certificate of completion attests.

3. Registered apprenticeship programs also have some advantages in gaining military deferment for apprentices. State selective service directors "are authorized to accept for deferment purposes apprentice training programs which meet its regulations. The request must be accompanied by a certification from the registration agency that the program has been in operation at least one year, and one or more apprentices have been in training during that time in each occupation covered."[3] Although deferment presumably can be granted to apprentices in nonregistered programs, those that are in the registered ones are automatically eligible for deferment.

4. There are also some miscellaneous advantages of registration. In Detroit, for example, only registered programs were permitted to use the public schools for related training purposes.

The foregoing advantages of registration seem to be of rather marginal importance to most unions and employers. The main impetus to apprenticeship is therefore given primarily by the advantages of this form of training to unions and some employers.

APPRENTICESHIP STANDARDS, QUALIFICATIONS, AND PROCEDURES

Many apprenticeship programs which did not previously have objective standards for admission have adopted formal procedures as a result of the growing technological requirements of their trades and the agitation to get more Negroes into these programs.

These standards, qualifications, and procedures for registered programs are established within the broad guidelines laid down by the FCA. Within the federal standards, local apprenticeship committees establish their own standards, either on the basis of general guides from national organizations to which they are affiliated or on the basis of local standards.

The standards prepared by the Electrical Joint Apprenticeship

[3] U.S. Department of Labor, *The National Apprenticeship Program* (Washington, D.C.: Government Printing Office, 1965), pp. 7–8.

15

and Training Committee, representing the National Electrical Contractors Association (NECA) and the International Brotherhood of Electrical Workers (IBEW), illustrate the general requirements of that industry. The electrical standards provide that the electrical trade "must select men who have a natural aptitude for using tools and at the same time, are gifted enough to master the intricacies of electrical science, who can and will keep up with the progress of the industry, and master a knowledge of the thousands of installation and maintenance procedures." The standards add that the electrical industry "places a high degree of personal responsibility on the individual journeyman." And "a faulty installation can prove extremely expensive and hazardous." The electrical standards require applicants to be between the ages of eighteen and twenty-four, high school graduates (mathematical and science backgrounds preferred), and physically fit. Applicants are required to submit to the electrical joint apprenticeship committee their birth certificates, transcripts of high school courses and grades, evidence of qualifying grades on an aptitude test, and a record of physical examination or satisfactory evidence of physical fitness. Once the electrical apprentice is indentured, he is required to work for not less than 8,000 hours and to undergo a minimum of 144 hours of related instruction each year away from the job, usually in a public vocational or high school.

The current apprentice selection process used by the electrical industry was adopted to meet the requirements of the Department of Labor's regulations (29 CFR pt. 30) made effective in January, 1964, in order to provide for nondiscrimination in apprenticeship programs. In a letter of June 3, 1966, explaining the new selection procedures, the National Joint Apprenticeship and Training Committee for the Electrical Industry explained to its affiliates that "A unified industry position is necessary if we are to continue to operate our own programs." The selection procedures provide for detailed record-keeping on each applicant and periodic rejection and notification of unqualified applicants. All applicants who are qualified are given an interview. The interviewers are asked to put the applicant at ease and ask him questions which will determine: whether or not he is really interested in the trade or just looking for a job; his attitude toward hard work and whether he has ever done any; his sense of responsibility for performance, materials, safety, and the like; his ability to work under supervision and take orders; whether he looks upon school as an opportunity or a requirement; and whether he understands what will be expected of him if he is accepted.

The interviewing committee grades the applicant on the basis of his education, with extra credit given for algebra and additional mathematics and science (physics is the preferred science course); marital status and dependents; financial condition (can he meet his obligations on the income of a beginning apprentice?); whether or not transportation is available to him; physical conditions and handicaps; such factors as interest, character, co-operativeness, and judgment brought out in the interview (the joint committees are asked to note that "interview factors should weigh heavily in the final grading").

The electrical industry standards require that applicants be selected according to the number of apprentices needed and on the basis of their grades, with a range from D to A+. The electrical standards also provide for an apprentice-applicant appeals procedure. The appeals committee is composed of one member appointed by labor, one member appointed by management, and a public member appointed by these members. It is provided, however, that no member of the apprenticeship committee may serve on the appeals committee. The grievant has a right to a hearing and the decisions of the appeals committee are final and binding upon the joint apprenticeship committee. On May 26, 1966, the electrical industry's standards were approved by the Under Secretary of Labor as being consistent with the Department of Labor's nondiscrimination regulations.

Illustrative of the standards of a local program, the Pittsburgh carpenters accept workers who are not high school graduates, but give extra points for high school graduation and good grades. The carpenters' standards provide the following points for different parts of their standards:

1. Education and training, maximum fifteen points.
2. Physical factors, maximum ten points.
3. Past working experience (credit given for vocational training related to the trade), maximum ten points.
4. References and conduct record, maximum ten points.
5. Test scores, maximum twenty-five points.
6. Military service (honorable discharge only), maximum five points.
7. Oral interview (sincerity of interest, attitude toward work, attitude toward related instruction, ability to work under supervision, understanding of responsibilities as an apprentice), maximum twenty-five points.

17

CHARACTERISTICS OF
APPRENTICESHIP PROGRAMS

While there is considerable diversity in apprenticeship training programs, we can make some generalizations about the factors determining whether or not an aspirant gets into this type of training and the usual procedures involved in becoming an apprentice. For some youngsters the selection process starts very early, because some trades and local unions have strong "father-son" relationships. Although we do not have current information on this point, a 1956 study by the BAT of the career patterns of 3,278 apprentices who had completed their apprenticeship training in 1950, found that the following proportion of craftsmen in the industries indicated were in the same trade as their fathers: construction, 32.0 per cent; metalworking, 14.0 per cent; mechanic and repair, 8.8 per cent; and printing, 9.3 per cent. But over half of the construction tradesmen typically had fathers in some of the skilled trades.[4]

However, father–son relationships apparently are breaking up in the skilled trades as craftsmen with higher incomes send their sons to college. As we shall see, moreover, various antidiscrimination measures have made nepotism more difficult.

Those aspirants who do not have friends and relatives in a trade get information on such matters as how to apply and apprenticeship qualifications from employers, unions, employment services, or other sources. Some industrial apprentices get into their training programs through the employers for whom they already work; others are recruited specifically for apprenticeship programs. In some major cities information may be secured from Apprenticeship Information Centers (AICs) operating jointly by the Bureau of Apprenticeship and Training and the Bureau of Employment Security through the state employment service. These Centers sometimes give certain testing and counseling services for the joint apprenticeship committees if they exist in an area. AICs were established because many youngsters without connections in the skilled trades often had real difficulties learning such elementary facts about apprenticeship programs as the qualifications required, how and where to make application, and when applications would be received.

The number of apprenticeship openings varies from trade to trade and city to city. Some trades, like electricians, plumbers, sheet metal workers, and printers, typically have long waiting lists, while

---

4 U.S. Department of Labor, Bureau of Apprenticeship and Training, *Career Patterns of Former Apprentices* (Washington, D.C.: Government Printing Office, 1956), p. 17.

others, like the roofers and carpenters, are more easily entered. The number of apprenticeship positions with any given employer depends upon how many journeymen he has, because agreements between unions and employers typically specify that an employer can have, say, one apprentice for each four journeymen. Although we really do not know what effect these so-called journeyman–apprentice ratios have on the number of apprentice openings, they apparently have considerable influence in specific cases, though, in the aggregate, employers do not seem to train as many apprentices as their ratios would allow. Of course, the main determinant of the number of journeymen who are employed is the demand for them, which is determined by business conditions. Technology also plays a part, because it destroys the demand for some crafts while increasing the demand for others. The level of employment in a trade is important, because journeymen obviously will resist adding apprentices if there are many unemployed journeymen.

It should be emphasized, however, that there are not very many apprenticeship openings in any trade in any given city. For instance, the electricians expect to take in about 4,000 apprentices in the United States during 1966. The total new registrations for some other trades in 1964 were as follows:

Bricklayers	2,588	Plumbers-pipefitters	5,755
Carpenters	10,301	Sheet metal workers	3,229
Cement masons	563	Structural ironworkers	1,831

Of 170,533 registered apprentices in 1964, 109,836 were in the construction trades, 27,960 were in the metal-working trades and 11,417 were in the printing trades. (See Table 2-1.)

In the District of Columbia during 1963, there were only the following openings for apprentices in construction trades shown:

Craft	Openings Each Year	Hourly Wages Apprentice	Journeyman
Ironworkers	15–20	$2.17	$4.45
Sheet metal worker	16–20	2.10	4.68
Electrician	about 35	1.88	4.70
Carpenter	about 60	2.12	3.90
Pipefitter	about 25	2.15	4.65
Plumber	about 20	2.15	4.65
Painter	6–10	1.77	3.94

Based on data from the District of Columbia Apprenticeship Information Center.

Table 2-1

Active Apprentices, New Registrations, Completions, and Suspensions,
Registered Programs, by State, 1964

State	Active at Beginning of Period	New[a] Regis-trations	Comple-tions	Cancellations[b] (including suspensions)	Active at End of Period
Total	*163,644*	*59,491*	*25,700*	*26,961*	*170,474*
Alabama	1,697	618	277	399	1,639
Alaska	260	160	47	22	351
Arizona	2,055	458	288	290	1,935
Arkansas	930	324	85	128	1,041
California	23,724	10,334	4,371	4,864	24,823
Colorado	2,256	714	271	467	2,232
Connecticut[c]	3,648	565	267	381	3,565
Delaware	670	171	66	36	739
District of Columbia	2,114	980	328	597	2,187
Florida	4,051	1,764	470	981	4,364
Georgia	2,245	656	192	436	2,273
Hawaii	989	461	160	318	972
Idaho	369	164	64	76	393
Illinois	9,374	2,432	1,274	1,790	8,742
Indiana	3,268	1,093	453	333	3,575
Iowa	1,405	294	234	182	1,283
Kansas	1,190	315	215	228	1,062
Kentucky	1,154	322	177	152	1,147
Louisiana	1,603	801	198	333	1,873
Maine	581	215	105	30	661
Maryland	2,120	756	244	442	2,190
Massachusetts	4,030	1,712	624	628	4,490
Michigan	7,986	4,041	1,558	509	9,960
Minnesota	4,390	1,043	736	279	4,418
Mississippi	788	192	66	102	812
Missouri	3,090	997	363	164	3,560
Montana	734	251	129	108	748
Nebraska	832	299	163	167	801
Nevada	807	198	104	84	817
New Hampshire	204	78	33	8	241
New Jersey	4,931	1,379	434	347	5,529
New Mexico	792	396	131	186	871
New York	21,710	6,844	3,767	3,389	21,398
North Carolina	2,804	1,676	441	992	3,047
North Dakota	374	220	45	69	480
Ohio	7,890	2,600	1,421	769	8,300
Oklahoma	1,563	978	180	815	1,546
Oregon	2,044	1,088	518	532	2,082
Pennsylvania	7,203	1,766	927	653	7,389
Puerto Rico	1,321	752	211	310	1,552
Rhode Island	1,195	119	31	10	1,273
South Carolina	1,179	198	50	100	1,227
South Dakota	353	58	32	50	329
Tennessee	2,942	1,114	603	481	2,972
Texas	5,262	2,112	806	1,141	5,427
Utah	1,095	427	201	210	1,111
Vermont	472	259	45	136	550
Virginia	2,981	1,794	427	850	3,498
Washington	3,660	1,178	746	728	3,364
West Virginia	825	242	118	77	872
Wisconsin	4,157	1,758	973	530	4,412
Wyoming	327	125	31	70	351

In 1964, there were only 54,491 new registrations in all apprenticeship programs in the United States, and over 10,000 of these were in California; 7,772 of the new registrants in California were in the construction trades.

Although we do not have much information on unregistered programs, a survey of training by the U.S. Department of Labor in 1963 found that 16.6 per cent of the 1.4 million workers taking formal training were in apprenticeship programs. The Labor Department's survey thus suggests that there were over 232,000 workers taking apprenticeship training, which is a much larger number than previous estimates had indicated. The 1960 census, for example, reported only 85,682 apprentices, 2.52 per cent of whom were nonwhites.

Although apprenticeship training was not very important for many occupations, it accounted for the following proportions of training, according to the 1963 Labor Department Survey:

	No. Taking Formal Training (000's)	No. Taking Apprenticeship Training (%)
Compositors and typesetters	171	30.6
Construction craftsmen	2,708	43.9
Linemen and servicemen, telegraph, telephone, and power	260	36.8
Machinists	732	34.9
Meat cutters	132	56.1

Based on data in *Manpower Report of the President, 1964,* Table F-9, p. 256.

The registered apprentices in selected construction trades are shown in Table 2-2. It will be observed that the ratio of new registrations to completions varies considerably from trade to trade. The carpenters have by far the most new registrants but had fewer completions than the electricians and the plumbers. The carpenters' programs have a high dropout rate partly because many apprentices are able to work at the trade without completing apprenticeships. The carpenters also have relatively low admissions standards as

---

Based on data obtained from U.S. Department of Labor, Bureau of Apprenticeship and Training.

a Includes reinstatements.

b Cancellations are not synonymous with "dropouts" since they include layoffs, discharges and out-of-state transfers as well as suspensions for military service and voluntary "quits."

c Data for the first six months of calendar year 1964 only.

Table 2-2

Apprentices in Selected Construction Trades Registered with State
Apprenticeship Agencies or the Bureau of Apprenticeship
and Training for the Calendar Year 1964

| | | Apprentice Actions for Period | | | |
Trade	Active at Beginning of Period	New registrations	Completions	Cancellations	Active at End of Period
Brick, stone, and tile	8,710	2,588	1,365	1,692	8,241
Carpenters	23,138	10,301	2,888	6,255	24,296
Cement masons	1,630	563	219	272	1,702
Electricians	20,332	6,595	3,884	2,525	20,518
Glaziers	1,078	357	266	183	986
Lathers	2,102	630	241	501	1,990
Painters	6,065	2,990	770	1,711	6,574
Plasterers	1,427	491	266	223	1,429
Plumbers, pipefitters	20,788	5,755	3,107	1,697	21,739
Roofers	2,624	1,385	282	1,500	2,227
Sheet metal workers	10,101	3,229	1,743	1,339	10,248
Structural ironworkers	4,813	1,831	729	751	5,164
Not classified above	4,294	1,619	526	687	4,700
Total	107,102	38,334	16,286	19,336	109,814

Based on data obtained from U.S. Department of Labor, Bureau of Apprenticeship and Training, Division of Research.

contrasted with the mechanical crafts. We also noted that the carpenters have in many places taken in relatively large numbers of Negro apprentices. Since carpenters' programs have a low completion rate and lead to lower-wage jobs, it obviously means less to get Negroes into the carpenters' than into the plumbers' or sheet metal workers' programs. However, those who complete the carpenters' apprentice programs apparently have better chances of becoming foremen than those who drop out.

Other factors influencing apprenticeship dropout rates include economic conditions (because apprentices must have jobs in order to stay in these programs), the desirability of the trade, and whether or not the length of time required for training is realistic. If the time period is unrealistic, the apprentice can drop out and work as a journeyman.

Of course, it might be argued that the number of apprentices should be expanded in order to provide training for a large proportion of the skilled work force—only about 10 per cent of whom currently get training through this means—but this is a point about which there is some disagreement.[5] Not only have a relatively small

[5] See George Strauss, "Apprenticeship: An Evaluation of the Need," in Arthur M. Ross (ed.), *Employment Policy and the Labor Market* (Berkeley and Los Angeles: University of California Press, 1965), pp. 299–332.

proportion of journeymen served apprenticeships, but the projections from 1960 to 1970 by the 1963 *Manpower Report of the President* suggest that relatively few craftsmen are likely to serve apprenticeships. Indeed, the crafts which meet the highest proportion of their needs through apprenticeship, the electricians, bricklayers, and sheet metal workers, are expected to meet only 36 per cent, 22 per cent, and 21 per cent, respectively, of their projected needs through apprenticeship.

If the applicant gets into a program, he often does so by taking written and oral examinations given by the employment service, a private testing agency, the employer, the union, or a joint apprenticeship committee. The JAC traditionally has constructed and administered its own examinations, but there appears to be a trend to the use of professionally developed tests.

The oral interview is designed to ascertain such matters as the applicant's interest in the trade, his physical and financial condition as they bear on his chances of completing his training program, and his attitude toward work. In general, the committee—which perhaps is going to allot a scarce position to the applicant and invest considerable resources and time in his training—is eager to be sure the apprentice stays in the program. The JACs also are concerned about dropouts because they are fearful of "flooding the market" with partially trained journeymen. Moreover, the committee is interested in getting the "right kind" of people in their training programs, which means persons who are socially acceptable as well as productive workers. There is a certain mystique and fraternal character about apprenticeship which the JAC expects the new apprentice to fit into. Part of the ritual in many trades takes the form of hazing and menial assignments to the new apprentices designed to "initiate" him into the trade. Some Negro apprentices have misunderstood this hazing at first and thought they were being mistreated because they were Negroes (see Appendix).

Once the apprentice is indentured, he is paid a progressively increasing proportion of the journeyman wage scale until he gets the journeyman's rate upon completion of his apprenticeship, at least one year and typically four years after he enters a program. In some cases, like that of the carpenters in San Francisco, the apprentice can get into the program by passing a simple aptitude test, but must find his own job. In other cases, like most electricians' programs, the JACs seem to be able to assure employment to the apprentice and take responsibility for finding him a job. Many in the apprenticeship establishment are fearful that the "hunting license" approach used by the carpenters in San Francisco and other places will bring too many people into the trade.

The apprentice probably will be expected to attend classes for related training to gain theoretical insight into his trade. This training may be conducted by the union at its own facilities, in a few cases through correspondence courses, but usually in a public vocational school. Some programs supplement the salaries of apprentice instructors and provide apprentice co-ordinators to supervise the apprentice's training, but over-all policy and guidance is established by the joint apprenticeship committee or other sponsor. The apprentice's wages often are paid by the employer while he attends classes during the day, but this practice varies considerably. In some cases related training classes are held in the evening.

Apprentices who complete their training usually stay in the trade and earn wages well above the average. Indeed, apprenticeship programs train many supervisors and managers. The 1956 BAT study of apprentices who graduated in 1950, cited earlier, reported that 19 per cent of former apprentices were working as supervisors and 8 per cent were in business for themselves as employers or contractors. The rate of upgrading into managerial positions in some trades is even greater than this: a skilled trades representative in the Detroit automobile industry said that 40 per cent of their apprentice graduates wind up in managerial positions within five years and a Houston electrical industry representative said that, within two years, 75 per cent of the apprentice graduates in his craft in Houston enter managerial positions. Obviously, therefore, apprenticeship training provides a means for advancement even beyond the skilled trades.

ADVANTAGES OF APPRENTICESHIP

Although we did not examine this question in detail, apprenticeship programs seem to have several advantages to all parties concerned over other means of acquiring skills. Not only do apprentices train for high-paying jobs, but they also seem to have greater stability of employment because their training is more general and not specialized narrowly on particular aspects of a trade. Flexibility is a particularly important advantage in a dynamic economy. When the task which the semiskilled worker has learned is automated out of existence, he is more likely to become unemployed than the apprentice who has learned a variety of skills and has mastered the theoretical aspects of his trade. The apprentice also earns while he learns the trade and gets first-hand experience in realistic settings which are likely to utilize the latest techniques. Moreover, the apprentice's training ideally is organized and more thorough than many other training techniques. The apprentice also has contractual assurance of a stated wage scale throughout his training, and is awarded a certificate as proof of his training by the state or the BAT.

Although we do not know the relative costs of apprenticeship training as compared with other methods of acquiring skills, apprenticeship representatives argue that the cost to society of training apprentices is probably much less than other forms of training. In 1963, for example, Charles F. Hanna, the head of the California Division of Apprenticeship Standards (DAS) estimated that in his state the public cost of training an apprentice was $130 as compared with $1900 a year for MDTA training in one California program.[6] Hanna termed the California expenditure "substantially more than is spent in any other state, but . . . substantially less than is needed." If the California experience is typical, apprenticeship training provides the nation with a supply of skilled manpower at relatively low direct cost to the public.

Although we have noted that employers' attitudes toward apprenticeship training vary depending upon their circumstances, they benefit by the apprenticeship system in that they get people who are trained according to methods and standards specified by the industry itself.

Although we have no reason to doubt the reality of the foregoing advantages of apprenticeship training, and accept them without question for the purposes of this study, there is very little detailed analytical information on the values of apprenticeship.

[6] Senate Committee on Labor and Public Welfare, *The Role of Apprenticeship in Manpower Development: United States and Western Europe*, pp. 1109, 1112.

CHAPTER III

NEGRO PARTICIPATION IN
APPRENTICESHIP TRAINING

EXTENT OF NEGRO PARTICIPATION

Although the statistics on apprenticeship in general are bad, and those on Negro participation in these programs almost nonexistent, the available evidence for the country and for particular areas demonstrates that, with recent exceptions, there have been very few Negro apprentices in the United States. The U.S. Census Bureau reported that Negroes constituted 1.90 per cent of apprentices in the labor force in 1950 and 2.52 per cent in 1960 (see Table 3-1). According to the census figures, there were 2,190 Negro apprentices in 1950 and 2,191 in 1960. It will be noted that the only apprenticeship classifications in which Negroes even approximated their proportions of the total work force in 1960 (10.6 per cent) were the building trades not elsewhere classified. Within the building trades, Negroes have been concentrated primarily in the laborers' jobs and in the so-called trowel (cement masons, plasterers, and bricklayers) and the carpentry trades.

Studies made in various states also confirm the virtual absence of Negroes from many apprenticeship programs until around 1960. For example, studies in California and New York found that Negroes constituted only 1.9 and 2 per cent of apprentices respectively; in New Jersey, Negroes held only about 0.5 per cent of apprentice positions.[1] The Connecticut Commission on Civil Rights reported Negroes to constitute 0.7 per cent of the apprentices in that state in 1960.[2] A survey of 1,000 apprentices in Tampa, Florida, by the Florida Advisory Committee of the U.S. Commission on Civil Rights failed to disclose a single Negro.[3] Although the count was admittedly only approximate, Maryland civil rights officials reported finding only twenty Negroes among approximately 2,400

[1] U.S. Civil Rights Commission, *Reports on Apprenticeship* (Washington, D.C.: U.S. Civil Rights Commission, 1964), p. 91
[2] *Ibid.*, p. 41.
[3] *Ibid.*, p. 57.

27

Table 3-1

Negro Apprentices, by Occupation, 1950 and 1960

Occupation	Total		Negroes in Experienced Civilian Labor Force				Negroes Employed			
			Number		Per cent of total		Number		Per cent of total	
	1950	1960	1950	1960	1950	1960	1950	1960	1950	1960
Total	*115,440*	*86,966*	*2,190*	*2,191*	*1.90*	*2.52*	*2,130*	*2,005*	*1.85*	*2.31*
Auto mechanics	3,660	1,761	120	40	3.27	2.27	120	40	3.27	2.27
Bricklayers and masons	6,810	3,257	270	350	3.96	10.75	270	288	3.96	8.84
Carpenters	10,350	6,660	60	122	.58	1.83	60	102	.58	1.53
Electricians	9,600	8,750	90	79	.94	.90	90	79	.94	.90
Machinists and toolmakers	14,940	14,606	60	245	.40	1.68	60	245	.40	1.68
Mechanics (except auto)	6,810	3,721	270	62	3.96	1.67	270	62	3.96	1.67
Plumbers and pipefitters	11,310	8,687	120	62	1.06	.71	120	62	1.06	.71
Building trades (not elsewhere classified)	3,900	2,791	180	207	4.62	7.42	150	145	3.85	5.20
Metal-working trades	7,470	5,706	150	141	2.01	2.47	150	141	2.01	2.47
Printing trades	14,490	11,722	270	206	1.86	1.76	240	206	1.66	1.76
Other specified	12,210	8,905	480	386	3.93	4.33	480	365	3.93	4.10
Trade not specified	13,890	10,400	120	291	.86	2.80	120	270	.86	2.60

Based on data from "Occupational Characteristics," in U.S. Bureau of the Census, *U.S. Census of Population, 1950* (Washington, D.C.: Government Printing Office, 1956), Vol. IV, Pt. 1, Chapter B; and "Occupational Characteristics," in U.S. Bureau of the Census, *U.S. Census of Population, 1960* (Washington, D.C.: Government Printing Office, 1963), p. 26.

apprentices.[4] Of some fifty apprenticeship programs in Tennessee, only four (bricklayers, carpenters, roofers, and cement finishers) were known to accept Negroes before 1960. In 1961, a breakthrough occurred when one Negro apprentice enrolled in each of the following trades in Oak Ridge: electrician, machinist, sheet metal worker, and millwright.

A 1965 survey of 989 construction industry contractors, 281 employer associations, and 731 unions by field teams from the President's Committee on Equal Employment Opportunity (PCEEO) is even more revealing. This survey found that in thirty Southern cities, of 3,696 apprentices selected for the five building trades unions, shown in Table 3-2, only twenty-six were Negroes and twenty of these were in the carpenters', a union which is relatively accessible to Negroes. Negroes were selected for the electricians' programs in Louisville and Huntsville, and for the plumbers' in New Orleans, but nowhere else in the South. The survey revealed not a single Negro among the 441 apprentices selected for the sheet metal workers' program and the 365 selected for the ironworkers'. The PCEEO survey also revealed, however, that very few Negroes were known to have applied for any of these apprenticeship programs in the South.

Table 3-3 shows the experience of the non-Southern cities: of the 5,908 apprentices selected for the five building trades surveyed in these cities, 133 were Negroes, 70 of whom were carpenters. Although these statistics do not show how many apprentices there are in these cities, they indicate the number of Negroes admitted to these programs in 1964. There undoubtedly were some programs that might have selected Negroes, that made no selections during the survey period. While these figures come from a *sample* and not the entire *universe,* they appear to reflect the patterns of Negro apprentices in all places except New York City, where a relatively significant number of Negroes got in before and after 1964.

A 1964 compliance survey of government contractors also found few Negro apprentices; of 21,500 apprentices only 483 (or 1.3 per cent) were Negroes.

REASONS FOR THE ABSENCE OF NEGROES FROM APPRENTICESHIP PROGRAMS

Although the reasons why so few Negroes are represented in apprenticeship training are easy to list, it is much more difficult to

4 *Ibid.,* p. 67.

29

Table 3-2

Negro and White Construction Apprentice Selections in Specified Construction Trades for Selected Southern Cities, 1964

City	Plumbers		Electricians		Sheet Metal Workers		Ironworkers		Carpenters	
	Total	Negro	Total	Negro	Total	Negro	Total	Negro	Total	Negro
Alabama										
Birmingham	0	0	15	0	0	0	20	0	16	0
Huntsville	5	0	33	1	6	0	18	0	12	0
Montgomery	0	0	—	—	—	—	—	—	6	0
Arkansas										
Little Rock	17	0	18	0	20	0	0	0	16	0
Florida										
Jacksonville-Gainesville	79	0	—	—	37	0	—	—	30	0
Miami–West Palm Beach	168	0	231	0	114	0	62	0	297	10
Orlando–Cape Kennedy	—	—	142	0	26	0	113	0	137	0
Pensacola–Panama City	47	0	92	0	14	0	—	—	—	—
Tallahassee	10	0	22	0	—	—	—	—	2	0
Tampa	121	0	120	0	54	0	0	0	117	0
Georgia										
Atlanta	33	0	38	0	28	0	29	0	24	0
Augusta	7	0	9	0	—	—	2	0	4	0
Columbus	6	0	2	0	1	0	—	—	9	0
Macon	10	0	14	0	1	0	—	—	8	0
Savannah	6	0	15	0	9	0	15	0	4	0

Kentucky										
Louisville	85	0	18	1	[a]	0	[a]	0	18	0
Louisiana										
Baton Rouge	—	—	0	0	—	—	4	0	15	0
Lake Charles	13	0	15	0	3	0	17	0	2	0
New Orleans	19	4	25	0	6	0	5	0	27	3
Shreveport	16	0	6	0	—	—	10	0	25	0
Mississippi										
Gulfport	5	0	13	0	—	—	—	—	5	1
Jackson	5	0	9	0	8	0	—	—	5	0
Oklahoma										
Oklahoma City	10	0	20	0	51	0	[a]	0	40	0
South Carolina										
Charleston	8	0	16	0	11	0	10	0	20	0
Texas										
Austin	4	0	5	0	—	—	2	0	20	0
Dallas	51	0	22	0	24	0	10	0	125	5
Fort Worth	13	0	10	0	6	0	15	0	39	0
Houston	40	0	39	0	15	0	25	0	50	0
Port Arthur	4	0	14	0	2	0	7	0	18	0
San Antonio	10	0	15	0	5	0	1	0	19	1
Total South	792	4	978	2	441	0	365	0	1,120	20

Based on data obtained from the President's Committee on Equal Employment Opportunity.

[a] The total number of applicants was unknown.

Table 3-3

Negro and White Construction Apprentice Selections in Specified Construction Trades for Selected Non-Southern Areas, 1964

City	Plumbers		Electricians		Sheet Metal Workers		Ironworkers		Carpenters	
	Total	Negro	Total	Negro	Total	Negro	Total	Negro	Total	Negro
California State (of)	264	7	162	5	200	6	33	1	2,047	35
Connecticut State (of)	—	—	16	0	00	00	00	00	24	3
Illinois Chicago	54	a	126	22	a	a	21	1	72	12
Indiana State (of)	55	a	67	a	30	a	14	a	38	a
Maryland Baltimore	50	0	45	4	11	0	—	—	53	3
Massachusetts Boston	14	0	45	0	23	1	35	0	64	7
Springfield	—	—	6	0	0	0	a	—	2	1
Michigan Detroit	a	—	85	0	—	—	4	0	250	0
Missouri Eastern	136	a	173	a	58	0	59	a	288	4
Western	31	a	14	a	—	—	—	—	45	a

New Jersey										
Newark	12	0	—	—	—	—	—	—	—	—
Northern N.J. (excluding Newark)	19	0	36	0	—	—	—	—	19	0
New York										
New York City	169	4	27	0	—	—	50	1	150	0
Long Island	—	—	—	—	—	—	—	—	2	1
Westchester Co.	—	—	—	—	—	—	—	—	36	0
Ohio										
Akron	13	0	8	0	5	0	12	0	12	0
Cincinnati	3	0	22	0	10	0	19	0	12	0
Cleveland	20	1	53	2	14	0	8	0	10	0
Columbus	12	0	10	0	19	0	17	0	14	1
Dayton	16	0	39	0	18	0	—	—	16	0
Pennsylvania										
Harrisburg	5	0	—	—	3	0	4	0	9	0
Philadelphia	16	2	30	0	15	1	15	1	65	[a]
Pittsburgh	—	—	15	0	20	5	—	—	25	3
Rhode Island										
Providence	5	0	6	0	2	0	—	—	16	0
West Virginia										
Parkersburg	12	0	11	0	4	0	10	0	4	0
Total Non-South	906	14	996	33	432	12	301	4	3,273	70

Based on data obtained from the President's Committee on Equal Employment Opportunity.

[a] The number of applicants was unknown.

assign weights to each of the factors in the complex constellation of causes. Civil rights groups have emphasized discrimination as a causal factor, while unions stressed lack of qualified Negroes. Specialized government agencies often add to the confusion by supporting the civil rights leaders (if they are antidiscrimination organizations) or the industry (if they are apprenticeship officials). Although there is an element of truth in all of these positions, they tend to be superficial and exaggerated.

Union and Management Attitudes

While there have perhaps been some significant changes in attitudes in recent years, there can be little question that racial prejudices and discrimination by unions and management (reflecting prevailing social attitudes) have been major reasons for the absence of Negroes from apprenticeship programs. Employers traditionally have felt that Negroes were "suited" mainly for hot, dirty, or otherwise disagreeable jobs. Historically, management has been willing to hire Negroes for "white" jobs only where they would work for lower wages than whites or would act as strikebreakers or otherwise help prevent unionization. But these latter motives became less important after the New Deal period when the new industrial unions championed Negro interests and the Negro community's allegiance shifted from employers and Republicans to unions and Democrats.

Of course, employment policies also are motivated by profit considerations. If employers fear boycotts by white customers or strikes by employees, they are reluctant to hire Negroes. Since many employers in the building trades rely on the union as a source of skilled manpower, and since union leaders have been able to refer better workers to preferred employers, management has had strong motives to maintain good relations with unions.

The supply of Negro craftsmen is an important determinant of the colored workers' ability to maintain jobs. White workers are not likely to attempt to prevent the employment of Negro workers who can supply the manpower needs of boycotted employers, and they are not likely to attempt to exclude Negroes who have sufficient supplies of competent workers to break strikes.

Attitudes toward hiring Negro workers seem to vary considerably between levels of management. Although top management people often agree to equal employment opportunity programs, lower-level supervisors and foremen are likely to be more opposed to hiring Negroes.

Although racial prejudice obviously continues to be an important factor in apprenticeship, little overt racial hostility seems to be expressed against Negro apprentices once they get in the programs. Indeed, there are many cases in which employers or union leaders have gone out of their way to see that Negroes "made it." Some Negro apprentices have been discriminated against in job assignments, a few have had trouble with journeymen which might have been racially inspired (although because of the hazing tradition it obviously was not entirely), but most seem to get along well with fellow apprentices or instructors. However, Negroes rarely feel completely accepted, even though there is outward cordiality.

Similarly, although some apprenticeship sponsors had trouble with tardiness, absenteeism, and sloppy work habits by Negro apprentices, most of them seemed to feel that Negroes perform at least as well as the average white apprentice.

While discrimination undoubtedly is responsible for the absence of Negroes from many construction apprenticeship programs, the unions' motives to exclude also are based on nonracial factors. For one thing, these unions attempt to control the supply of labor in order to maintain their wage rates. The construction industry is plagued by a sense of job insecurity stemming from rates of unemployment which are consistently much higher than the average rates. Indeed, construction unemployment rates typically are higher than the general unemployment rates of nonwhite males. In order to protect their jobs, therefore, most skilled construction unions attempt to control the supply of labor through a variety of means. Some of them operate hiring halls, most of them refuse to work with nonunion workers, and most of them control entry into their apprentice programs.

As noted in Chapter II, craft unions also are interested in the qualifications of apprentices because they realize that job control requires a supply of competent workers. As George Strauss has emphasized, unions also want well-trained men because "the presence of unskilled men in the union makes the business agent's life more difficult, unskilled men are harder to place, unskilled men are far more likely than skilled men to insist on various types of featherbedding, and internal schisms develop as the unskilled insist that job opportunities be shared equally."[5]

Local union leaders also have political reasons for controlling apprenticeship training and resisting the entry of Negroes. For one

[5] George Strauss, "Apprenticeship: An Evaluation of the Need," in Ross (ed.), *Employment Policy and the Labor Market,* p. 320.

thing, because the union is a source of jobs, local building trades organizations have been closely controlled by their members and business agents and therefore have been very reluctant to accept any apprentice who would not be acceptable to their members.

Another important motive behind the pattern of racial exclusion in craft unions has been nepotism. Although it appears to be diminishing, the father-son relationship has been particularly strong in some of the building trades unions and is defended on the grounds of assuring a supply of competent craftsmen; the unions argue that one of the assurances that apprentices will not drop out of their training programs is the craft tradition which comes from having relatives in the trades. In addition, it is argued that a strong sense of craftsmanship which comes from long association with the trade is a prerequisite to excellence in any skilled trade. Craft unionists argue that their sons and relatives are more likely to have this feeling of craftsmanship than a youngster "off the street" who is merely looking for a job. Many Negro youngsters are indeed merely looking for jobs and often have been marked down on this point by apprentice-selection committees.

Craft unionists also often defend nepotism as morally justified. "After all," they argue, "we have struggled to build our trades; why shouldn't we be able to pass them on to our children just as wealthy individuals pass on their wealth?" Of course, nepotism also has become a part of the political system in some unions. Apprenticeship positions and summer jobs have been used by business agents to reward their supporters.

The main objection to nepotism from the point of view of the Negro, of course, is that few Negroes are in some of the crafts and, although discrimination might not just be against Negroes per se, they are barred from apprenticeship training by this system. However, there is some evidence that Negroes as well as whites are more likely to get into trades where they have friends and relatives (see Appendix). IBEW Local 3 in New York has permitted its noncraft members to recommend their sons for the craft apprenticeship programs.

Although discrimination is undoubtedly involved in their attitudes, many craft unions, particularly in the building trades, seem to have been unco-operative in lowering racial barriers—or have actually adopted "standards" which tend to perpetuate exclusion—because of a defensiveness stemming from the belief that much of the criticism of them is unfair and based on ignorance of the industry. Many building trades leaders particularly resent the implication that apprenticeship training is a place for dropouts, pointing out that this attitude has contributed to the weakness of vocational education in this country. These leaders also resent what they consider to be governmental efforts to require them to give preferential treatment to Negroes which would require them to discriminate against their own members. They also resent the implications that their qualifications are designed solely to exclude Negroes from membership. Such an implication is, they argue, due primarily to ignorance of the apprenticeship system and the requirements of the skilled crafts. Even those unionists who admit discrimination in the past argue that the present paucity of Negroes in some apprenticeship programs is due primarily to the lack of qualified applicants. Their convictions on this point are strengthened by the meager results of the recruiting campaigns undertaken in various Northern cities during the early 1960's. The building trades' defensiveness likewise is strengthened by the paucity of valid complaints of discrimination in apprenticeship programs filed with government agencies and the small number of qualified Negro applicants for apprenticeship training. Union leaders also resent the implication that the absence of Negroes from a program *proves* discrimination and are critical of government officials who sanction action to get Negroes in by "whatever means."

Cultural Factors

Of all the factors tending to perpetuate the exclusion of Negroes from apprenticeship programs, the most important have been those which relegated the Negro to inferior occupations. The Negro's main problem historically is that he lacked the political and economic power to force whites to share their job opportunities with him. Indeed, apparently the only time Negroes were able to enter the skilled trades with relative ease was under slavery, when slave craftsmen were protected from hostile whites by the powerful slave-owning class.

After emancipation, however, the only skilled occupations in which Negroes were able to maintain their positions with any success were those in which they performed services in the Negro community or in which Negroes were too numerous to be excluded by whites. The main crafts which Negroes continued to practice were those which had relatively stable technologies. For example, Negroes have held a relatively significant share of older trowel crafts, but have had a very low proportion in such newer occupations as electricians, sheet metal workers, elevator constructors,

plumbers, and pipefitters. These occupations often required training, experience, and skills which were beyond the Negro's reach.

Status also has been an important factor in racial exclusion. In
the hierarchy of jobs in each industry it has generally been understood that, with few exceptions, certain inferior jobs would go to
Negroes. Because of the racial prejudices of the white community,
Negroes were excluded from certain "status" jobs such as electricians, locomotive engineers, and supervisors of all kinds. Many
craftsmen whose status has been due to daring and risk as well as
skill—such as ironworkers—have excluded Negroes because of the
stereotyped idea that Negroes were afraid of heights or other
dangers. As might be expected, experience shows these stereotyped
ideas to be completely unfounded.

As a consequence of these job limitations, Negro employment
patterns have become deeply entrenched and are therefore difficult
to change. Not having worked in a variety of skilled, technical jobs,
Negroes became stereotyped for certain jobs by employers, white
workers, and even themselves. Since Negroes usually live in segregated neighborhoods and go to segregated schools, they rarely learn
about occupations with few or no Negroes in them, and they apply
for the kinds of jobs they know they can get. Since aspirations are
conditioned by one's associations, few Negroes are motivated to
apply for jobs from which they are excluded.

As a consequence of these historical and cultural forces, as well
as for a variety of other reasons, Negroes often have not applied for
apprenticeship openings which have been opened to them. For one
thing, very few Negroes have known much about apprenticeship
programs, in spite of the publicity given them by the civil rights
movement. Indeed, racial demonstrations in some cases, while un-
deniably contributing to the lowering of racial barriers, or the sub-
stitution of tokenism or more subtle forms of discriminations, have
tended to symbolize to Negro youngsters the obstacles to becoming
apprentices. Very few school counselors have advised Negro youngsters to apply for apprenticeship openings, either because of ignorance of apprenticeship or because they thought that Negroes could
not get in. Moreover, many employment counselors apparently have
low opinions of the skilled trades and have therefore discouraged
the more qualified Negro youngsters from entering apprenticeship
programs. In some cases the counselor's attitudes are based on the
reality of the situation and prevailing community prejudices against
manual work. This is poor counseling if the youngster has an apti-

tude for the skilled trades, because apprenticeship training often leads to satisfying work and high-paying supervisory jobs.

Civil rights and union leaders have been surprised at the apathy shown by Negro youngsters toward apprenticeship programs even when they had a chance to get in. Of course, the main reason for this is that Negro youngsters apparently do not aspire to the skilled trades. Many of those who are qualified to enter these programs either aspire to white-collar jobs or wish to get jobs with immediate earnings. In some of the latter cases, Negro youngsters take jobs out of necessity, but in some cases it is because they are not interested in the trades. The findings of our study confirm those of B. A. Turner, who studied the occupational choices of 2,012 high school seniors in fourteen Negro, two all-white, and two integrated schools.[6] Only 3.2 per cent of these students aspired to the skilled trades and expressed interest mainly in the trades Negroes have traditionally been able to enter. The most popular first and second choices of these 2,012 seniors were:

| | Choice | |
Occupation	1st	2nd
Business	140	115
Nurse	203	74
Secretary	36	64
Teacher	171	161
Engineer	54	19
Home economics	59	62
Mathematics	53	40

The occupational choices by broad groups were:

	No.	%
Professional and managerial	1332	66.2
Clerical and sales	283	14.1
Service	75	3.7
Skilled	65	3.2
Agriculture	17	0.9
All other	36	1.8
Not classified	204	10.0

Some observers have been surprised that qualified Negro youngsters have taken nonskilled jobs instead of apprenticeships which,

[6] B. A. Turner, *Occupational Choices of High School Seniors in the Space Age* (Houston: Texas Southern University, 1964).

on the average, pay more than the average nonskilled Negro youngster can hope to make. But youngsters who are otherwise qualified
for apprenticeship are above average and have been able to earn
more than the beginning rates for apprenticeship programs. The
wage factor is particularly important in the more desirable occupations for which there are typically many more applicants than jobs.
In these trades, the wages of apprentices typically are lower relative
to journeyman rates than in carpentry and other occupations which
are likely to have lower qualifications for entry. Wages are likely
to be more important to Negro apprentices, who seem older on the
average than their white classmates.

Dissatisfaction among Negro youngsters is likely to be prevalent
among those who are overqualified for occupations as well as among
those who are underqualified. Highly qualified Negroes and whites
get bored with even those apprenticeship programs which have the
highest qualifications. Some of these apprentices would be in college
if they had the financial resources to pay their way. Some of those
who failed to follow through on their applications for apprenticeship programs go to college rather than become apprentices, and
others drop out for this reason.

The Negro's low degree of aspiration for apprenticeship training
programs seems to contradict the emphasis given these programs
by the civil rights movement. In some sense this contradiction is
based on different objectives. Many Negro adults compare the
skilled trades with the jobs they now hold and consider apprenticeship programs to be highly desirable, while Negro youngsters who
are otherwise qualified compare apprenticeships with their aspirations and consider them undesirable. Many civil rights leaders, who
sometimes are intellectuals with little understanding of apprenticeship programs, approach the apprenticeship problem symbolically.
They reason that some Negro youngsters ought to go into these
programs and are incensed by the manifestations of discrimination
which have barred Negroes from skilled occupations. The con-
spicuousness of construction projects and the fact that many of
them are financed by government funds make the building trades
apprenticeship programs logical targets for civil rights organizations. But, since many Negro youngsters apparently are not eager
to enter these programs, and since, as we shall see, very few jobs
are involved, the emphasis on apprenticeship training often either
is symbolic or is based on a misunderstanding of realities. However,
many civil rights leaders have learned more about apprenticeship
programs as a result of the conflicts of the early 1960's and take a

more realistic approach. They realize that not many jobs are involved but that they are good jobs. They also realize, of course, that symbolism also is important for the civil rights movement.

The foregoing is not intended to imply that there are not more qualified Negro youngsters who would like to get into apprentice-training programs if they knew about them. Some high school counselors have been successful in getting Negro youngsters to apply to these programs and, although much effort was required, some organizations have succeeded in recruiting Negro youngsters for apprenticeship programs.

Negro youngsters who apply for apprenticeship programs often do not follow through for a variety of reasons which do not follow any particular pattern (see Appendix). Some applicants are discouraged by fees charged either to take the tests or to enter the unions. Many of those youngsters who have persevered through the difficult process of finding out about the qualifications, starting times, and application procedures for apprenticeship programs have failed to appear for tests or avail themselves of opportunities to enter these programs because of the time delays and uncertainties involved. As a consequence, many of them are drafted, find other jobs, or move away before the time comes for them to enter apprenticeship programs.

Some Negro youngsters fail to follow through with these programs because of poor discipline. We have no way of knowing how these compare with whites, but some of the reasons given by Negro youngsters for their failure to follow through with their applications seem very trivial: some "forgot," others overslept, and still others had no excuse at all. It is often necessary for some organization to see Negro youngsters through the difficult and uncertain process of making proper application to apprenticeship programs, preparing them to take the tests, and seeing to it that they develop proper work habits once they are on the job. Of course, white youngsters also need this kind of attention, but they are more likely to get it from friends or relatives in the trades.

Lack of Qualifications

As we shall see in our discussions of the apprenticeship experience of Negroes in the various cities, a large proportion of Negroes recruited for apprenticeship programs are found to be unqualified. Although Negroes often feel that the tests and qualifications are designed to keep them out, there is also agreement that for many reasons Negroes are not likely to do as well as whites on paper-and-pencil tests designed to discover aptitudes and abilities.

Education

A larger proportion of Negroes than whites are barred from apprenticeship programs by educational standards. As noted in Chapter II, almost all apprenticeship programs require that applicants be high school graduates and some require, or give extra credit for, specified courses in mathematics and sciences. Although there is a marked increase in the trend for Negroes to complete high school, in October, 1965, 60 per cent of whites but only 37 per cent of nonwhites in the labor force had completed four years of high school or more. Median nonwhite education lagged 3.8 years behind whites in 1952; 2.6 years in 1962, and only 1.8 years of 1965. Nonwhite male education levels lag significantly behind other groups; the median years of education they completed in 1965 was 10.2 as compared with 12.2 for white males, 12.3 for white females and 11.1 for nonwhite females.

These statistics do not tell the whole story, however, because it is well known that Negro education has been inferior to that of whites in all sections of the country. According to a 1966 report by the U.S. Office of Education, Negroes in the metropolitan Northeast in the sixth grade were about 1.6 years behind whites; at Grade 9, 2.4 years behind whites, and at Grade 12 Negroes were 3.3 years behind whites.[7] The report also concludes that "by grade 12, both white and Negro students in the South score below their counterparts—white and Negro—in the North. In addition, Southern Negroes score farther below Southern whites than Northern Negroes score below Northern whites."[8] Although these tests measure educational achievement, the report emphasizes that they "do not measure intelligence, nor attitudes or character."[9]

Professor Kenneth B. Clark's conclusion concerning employers is equally applicable to apprenticeship programs:

The fact is that the massive inefficiency of the public schools where the masses of Negroes go, does the discriminating for any prejudiced employer, so that he doesn't have to do it himself.

All he has to do is maintain even minimum standards of qualifications in such basic subjects as reading or arithmetic, and as things now stand,

---

[7] U.S. Department of Health, Education, and Welfare, Office of Education, *Equality of Educational Opportunity* (Washington, D.C.: Government Printing Office, 1966), p. 20.

[8] *Ibid.*, p. 21.

[9] *Ibid.*, p. 20.

the vast bulk of the Negro youngsters from the working class, the lower middle class, are unable to meet minimal standards for employment in other than menial lower status jobs.[10]

Vocational schools, which might be expected to give youngsters an advantage in applying for the skilled trades, actually seem to put them at a disadvantage in applying for apprenticeship training (see Appendix).

Many Negro youngsters have not had such courses as algebra, trigonometry, and physics, all of which were emphasized by the electrical, plumbing, sheet metal, and other apprenticeship programs.

The Problem of Testing

Negro youngsters attempting to enter apprenticeship programs sometimes are barred by the tests used to select apprentices. Although there has been a long-run trend in the use of tests, there seems little question that the civil rights movement's demands for better job opportunities have accelerated the use of these selection devices. It is therefore understandable that Negroes and civil rights leaders suspect the tests were introduced as a means of continuing discrimination under the guise of maintaining standards.

Although it was not our purpose to appraise either the validity of the tests or the reasonableness of the qualifications and standards imposed by the unions, because of its importance to Negro participation in apprenticeship programs we sought some answers to the question of the fairness of the tests given. Except in a few cases, the tests seem to have been fairly administered, but there is some question concerning the weight given certain parts of the tests, especially the heavy reliance on oral interviews.

Some interviewees suggested that oral interviews should be eliminated or their weight should be no more than, say, 5 per cent of the test. Industry interviewees reject this suggestion, arguing that many attributes which indicate probability of successfully completing a program can be determined only by oral interviews. Moreover, our evidence indicates that written tests are more likely to exclude Negroes than oral interviews. The interviews obviously are flexible enough to permit the examiners to do whatever they want to do. Negroes also can be tutored to improve their chances of making good impressions in oral interviews.

[10] Kenneth B. Clark, *Social and Economic Implications of Integration in the Public Schools,* Seminar on Manpower Policy and Program (Washington, D.C.: Department of Labor, Manpower Administration, Office of Manpower, Automation and Training, 1964), p. 6.

Efforts to get Negroes into apprenticeship programs also raise the question of whether or not written selection tests are inherently biased against Negroes. Most of the JACs apparently make up their own written tests which supplement oral interviews in order to make better selections and reduce dropouts.[11] The testing question has received considerable publicity as a result of the famous Motorola Case, in which the Illinois Supreme Court (in March, 1966) reversed a ruling by that state's FEP Commission holding that the Motorola Company had discriminated against a Negro by giving an aptitude test. The hearing examiner had ruled that the test was normed on advantaged groups and therefore did not "lend itself to equal employment opportunity to qualify" by "culturally deprived disadvantaged groups." The publicity given the Motorola Case led to the so-called "Tower Amendment" to the Civil Rights Act of 1964 which provides that it shall not be unlawful to rely and act on the results of a "professionally developed" ability test that is not "designed or intended" to be used to discriminate.

Although testing is a complicated question on which professionals disagree, there seems to be some consensus on several general conclusions. There is agreement, for example, that, in spite of considerable overlap in individual cases, Negroes usually have lower scores than whites on written tests. These differential results are thought to reflect cultural or background differences as compared with the populations on which the tests were standardized. Such tests, therefore, will not be accurate predictors of performance on the job or in the training program. Psychologists have attempted to get around this problem by devising "culture-free" or "culture-fair" tests which would hold culture constant either by using test items which are equally novel or equally familiar to all cultures. As a practical matter, however, psychologists apparently have not succeeded in developing "culture-free" performance tests which are correlated with the more comprehensive verbal scales.

Some psychologists have suggested using different racial standards for evaluating test performances. Where the tests are biased against Negroes, lower standards are justified in order to correct for the bias. It has been very difficult, however, to determine the extent to which the tests are biased against Negroes. The use of separate standards also has the disadvantage of perpetuating the idea of racial inferiority. There is, however, some precedent for the use of different standards, because several widely used tests, such as the

[11] Minutes of the Advisory Committee on Equal Opportunity in Apprenticeship and Training, 10th Meeting, June 29, 1965 (dittoed), pp. 4–5.

Benet, Wonderlick, Minnesota Paper Form Board, and the Thurstone Temperament Schedule, provide different norms for males and females.

Whatever conclusion one reaches on adjusting to the testing bias, there is little question that tests should be used with care and must be interpreted by qualified persons.

Moreover, tests should rarely be used as the only standard for selecting trainees or employees, because other criteria usually will be important in determining successful training or job performance. It is also important for employers and training directors to check the validity of their tests by examining the correlation between test scores and performance in their specific jobs or training programs.[12]

Although our evidence is far from conclusive, we are persuaded that fairly administered tests are not insurmountable obstacles to the entry of Negroes into apprenticeship programs. The experience of the Workers Defense League in New York suggests that, with proper selection and tutoring, Negroes can perform at least as well as whites on apprenticeship selection tests.

---

[12] In August, 1966, the Equal Employment Opportunity Commission adopted guidelines on testing and advocated:

    I. Use of a *total personnel assessment system* that is nondiscriminatory within the spirit of the law and places special emphasis on:

      (a) *Careful job analysis to define skill requirements.* . . .

      (b) *Special efforts in recruiting minorities.* . . .

      (c) *Screening and interviewing related to job requirements.* . . .

      (d) *Tests selected on the basis of specific job-related criteria.* The Commission views tests as only one component of the personnel system —no better or worse than the selection system of which they are a part. "It is quite possible to take a test that has been professionally developed in one situation and misuse it in another situation." The characteristics of a test, apart from the situation in which it is used, are not sufficient evidence on which to judge its quality.

      (e) *Comparison of test performance versus job performance.* . . . Since cultural factors can so readily affect performance on so many tests, it is recommended that the test be judged against job performance rather than by what they claim to measure.

      (f) *Retesting.* Mindful of the special problems of minorities, employers are encouraged to provide an opportunity for retesting to those "failure candidates" who have availed themselves of more training or experience.

      (g) *Tests should be validated for minorities.*

    II. *Objective Administration of Tests.* . . . Members of disadvantaged groups tend to be particularly sensitive to test situations and those giving tests should be aware of this and be able to alleviate a certain amount of anxiety.

CHAPTER IV

NEW YORK

Because of the size and diversity of its population, New York has had a greater variety of minority group employment problems than any other city. Equally significant for our purposes, New York also has had a wide variety of programs designed to improve the employment conditions of minorities.

New York's large nonwhite population is highly concentrated within certain areas of the city. In 1960, for example, although only 14.7 per cent of New York's 7.8 million people were nonwhite, nonwhites constituted over 25 per cent of the population of the Borough of Manhattan. While the proportion of nonwhites in New York was lower than that in any of our survey cities, New York's total nonwhite population—1,167,298—was larger in absolute terms in 1960 than the nonwhite population of any of our other ten cities.

The construction industry, which gives employment to more people than any other industry in New York, has been a major target of attacks by civil rights groups because it has had a relatively low proportion of nonwhites. As shown in Table 4-1, 92.1 per cent of the 189,122 construction workers were white. This percentage was exceeded by only one other city (Pittsburgh) included in this study.

Because of their size and importance, the New York building trades unions have exerted considerable influence in the city, state, and national labor movements. The president of the state AFL-CIO, Raymond Corbett, is also the business agent for New York Ironworkers Local 40. Likewise, Peter J. Brennan is chairman of both the state and city building and construction trades councils, and George Meany, president of the AFL-CIO, is a member of Plumbers Local 2 in New York and a former president of the New York Federation of Labor.

Table 4-1

Employment in Selected Occupations by Race, 1960—New York Metropolitan Area

Occupation	Number Employed				Percentage Distribution			
	Total	White	Negro	Other nonwhite	Total	White	Negro	Other nonwhite
Selected occupations								
Carpenters	34,483	32,713	1,725	45	100.0	94.9	5.0	0.1
Plasterers and cement finishers	4,688	4,383	305	—	100.0	93.5	6.5	—
Structural metal workers	3,586	3,352	174	60	100.0	93.5	4.9	1.6
Electricians	19,090	18,346	712	32	100.0	96.1	3.7	0.2
Plumbers and pipefitters	18,777	18,247	527	3	100.0	97.2	2.8	<0.005
Construction laborers	34,584	27,714	6,795	75	100.0	80.1	19.6	0.3
Total employed	2,842,283	2,548,517	272,465	21,301	100.0	89.7	9.6	0.7
Total construction industry	189,122	174,273	14,581	268	100.0	92.1	7.7	0.2

Note: Percentages may not add to total because of rounding.
Based on data in "Detailed Characteristics," in U.S. Bureau of the Census, *U.S. Census of Population, 1960*, Parts 6, 10, 12, 24, 34, 37, 40, and 45.

THE EXTENT OF NEGRO PARTICIPATION
IN UNIONS AND APPRENTICESHIP PROGRAMS

A study on the degree of Negro participation in apprenticeship programs, released in 1960 by the New York State Commission Against Discrimination (SCAD), disclosed that (1) "both historically and currently Negroes have not been utilized by industry [in New York] in the skilled craft components of the labor force"; and (2) that "apprenticeship has not been, nor is it presently, a significant mode of entry for Negroes into skilled-craft occupations."[1] With reference to the entire state, the report stated that in 1940 there were 36 Negroes out of 7,421 apprentices (or about 0.5 per cent); by 1950, there were 152 Negroes out of 10,000 apprentices (or about 1.5 per cent); in 1960 there were about 300 Negroes out of 15,000 apprentices (or about 2 per cent).[2] About 73 per cent of the total number of apprentices in the state was in New York City, with the bulk of this proportion concentrated in the construction and printing trades. SCAD found that "of the relatively few Negro apprentices in the state, nearly all are located in the New York City region,"[3] and primarily in the electrical, bricklaying, painting, and "possibly carpentry trades."[4] Similarly, the report stated that there were no Negro apprentices in the city in the following trades: plumbers, steamfitters, sheet metal workers, structural and ornamental ironworkers, plasterers, and mosaic and terrazzo workers.[5] SCAD attributed the lack of participation to a variety of causes: the lack of information concerning the general nature of apprenticeship and the specific details of how to gain admission to specific programs; the availability of alternative training opportunities; the limited number of apprenticeship openings (given set journeyman–apprentice ratios and strong competition from many white youths seeking these positions); the low wages of apprentices (a youth can often earn more as a helper than as an apprentice); the standards for selection (a high school diploma, written test performance, and subjective evaluations); management prejudice about Negro job performance; anticipated objections by other employees of an enterprise; overt acts of discrimination by trade unions; and the nature

[1] New York State Commission Against Discrimination, *Apprentices, Skilled Craftsmen and the Negro: An Analysis* (April, 1960), p. 13.
[2] *Ibid.*, p. 15.
[3] *Ibid.*, p. 64.
[4] *Ibid.*
[5] *Ibid.*

of internal union structure wherein the union leader (unlike management) is responsible to the membership for its actions.[6]

In spite of these findings, the Commission reported very few cases involving discrimination by apprenticeship programs, in violation of the New York State Law Against Discrimination. The reasons for this paucity of cases, according to SCAD, included the following: the Commission could not initiate investigations, but relied on complaints of aggrieved parties; discrimination in apprenticeship training is difficult to prove; few Negroes apply for apprenticeship positions; many people do not know that they have the right to file a complaint with the Commission (a conclusion that has been verified many times over during the course of our study).

Another study was released during the height of the 1963 summer demonstrations by the New York Advisory Committee to the U.S. Commission on Civil Rights, and concluded that "Negroes are denied access to employment in most of the building trades in New York City. The study further indicates that retention of present practices in admission to apprenticeship programs will mean that Negroes can expect no more than token participation in most of the building trades in the future."[7] The format of the 1963 report was similar to the earlier SCAD findings except that it indicated little had been done since 1960, except the notable action by IBEW Local 3—to be discussed below—about which the report is highly complimentary but pessimistic in its expectation that other unions might follow the example.

The third study, which was an outgrowth of the investigations begun by the New York City Commission on Human Rights (CCHR) during the 1963 street demonstrations over the issue of Negro participation in the building trades and released in December of that year, concluded:

The City Commission on Human Rights finds a pattern of exclusion in a substantial portion of the building and construction industry which effectively bars nonwhites from participating in this area of the city's economic life.

---

[6] In this regard, the Commission reported: "it appears that most indenturing units use criteria which do not lend themselves to objective measurement. Proper attitudes, correct motivation, a sense of responsibility, job interest, and general intellectual skills are deemed more valuable than specific attainments" (p. 87).

[7] "A Report of the New York Advisory Committee to the U.S. Commission on Civil Rights," reprinted in Senate Committee on Labor and Public Welfare, *The Role of Apprenticeship in Manpower Development: United States and Western Europe*, p. 1250.

The Commission finds the foregoing condition is the result of employer failure to accept responsibility for including minority group workers in the staffing of his projects, union barriers to Negro admittance, and government failure to enforce regulations barring discrimination.[8]

The CCHR recognized that "the city has no authority to enact legislation to outlaw race discrimination by trade unions"[9] but it felt that it was incumbent upon the state agencies to enforce the state laws in earnest. The CCHR report also criticized unions for not relying on vocational students: "It was shocking to hear from Board of Education representatives that many union officials did not seek apprentices, or permit realistic applications from graduates of training schools in the very area of the unions' jurisdiction. Since many nonwhites attend such schools before they learn the true state of affairs, the union rejection of this source of apprentices is most destructive."[10] As will be indicated shortly, however, academic students seem to perform much better than vocational students on apprenticeship tests.

Since 1963, the Building and Construction Trades Council has released figures indicating the number of nonwhites admitted to various apprenticeship programs. Table 4-2 shows the number of apprentices and Table 4-3 shows the number of nonwhite journeymen admitted over the same time span. Care must be taken in evaluating these figures, since Puerto Ricans are often included as nonwhites in New York City statistics, and these tables do not indicate the number who have dropped out after having been admitted.

Nevertheless, there can be little question that in spite of uneven progress in some apprenticeship programs, developments since 1961 have caused considerable change in New York programs. We turn our attention next to some of the more important of these developments.

THE 1963 DEMONSTRATIONS

On May 15, 1963, a civil rights group, known as the Joint Committee for Equal Employment Opportunity (JCEEO),[11] announced plans to picket the construction site of the Harlem Hospital to pro-

---

[8] The City Commission on Human Rights, "Bias in the Building Industry: An Interim Report to the Mayor" (December, 1963), p. 10.

[9] *Ibid.*, p. 23.

[10] *Ibid.*, p. 15.

[11] JCEEO's membership was composed of representatives of the New York chapter of CORE, the Negro-American Labor Council, the Workers Defense League, the Urban League of Greater New York, and the Association of Catholic Trade Unionists.

Table 4-2

Nonwhite Participation in Apprenticeship Programs in Selected
Building Trades Unions since March, 1963

Union	Nonwhite Apprentices Admitted		Total Nonwhite Apprentices Admitted
	1963–65	1965–66	1963–66
Carpenters District Council	623	7	630
Operating Engineers 15	7	(no program)	7
IBEW 3	240	35[a]	275
Ironworkers 361	8	N.A.	8
Ironworkers 40	N.A.	14	14
Elevator Constructors	N.A.	2	2
Plumbers 1	16	6	22
Plumbers 2	9	0	9
Sheet Metal Workers 28	0	12	12
Steamfitters 638	9	6[b]	15

[a] Data supplied by Workers Defense League.
[b] Data supplied by Area Coordinator for the U.S. Equal Employment Opportunity Commission.
N.A., not available.
Based on data obtained from N.Y. City Building and Construction Trades Council (except where indicated).

test discrimination in the building trades. The committee demanded that 25 per cent of the employees at the job site be Negroes or Puerto Ricans (at the time, nine of the sixty-four employees, or 14 per cent, were Negroes). JCEEO had asked for a meeting between all parties to discuss the subject. Although Acting Mayor Paul R. Screvane offered to meet with them, the unions and the contractor refused to do so and the Joint Committee started picketing the site in June. After two days of intermittent clashes with police, the Acting Mayor ordered the suspension of the construction work "in order to develop a climate" to study the charges. During the period of cessation, the city was liable for $3,000 to $4,000 a week in payments to the contractor for maintenance and protection costs.

The demonstrations at the Harlem Hospital project were part of an attempt to shut down all publicly aided construction in the city until 25 per cent of the jobs were filled by Negroes and Puerto Ricans. Accordingly, demonstrations began during the summer at the Rutgers Housing Project (on the lower East Side), the Downstate Medical Center (in Brooklyn), at Rochdale Village Housing

Table 4-3

Nonwhite Journeymen Admitted to Selected Building Trades Unions
between March, 1963, and March, 1966

Union	Nonwhite Journeymen Admitted		Total Nonwhite Journeymen Admitted
	1963–65	1965–66	1963–66
Carpenters District Council	276	146	422
Operating Engineers 15	55	N.A.	55
IBEW 3	N.A.	N.A.	
Ironworkers 361	N.A.	N.A.	
Ironworkers 40	N.A.	7	7
Plumbers 1	14	1	15
Plumbers 2	10	2	12
Sheet Metal Workers 28	0	0	0
Steamfitters 638	N.A.	N.A.	
Elevator Constructors	3	N.A.	3

N.A., not available.
Based on data obtained from N.Y. City Building and Construction Trades
Council.

Project (in Jamaica), and Madison Houses (in Harlem). Blocking access to job sites, daily sit-ins at the Mayor's office (lasting ultimately for forty-four days), sit-ins at the Governor's office in the city, clashes with police, and over 650 arrests of demonstrators at those sites kept the issue in the headlines. Meetings were held between union, civil rights, and city and state government officials.

The first indications of progress toward a settlement came on July 23, 1963, when the city's Building and Construction Trades Council announced a plan to establish a specific referral committee (to be discussed below) to assist in processing applications from nonwhites. Shortly afterward, on August 1, 1963, Plumbers Local 1, which was all white in membership, announced that it would admit two Negro "helpers" at the Downstate Medical Center.

In mid-August, 1963, the City Commission on Human Rights began public hearings on the issue of racial bias in the construction industry. The union officials were subpoenaed to appear after they ignored requests to meet informally with minority groups and local government officials, an action seen as a "snub" by the demonstration leaders, who then intensified their efforts. Against this backdrop, the first tangible results of the demonstrations began to show.

During the second week of August, 1963, a special referral program was established for the purpose of compiling a list of qualified Negro journeymen and Negro apprentice-applicants. The immediate impetus for the committee's formation was an accord reached between Governor Nelson Rockefeller and a group of Brooklyn ministers (known as the Committee for Job Opportunities in Brooklyn) who had participated in the demonstrations at the site of the Downstate Medical Center. The Governor ordered the New York State Employment Service to assign special "consultants and advisers" to two recruitment centers to be opened by the ministers. In return, the ministers withdrew their moral and financial support from the demonstrations. The list of names was to be forwarded to the Referral Committee of the Building Trades which had been established a few days earlier. The recruitment centers—which turned out to be three in number—were opened on August 12, 1963.

Within a week after Rockefeller's plan was made operative, Mayor Robert Wagner announced, in a top priority "directive," that the city would open seventeen offices on August 19, 1963, for the registration of Negro and Puerto Rican applicants for jobs in the construction industry. The city's Department of Labor was assigned the responsibility for co-ordinating the effort. City residents who signed up at one of these were sent to the Referral Committee of the Building Trades for interviewing. At the same time, the Mayor announced the city's appointment of Morris Tarshis—a personal aide to the Mayor on labor matters—to serve on the three-man appeals panel for those who felt unjustly treated by the Referral Committee.

There was apparently some competition for political visibility between the Governor's office and the Mayor's office in setting up these dual channeling bodies. In fact, in Brooklyn the Mayor's program set up shop *in the same office* in the Bedford YMCA Building in which the Governor's program was recruiting. One of the ministers for the Governor's group stated: "In order to keep peace we moved out into the hall."[12] There was never any effort to co-ordinate the two drives. Indicative of the hasty preparations involved, the city's application forms did not solicit the age of the applicant, which is almost always necessary for entry decisions into apprenticeship programs.

12 *New York Times,* August 20, 1963.

THE RODGERS COMMITTEE

On August 9, 1963, a special biracial committee was formed to screen and interview Negro and Puerto Rican applicants who believed themselves qualified for journeyman or apprentice status in the construction industry. Known as the Building Industry of New York City Referral Committee (or as the Rodgers Committee, after its chairman), the six-man committee was appointed by Peter Brennan, President of the New York City Building and Construction Trades Council, who was an ex officio member of the Committee. The Committee interviewed and screened applicants referred to it by civil rights groups, the State Employment Service, the two special governmental recruitment programs discussed above, or by individuals through written application to a special post office box. The interviews were held at a downtown hotel, rather than in a union hall, to overcome any hesitancy that any applicant might have. The members of the committee served without pay and the cost of the operation (about $9,000) was paid entirely by the Building Trades Council. The findings and results of the efforts were released in a report issued in December, 1963.[13]

To be interviewed by the committee, an applicant (1) had to be either Negro or Puerto Rican and (2) had to have lived in the city for at least two years. After he was interviewed, the applicant was either rejected or referred to the local union in the trade applied for. Referral did not constitute admission; those rejected, on the other hand, had the option to appeal to a special three-man committee (one man appointed by the Governor, one by the Mayor, and one by the Secretary of Labor). The referral committee met twenty-four times between August 9 and October 26, 1963.

A total of 1,624 Negroes and Puerto Ricans expressed an interest in apprenticeship. Of this number 528 were rejected before being interviewed (129, because they were nonresidents; 202, because they were either over or under age for apprentice programs; and 197, because they lacked minimal education). Thus, 1,096 were scheduled to be interviewed. Of this number 426 (or 39 per cent) did not appear. The remaining 670 were personally interviewed with the result that 573 (or 85 per cent) were referred and 97 were rejected for the following reasons: lack of minimal education—21; over- or under-age—20; nonresidents—6; not Negro or Puerto Rican—50.[14]

The Rodgers Committee also attempted to refer journeymen. A

[13] "Report of the Building Industry of New York Referral Committee" (December 18, 1963).

[14] All figures in this paragraph are taken from *ibid.*, pp. 4 and 5.

total of 494 individuals applied to the committee for journeyman positions: 243 were rejected (57, because they were nonresidents; 54, because they had no construction experience; and 132, because they had no journeyman experience). Accordingly, 241 were to be interviewed, but 72 did not show up (or 28 per cent). Of the 179 actually interviewed, 109 (or 61 per cent) were referred and 70 were rejected. The 70 rejectees were disqualified on the following grounds: 23 had no journeyman experience, 21 had no construction experience, 2 because of age, 24 were not Negro or Puerto Rican.[15]

The specific unions to which the referrals were made are shown in Table 4-4. Of the 682 referred, the information provided on

Table 4-4

Referrals Made by the Rodgers Committee to Specific
Building Trades, 1963

Trade	Apprentices	Journeymen	Totals
Boilermakers	3		3
Bricklayers	110	4	114
Carpenters	135	13	148
Cement Masons	12	10	22
Electricians	139	23	162
Elevator Constructors	10		10
Operating Engineers 15	16	3	19
Operating Engineers 30	2		2
Operating Engineers 94	1		1
Glaziers	4		4
Ironworkers 40	14	2	16
Ironworkers 580	6		6
Lathers 46	4	2	6
Lathers 308		1	1
Painters	39	19	58
Plasterers	4	8	12
Plumbers 1	14	7	21
Plumbers 2	5	9	14
Roofers	14	1	15
Sheet Metal Workers	28	3	31
Steamfitters	8	1	9
Stone Setters	1		1
Tile Layers	4	2	6
Waterproofers (Roofers)		1	1
Total	573	109	682

Based on data in "Report of the Building Industry of New York Referral Committee" (December 18, 1963), p. 7A.

---

15 *Ibid.*, pp. 4 and 6.

actual placement is somewhat sketchy. A total of 111 referrals was accounted for in the report, and action was still pending on many applications at the time of issuance of the final report. In aggregate terms, 81 of the 111 were accepted; 28 (or 25 per cent) failed to appear at the union halls; and only two were rejected who actually applied to the unions. It is clear, however, from a review of Table 4-5 that many of those whom the unions had accepted decided not to avail themselves of the opportunity once it was offered to them.

Table 4-5

Specific Placements of Initial Referrals by the Rodgers Committee

Cement Masons	9 accepted (no break-down between apprentices and journeymen)
Elevator Constructors	9 accepted (no break-down between apprentices and journeymen)
Operating Engineers 15	4 apprentices accepted (10 more placed on list for consideration for next class)
	3 journeymen accepted
Operating Engineers 30	1 apprentice accepted
Glaziers	4 apprentices accepted
Lathers 46	4 apprentices accepted
Painters	18 apprentices accepted
	3 journeymen accepted (4 others accepted, but they declined)
Carpenters	3 journeymen accepted
	43 apprentices accepted
	(a) 5 did not show up to the District Council to be interviewed
	(b) 2 declined membership
	(c) <u>36</u> were referred to locals
	43 (subtotal)
	36 referred to locals
	(a) 22 failed to report to the local
	(b) 7 reported but failed to return for initiation and placement
	(c) 1 reported but declined membership
	(d) <u>6</u> reported and were employed
	36 (subtotal)
Operating Engineers 94	1 apprentice selected
Structural Steel and Bridge Painters 806	7 journeymen accepted 1 apprentice accepted
Painters 1456	2 accepted (no break-down between journeymen and apprentices)

Based on data in "Report of the Building Industry of New York Referral Committee" (December 18, 1963), pp. 15–18.

Such is clearly the case with the carpenters' experience. Accordingly, actual placements were far fewer than the number of referrals.

In passing it should be noted that IBEW Local 3 did not take any of the referrals since their class was full (details to be discussed below); Sheet Metal Workers Local 28 informed the committee that it would postpone action on any referrals until after the outcome of a pending legal suit on a charge of discrimination (also discussed below); and the bricklayers' district council reported that due to high unemployment in the trade it would take no action on referrals until employment conditions improved.

As indicated above, 1,624 originally applied to be interviewed for apprentice positions, and 494 applied for journeymen positions in the building trades. The work of the Rodgers Committee, however, was delayed by the fact that it had to process an additional 1,003 applications of individuals who were not Negroes or Puerto Ricans,[16] who were applying for apprenticeship positions in occupations outside of the building trades, or who were simply looking for jobs.

The Rodgers Committee drew two important conclusions from its efforts. First, massive campaigns to recruit applicants can be a fruitless undertaking: 498 (or 25 per cent) of the applicants for apprentice and journeymen positions did not show up for the referral interview[17] and many others failed to apply once referred. Secondly, the Committee came to the following critical conclusion on the preparation of the youths who appeared before it:

One of the greatest eye openers to this Committee was the apparent abandoning of many youths in our school system. Most of the Committee was shocked that boys who were graduates of our vocational high schools or who had at least two years in these schools could not spell such words as "brick," "carpenter," "building," etc., or could not add inches and feet. . . . It is quite apparent that they are the product of a social system that pushed them through the earlier grades of school without insuring that they had the basic tools necessary for a minimal academic education. They were shunted to the dumping ground of the "vocational school."

We call attention to this problem because the apprentice in any trade must come equipped with these tools. It has been the experience of many who direct apprentice programs that the apprentice with a firm academic schooling fares better than the vocational trained apprentice. We see a

---

16 Interestingly, the rejection of white applicants led to four separate discrimination charges against the Committee with the city and state human relations committee.

17 These figures do not include those who could not be interviewed at prescribed times. All of those who notified the Committee of time conflicts had new appointments made at convenient times. Two applicants of this broad recruitment effort stated "they were recruited in the park [and] did not know what it was all about and had no desire for any training" (ibid., p. 12).

very good lesson for those who are interested in minority groups entering the skilled crafts.[18]

Summing up its work, the Committee stated: "We had been led to believe that there were thousands who couldn't gain admittance into the building trades unions. As a committee we felt that the numbers who came forward were small and those qualified were even smaller in number."[19]

In April, 1964, the Appellate Division of the State Supreme Court reversed a lower court ruling and dismissed unanimously an NAACP suit to halt $10 million in state and city construction work. Ten construction unions in New York City whose practices the NAACP believed to be discriminatory were the indirect targets of the action. However, the Court warned that the racial exclusionary policies of some of these unions "are of so long duration and so widely known that courts might, if they so elected, take judicial notice of the fact."[20]

During 1965, the apprenticeship issue temporarily receded in New York—as it did in Cleveland—due to the fact that municipal elections were to be held in both cities in November. No party wished to play into the hands of the other nor to offend any major power group. In New York, the Republicans captured the Mayor's office and restaffed the City Commission on Human Rights (CCHR). The issue of minority participation in apprenticeship programs—in the spotlight so frequently over the past few years—was involved in the campaign. In 1966, the CCHR announced its intention to investigate the issue thoroughly. William H. Booth, formerly an official of the NAACP and the new director of the CCHR, announced that public hearings would be conducted and a report would be issued. But after an initial uproar and a near confrontation, it was decided that for the time being attention would be focused primarily on Plumbers Local 2, which (as reported by BAT) was the only construction apprentice program of the 106 in the city not in compliance with the state's apprenticeship standards. The only other apprenticeship programs investigated during the hearings were Plumbers Local 1 and Steamfitters Local 638. The CCHR also decided to give more concern to the issue of placement of qualified minority journeymen on jobs and watch developments in the apprenticeship area for a while. It is reported, however, that one out-

[18] Ibid., pp. 12–13.
[19] New York Times, December 19, 1963.
[20] New York Times, April 22, 1964.

growth of this latest near-showdown between the city and the unions has been an agreement that all unions will give open tests for apprenticeship classes. The use of tests would include IBEW Local 3, which has admitted the most Negroes—all of them without being given a formal written test.

IBEW LOCAL 3

IBEW Local 3's experiences with Negro apprentices have been without parallel in the electrical industry. With over 34,000 members, Local 3 is one of the largest single locals in the construction trades. The union has two broad categories of members: "A" Division, which does the construction work, and "BA" Division, which does manufacturing work. About 30 per cent of the membership is in "A" Division and 70 per cent is in "BA" Division. Prior to 1962, almost all minority members were in "BA" Division—mostly holding semiskilled and unskilled jobs. Minority representatives in 1961 totaled 1,500 Negroes and 3,000 Puerto Ricans, or 4,500 in all.

Traditionally, eligibility for apprenticeship in the New York electrical industry was based upon a father–son relationship. In the early sixties, however, Harry Van Arsdale, Local 3's business representative, sought to broaden the opportunity base for admission by also making sons of its "BA" members eligible for apprentice positions in the "A" Division. In this way, the sons of the 4,500 minority members were also made eligible.

In 1961, when the local had 900 apprentices, Edward Mays became the first Negro to graduate from the industry's five-year apprentice-training program.

However, Local 3's past apprentice recruitment pattern underwent a drastic reversal during 1962. As an outgrowth of contract negotiations in which the twenty-five-hour week was established, Van Arsdale announced that his union would increase sharply the number of apprentices selected for the next class and that every effort would be made to assure substantial minority participation.

In complying with the terms of the contract, Local 3 sent out 2,000 letters on April 3, 1962, requesting the submission of applications. Civil rights groups, employers, vocational high schools, and other unions in the city were all notified. The Urban League responded with fifty-one names and the NAACP with fifty-seven. A total of 1,600 completed applications was received. To review the applications, a special three-man screening committee was established, consisting or Dr. Harry J. Carman, Dean Emeritus of Columbia College; Robert McCormick, Director of Apprentice Training of the Joint Industry Board; and Edward Mays, Assistant to McCormick and, as mentioned above, the first Negro ever to graduate from the apprentice program and receive an "A" journeyman's card. The qualifications established by the committee were a high school diploma, a desire to go to college, and age of eighteen to twenty-one. There was no written test given to any applicant. In fact, no written tests had ever been given for admission into the local's apprenticeship classes before the 1966 changes mentioned above.

The class selected in 1962 totaled 1,020 new first-year apprentices (more than the total number in the entire five-year program at that time). Of this number, 240 were Negroes and 60 were Puerto Ricans.[21] The 300 minority apprentices were placed in the regular apprenticeship training class which would lead to full journeyman status with Class "A" membership. The significance of this event cannot be stated in strong enough terms; its importance can be gauged by the fact that the U.S. Census of 1960 reported only 79 Negro electrical apprentices in the entire nation.

Our attempts to find details on the progress of the class have not been particularly successful. But the limited information available shows that about 20 per cent of the minority members dropped out by January, 1966, which is above the IBEW's national average of about 5 per cent dropouts.[22] Of the 1,020 admitted in 1962, 100 had dropped out by the end of 1965, about 50 of whom were reported to be Negroes.

On January 14, 1966, almost 200 apprentices became journeymen. Of this number 7 were reported to be Negroes. The large class of 1962 is scheduled to graduate in 1967.

The Workers Defense League, which has devoted considerable attention to efforts to increase nonwhite participation in apprenticeship programs, reports that it has had excellent co-operation with the union in general and with Van Arsdale in particular. During 1965, in fact, the League reports that the local accepted thirty-five minority applicants recruited by the WDL.[23] All were admitted

[21] The figures showing the number of Negroes admitted in 1962 were supplied by officials of the WDL, the Building and Construction Trades Council, and other interviews in the city. This figure is higher than that reported in "The Report of the New York Advisory Committee to the United States Commission on Civil Rights," reproduced in Senate Committee on Labor and Public Welfare, *The Role of Apprenticeship in Manpower Development: United States and Western Europe*, pp. 1253–54. That report showed only 140 Negroes admitted. *All* other sources interviewed have reported 240 Negroes were admitted.

[22] Field interviews with IBEW Local 3 officials.

[23] Field interviews with WDL officials.

without being required to take a written examination. One of the thirty-five has subsequently been elected vice-president of his apprenticeship class. In addition to these thirty-five registered apprentices, the WDL has been able to place fifteen Negro college students in the local as third-year apprentices at $3.50 an hour. They are able to return each summer as fill-ins for vacationing journeymen. Moreover, Van Arsdale has personally intervened with other unions (specifically the Machinists District Council 15, the Utility Workers, the Communication Workers, and the Painters District Council) on behalf of WDL programs.

Negroes within the IBEW formed a special club in 1958, known as the Lewis Howard Lattimer[24] Progressive Association, which serves as an ethnic-fraternal-civil rights group. Its specific objectives are:

1. to encourage Negroes to become instructors at the apprenticeship school (there is only one Negro instructor currently on the staff);
2. to encourage Negro apprentices to help each other to stay in the program;
3. to encourage other Negro youths to enter the program; and
4. to contribute money to civil rights groups for worthwhile projects.

It is estimated that there are about 200 members in the club, presumably all Negro Local 3 members.

SHEET METAL WORKERS LOCAL 28

In March, 1964, the State Commission for Human Rights (NYSCHR, formerly the State Commission Against Discrimination) ruled that Sheet Metal Workers Local 28 had systematically barred Negroes throughout its seventy-six-year history. Although the NYSCHR's action was based on a verified complaint of James Ballard (a Negro apprentice applicant) filed by the State Attorney General with the State Commission in late 1962, the decision was seen as revolutionary in that it was based upon the existence of a historical pattern of exclusion rather than relying entirely on a specific complaint.

The union appealed the NYSCHR decision that it was guilty of discrimination, and on review the Supreme Court of New York

[24] Lattimer was a Negro electrical engineer who worked with Thomas Edison and Alexander Graham Bell.

County upheld the Commission's findings *in toto*.[25] The Court out-lawed as "illegal and unconstitutional" the union's customary father-son preference. The Court also agreed with the Commission's proposal that affirmative relief be taken by the union to open up its membership ranks to all qualified applicants. Shortly after-ward, the Court accepted a plan drawn up by the industry concern-ing the selection methods for the next class of apprentices. It was agreed that sixty-five apprentices were to be admitted into a class to be formed not later than March 15, 1965. As a further stipulation, the Court stated that it expected that new classes would be formed thereafter on a regular basis. After forming the spring class of 1965, however, the union announced that it would not form its customary fall class of sixty-five apprentices. The union, however, later agreed to form a new class but balked over being told how large it was to be. Hence, the Court, on October 30, 1965, issued a second order directing that a class of sixty-five be formed on or before October 30, 1965. Both the employers and the unions appealed this order, claiming that it represented judicial interference. Class size, they contended, had nothing to do with the discriminatory practices condemned in the original ruling. On December 10, 1965, the New York Supreme Court, Appellate Division, affirmed the lower Court's ruling that a second class be formed in 1965 and that it consist of sixty-five apprentices. As will be discussed shortly, this class ulti-mately had eleven Negroes in it. The Court's decision included the following important comment: "There is a distinction between compelling integration and the termination of discrimination. A party has the right not be excluded from the union because of race, creed or religious persuasion. Quite different would be the asser-tion of a right—non-existent under the Law Against Discrimination—to have the union take affirmative steps looking toward integra-tion."[26] The Court clearly distinguishes between "integration" and "discrimination"—a distinction that has important implications for the legality of so-called affirmative action proposals to correct past discriminatory practices or patterns.

With respect to the successful WDL Negro recruitees for the sheet metal program, our interviews with union and employer apprentice-ship officials have had somewhat polar evaluations. One union official caustically concluded that "some of the group don't pay fees on time, come late to the job and school, and miss school; some are O.K." On the other hand, the president of a large sheet-metal

25 *State Commission for Human Rights* v. *Farrell,* 252 NYS 2d 649.
26 *Daily Labor Report* No. 236, December 8, 1965, p. A-1.

company with over 400 employees stated: "This [WDL] experiment brought about substantial improvement in the quality of applicants in general, including whites. If the WDL operation continues, there may well be both an influx of Negroes along with a raising of the quality of apprentices." In passing it is useful to add the comments of this same employer spokesman concerning the oral interview part of the admission procedure: "The personal interview section of the application process was not professional enough; it was too subjective. Monkey business could take place here. Trained professionals should be in the picture. This was a burden to the JAC members. We gave almost everybody the same personal interview score because we over-reacted to a sensitive issue."

PLUMBERS LOCAL 2

In April, 1964, the spring building season in New York was ushered in with a new confrontation that centered upon minority participation. On April 30, 1964, all the plumbers on a $25 million city construction site, the Terminal Market, in the Bronx, struck when three nonunion Puerto Rican and one nonunion Negro plumber reported to work. The nonunion plumbers had been hired by a contractor who had made an agreement with the City Commission on Human Rights (CCHR) to hire from minority groups. The four men were interviewed in late April, 1964, and told to report to work on April 30. Following the union walkout, the four filed charges with the CCHR alleging that they were being discriminated against by Plumbers Local 2. Labeling the Plumbers' action a "disgrace to unionism," the *New York Times* editorialized:

> Their [Local 2] racial boycott is doubly shameful because they belong to the local that gave George Meany his start toward the presidency of the AFL-CIO. Mr. Meany has labored hard to translate into actuality the pledges of racial equality contained in the federation's constitution. Peter T. Schoemann, the plumbers' international president, has repeatedly told all the union's locals that their function is to organize, not to exclude, and their charters will be revoked if units persist in Jim Crow policies.[27]

On May 1, 1964, the plumbers again refused to work, claiming that they would not work with nonunion men. The CCHR began proceedings to cancel the building contract because of discriminatory practices. It was the first time that any governmental agency in the state had initiated such a step. As the stalemate entered its seventh working day, President Lyndon Johnson requested that

[27] *New York Times,* May 2, 1964.

Secretary of Labor Wirtz investigate the matter. At the same time, AFL-CIO President Meany dispatched two aides from the AFL-CIO Civil Rights Department to gather the facts concerning the dispute. On May 11, 1964, CORE started picketing in front of Local 2's headquarters and staged a sit-in inside the lobby of the union's office building. Finally, on May 15, 1964, after the walkout had lasted two weeks, an accord was announced by Mayor Wagner, accompanied by George Meany. It was agreed that the regular journeyman's examination would be given the four men, and, if they passed, their applications would be accepted so that they could go to work immediately. Although Meany criticized the CCHR for forcing the company to hire the four men and was quoted as saying on the same day that the action of the local "was completely justified," since it "is the practice of American labor to work with union men,"[28] he was nevertheless instrumental in the settlement.

Mayor Wagner also sharply rebuked the CCHR for its role in the affair, claiming that the dispute had gotten out of hand and the CCHR was "never again to act as an employment agency for minority groups."[29] As of that date, in fact, the CCHR was removed as a party to the subsequent proceedings by directive from the Mayor.

Hopes for an end to the impasse were soon dashed, however, because the four workers refused to take the examination. The attorney for the group said that it was illegal (allegedly violating the Taft-Hartley ban on the closed shop since only the employer has the right to determine the qualifications of his employees) for the union to give the test. On May 18, 1964, when the four showed up for work they were told they were "not hired" by the contractor since they refused to take the test.[30] Work was resumed by the other union members. Commenting on the developments, Meany stated he wished "they would take it and pass it."[31] On the evening of May 18, three of the nonunion plumbers relented and, in the presence of the CCHR representatives and the press, took the journeyman's test. They all failed. Subsequently, the three filed charges with NLRB alleging that the union had violated the Taft-Hartley Act by causing the employer—through the strike—to discontinue the employment of the Negro and Puerto Rican employees.

28 *New York Times*, May 16, 1963, pp. 1 and 38.
29 *New York Times*, May 23, 1964.
30 *New York Times*, May 17, 1964.
31 *New York Times*, May 19, 1964.

On June 5, 1965, the NLRB ruled against Plumbers Local 2 by holding that in no instance may union membership be a condition of employment prior to the expiration of the seven-day grace period allowed by the NLRB (after which time the union may admit them or else they can stay on the job as nonunion employees) and that standards for judging competency for admission to the union cannot be limited to the passing of a particular union's test.[32] While the decision did not pertain specifically to racial discrimination, it was heralded by an NAACP spokesman as "a real breakthrough against the discriminatory practices of unions."[33]

DEVELOPMENTS IN THE PRINTING INDUSTRY

In New York, printing is a major industry. Indeed, the industry's trade association claims that printing is the second largest industry in the city.

In appraising the degree of minority participation, the 1960 SCAD report (mentioned earlier) stated that "in the printing trades (with the exception of the Printing Pressman's Assistants Union), Negroes either serve in insignificant numbers or not at all."[34] Printing apprentices traditionally have been drawn from a class of shop employees who perform utility work.[35] Prior to 1964, apprentices were selected on the basis of the length of time they had been employed in a shop and on the basis of performance on an examination conducted by the New York School of Printing until 1961 and thereafter by the New York State Employment Service.

During contract negotiations in 1962 and 1963, the issue of the supply of qualified apprentices was raised by representatives of both Typographers Local 6 and management. The long period that many employees had to work in utility jobs until apprenticeship openings, averaging about one hundred a year, occurred sometimes lasted up to eight years. It was felt that many promising workers consequently became dissatisfied and left the industry. Such was especially the case of disadvantaged youths, since they more frequently had to help supplement a low family income and were more susceptible to the inducement of higher-paying short-run job offers.

[32] 59 *Labor Relations Reference Manual,* pp. 1234–38.

[33] *New York Times,* June 6, 1965.

[34] New York State Commission Against Discrimination, *Apprentices, Skilled Craftsmen and the Negro: An Analysis,* p. 64.

[35] "Public Report of the Joint Printing Industry Board on the Selection of Apprentices," compiled by Theodore W. Kheel (undated mimeographed material), pp. 2–3.

In 1963, Typographers Local 6—the largest local in the industry with close to 10,000 members—reported that it had about 42 Negroes and Puerto Ricans out of the 600 apprentices in its six-year program.[36]

Local 6's 1963 collective bargaining contract amended the apprentice-selection procedure and added a nondiscrimination pledge. The parties sought to implement this pledge by agreeing to give an annual "industrywide" written examination and made the practice of selecting apprentices from "helpers" who had been in the utility pool for at least six months a formal requirement for apprentices. This requirement conforms with the New York apprenticeship regulations and was thought to be beneficial to minorities who were well represented in the helper classification. In the summer of 1966, for example, the pool consisted of about 1,000 utility workers, of whom about 400 were from minority groups. The WDL program placed five Negroes in this pool in 1966. In addition, "an appropriate impartial agency" was to conduct and grade the examination. An appeals procedure under which cases were sent to an outside arbitrator was also included in the plan. The 1963 contract also provided that the number of apprentices to be selected would be announced prior to the day of the test and that the examination subjects to be included would be specified. The written test covered reading comprehension, grammar, spelling, mathematics, general aptitudes, and knowledge of the trade. All successful applicants would be ranked in order of their scores and indentured as vacancies occurred.

The testing procedure included three stages: (1) an aptitude test and an appraisal interview given by the New York State Employment Service; (2) a series of written examinations over subjects and material specified in the contract, administered by the New York City School of Printing; and (3) service credits awarded for length of service. The points given at each stage were as follows:[37]

1. Aptitude test and interview	0	OR	40 points
2. Educational skills (reading, spelling, grammar)	0	OR	10 points
3. Arithmetic ability	0	to	30 points
4. Trade knowledge	0	to	20 points
			100 points

36 *Ibid.*, p. 2.
37 *Ibid.*, p. 10.

In addition to the 100 points set forth in the aforementioned program, each applicant received 3.33 points (up to a maximum of 15 points) for each year he had been in the union.

The aptitude test points were given on an "all-or-nothing" scoring basis. Its purpose was to be a "hurdle" over which all who demonstrated an ability to learn could pass, but which would virtually assure that all those who did not pass would be disqualified. If an applicant performed poorly on the written aptitude tests but showed great potential during the interview he could be awarded the full 40 points given for the aptitude test and would progress to Stage Two. The written examination, on spelling, grammar, and reading, "was a demonstration of a sufficient level of educational skills to profit from apprenticeship."[38] The level of proficiency required was set at the eighth-grade level.[39] The remainder of the examination was on arithmetic and on trade knowledge. The entire compilation and ranking process was done by Professor Albert Thompson of Teachers College, Columbia University.

Prior to the test, a briefing meeting was held to inform all interested parties of the procedures. At that time, sample tests were given out. According to one interviewee, many minority people looked at the examination and became discouraged over their ability to pass it. For this reason, they failed to pursue the opportunity further. The most awesome part of the examination, according to the interviewee, was the arithmetic section. Ironically, the heavy weight given to mathematics over the verbal skills section (30 points as opposed to 10) was due to the expressed belief that math "is less influenced by language performance"[40] and would be less of an obstacle to those with poorer educational backgrounds.

The first test under the new procedures was administered on October 31, 1964. Of the 1,000 employees in the pool, about 350 were Negroes and Puerto Ricans. A total of 602 individuals requested application blanks; of this number 456 were screened (of whom only 36 were Negroes and Puerto Ricans) by the employment service at the first stage of the admission procedure; 350 actually took the written test given at the second stage. Ultimately, once the ranking process was complete, 71 persons appeared on the eligible list—two were Negroes and one was a Puerto Rican.

In assessing the outcome of the first program, the industry felt

38 *Ibid.*, p. 9.
39 *Ibid.*
40 "The 1966 Testing Procedure," compiled by Theodore W. Kheel (undated mimeographed material).

that the most significant explanation for the lack of successful minority applicants was that so few actually availed themselves of the opportunity (only 36 of approximately 350 eligible minority people participated in the first step of the procedure).[41]

The second industrywide examination was given in the spring of 1966. With only minor exceptions, the testing procedure was identical to that followed previously. About 400 applicants attended the briefing session (of whom 150 were estimated to be Negroes), and prior to the test 300 applicants attended two weeks of special review classes sponsored by the union (about 125 of whom were estimated to be Negroes).[42] Approximately 250 individuals actually took the examination. A total of 58 applicants successfully completed the testing procedure and were admitted into the program. Twelve of the 58 were Negroes.

Although our interviewees generally thought the printing industries procedure was "fair," one said it was either very fair or the "greatest dodge" yet devised. The implication of his remark was that the formulators of the plan, which is permissible under New York's nondiscrimination standards as an alternative to selection on the basis of qualifications alone, knew that few Negroes or Puerto Ricans would qualify. However, a more representative comment came from another interviewee: "it [the examination] is open to everybody. If a guy doesn't want to take the test, it is absolutely his fault . . . it is absolutely fair."

APPRENTICESHIP TRAINING
INFORMATION CENTER

On September 17, 1962, the first Apprenticeship Training Information Center (ATIC) in the nation was formally opened in New York City. This center, not to be confused with the Apprenticeship Information Centers discussed in the other survey cities, was established by the city itself and is an organ of the New York City Department of Labor. The impetus for its establishment was an earlier recommendation made by the Mayor's Committee on Exploitation.[43] Information was made available about fifty-four ap-

[41] All figures presented in this paragraph are from "Public Report of the Joint Printing Industry Board on the Selection of Apprentices," compiled by Theodore W. Kheel, pp. 11–14.

[42] All estimates in this sentence were supplied by representatives of the Workers Defense League.

[43] A committee established to hear various complaints of individuals involving AFL-CIO-affiliated unions which were not satisfactorily adjusted in a two-week period and to offer suggested remedies.

prenticeship programs, including many building trades programs. Specifically included were those of the bricklayers, carpenters, electricians, glaziers, ironworkers, plasterers, painters, plumbers, roofers, sheet metal workers, and steamfitters. In its first year of operation it had 2,952 applicants, of whom 1,172 were Negroes. Information on subsequent years was not available but it seems that most referrals have been to apprenticeship programs outside the building and printing trades. Since the Center has no follow-up procedures, it is impossible to assess its success. But from the interviews conducted in the city with BAT, civil rights, union, and city and state antidiscrimination officials, the conclusion was unanimous that the center has had little if any impact on Negro participation in apprenticeship in the building and printing trades. In fact, several knowledgeable officials inquired as to whether it still existed. As for the interviews of Negro apprentices and apprentice applicants, there is no indication of the slightest awareness of the Center.

THE NEW YORK APPRENTICESHIP LAW

With the case of Sheet Metal Workers Local 28 in the headlines in early 1964, the apprenticeship issue was rekindled in the state legislature. Acting on the recommendation of the state Attorney General, a measure was introduced to make it "an unlawful discriminatory practice" to select persons for apprenticeship programs on any basis "other than their qualifications." The language of the proposed act had been composed by the State Civil Rights Bureau. The bill was brought before the lower house from the rules committee "in a surprise move" only a few days before the scheduled adjournment of the session. Immediately before the vote was taken a memorandum was circulated to many legislators from Raymond Corbett, President of the state AFL-CIO, indicating his organization's opposition to the proposal. The bill consequently was defeated by ten votes. Ostensibly, the opposition was concerned with the question of how the concept of apprentice selection "by objective criteria which permit review" would be enforced.

The state AFL-CIO's action drew immediate protests from civil rights, government, and even union representatives. Civil rights groups denounced Corbett's stand and threatened to renew their picketing of construction sites. The speaker of the Assembly, Joseph F. Carlino, joined in the criticism. A few days later, Corbett announced that the state AFL-CIO would withdraw its opposition since "our reasons for objecting to this bill have been misunderstood."[44] On March 24, 1964, shortly after Corbett's announcement, the bill was passed by a vote of 135 to 10 (out of 150 possible ballots).

Although the bill became law a few days later and was to become effective on September 1, 1964, a one-year grace period was allowed for apprenticeship programs to be brought into compliance. It is understood from our field interviews with state BAT officials in New York as of June, 1966, that all major programs in New York City, except that of Plumbers Local 2, were in compliance with the New York apprenticeship law. Plumbers Local 2 had not formed an apprenticeship class since the state provisions became effective, so there was a question concerning the legality of the noncompliance status of the union.

The New York regulations for equality in apprenticeship programs provide less latitude to the industry than the federal regulations in 29 CFR 30 (discussed in Chapter XIII). The New York regulations require the selection of apprentices "after full and fair opportunity for application on the basis of qualifications not based upon race . . . in accordance with objective standards which permit review." New York did not follow the federal example of permitting selections which "demonstrate results." Under the federal regulations, no control is exercised over the selection standards so long as they are objectively administered, but the New York regulations provide that "No program may be or remain registered unless it includes an acceptable selection procedure and acceptable standards for admission." The New York law also specifies that to be acceptable, tests must be reasonable, meaning "reasonably related to general intelligence and/or job aptitude and is developed and administered by competent organizations." In addition, the New York law requires apprenticeship sponsors to give applicants written statements of qualifications for admission and specify in writing the reasons why applicants are not appointed. Any applicant who is rejected must be notified that he may register a complaint with the NYSCHR "if he believes that his failure to qualify on the applicant list, or his ranking on such list, or his failure of appointment was caused by discrimination."

The penalties under the New York law are limited to deregistration. Program sponsors may have a hearing before programs are deregistered except where the NYSCHR has found discrimination. In that case the program may be deregistered without a hearing.

[44] *New York Times,* March 24, 1964.

THE WORKERS DEFENSE LEAGUE

The nucleus about which almost all activity for recruiting, preparing, and referring Negroes for apprenticeship openings has revolved in the city has been the pioneering effort of the Workers Defense League (WDL). Founded shortly before World War II as a human rights organization, the WDL moved into the apprenticeship area in 1963 as a participant in the JCEEO demonstrations. After the construction site was closed, it became very apparent to the civil rights leaders in general and the WDL staff in particular that they had no way to fill vacancies in apprenticeship programs even if they were made accessible. As a result, WDL decided to concentrate on the apprenticeship problem as one of its primary missions. At first it planned to do a case study of the reversal experience of IBEW Local 3. Instead, however, it decided to assume the more ambitious task of recruitment. But in order to accomplish this objective, it was first necessary for the League to determine the unions' admission standards. Information was not available from most of the unions, the state apprenticeship offices, or the ATIC (which apparently had more information on where and when to apply than on the actual standards for admission).

Thus, the WDL decided to begin its work by gathering and publishing a guide to the entry requirements of New York apprenticeship programs. After months of fruitless efforts to uncover these standards, the League found a man in the New York State Employment Service who had such a listing in his files. Once secured, the data was published and widely distributed by the WDL in a booklet entitled *Apprenticeship Training in New York, Openings in 1963.* The booklet listed 3,000 openings for apprentices and told exactly where and how to apply and—most important—what qualifications were prerequisites for application. Since many Negroes from the ghettos know what a carpenter is but have no idea what a sheet metal worker does and therefore would never apply to one of these unknown trades, each trade was carefully explained so that the reader would know exactly what the trade did. The handbook also sought to entice presently qualified minority people to apply for apprenticeship openings and to encourage potential applicants to acquire the necessary qualifications.

Early in 1964, the WDL received grants from the Taconic Foundation to undertake more extensive operations. In May, 1964, Ray Murphy, a New Jersey employment specialist with a Master's degree in psychology, became director of the WDL's apprenticeship program. Ernest Green joined him as his assistant. Full-scale operations commenced on June 1, 1964, with the opening of a special office in the Bedford-Stuyvesant section of Brooklyn, which is convenient to the heart of New York's minority community. After serving as a volunteer for several months, Dennis Derryck joined the staff in June, 1966, to take charge of the tutoring program.

Recruitment efforts and the dissemination of information have been the cornerstone of the WDL's efforts. A group of Brooklyn ministers had promised the WDL a list of 600 applicants for apprenticeship gathered in conjunction with the construction site demonstrations of the preceding year, but the ministers never made the list available, despite continual efforts to secure it. It was therefore necessary for the apprenticeship program to begin its work from scratch. Contact was established with other youth employment organizations in the city who were requested to refer all young people eligible and interested to WDL; information channels were established with various community organizations (such as churches, fraternal, and civil rights groups) through mailings and direct talks to meetings; membership was established with the Central Brooklyn Coordinating Council in order to co-ordinate WDL's work with the broader antipoverty program for the area; and liaison was begun with the school system, and with local school officials and counselors. WDL staff members made speeches to the students and conducted apprenticeship conferences at local schools.

In its initial efforts to collect a list of available applicants, the WDL staff gathered a list of 700 names from vocational schools in the area. Since many of the 300 applicants who actually presented themselves to the WDL for testing and screening were not qualified, the WDL found itself in the awkward position of being forced to tell many of the minority group respondents it had recruited that they were not eligible to enter an apprenticeship program. Such blanket efforts, therefore, have been replaced by new approaches which emphasized more selective recruitment.

In addition to locating minority applicants, an important explanation for the success of the WDL's work has been its ability to win the confidence of many union officials in the community. Initially, some local union officials thought that the League was "some Communist group," but their fears were quickly dissipated, because the League, unlike some other groups, was obviously more interested in getting Negroes and Puerto Ricans into apprenticeship programs than in embarrassing the unions. From the inception of its Apprenticeship Program, WDL has sought and has received consultative advice from local and national AFL-CIO civil rights staffs. Moreover, local union officials were contacted and informed of the League's objectives and methods. Its efforts are designed explicitly to avoid direct and dramatic public confrontations with the unions. In fact, the WDL reports that "the emphasis of the apprenticeship program has always been on placement of applicants (rather than on 'cases,' or education, publicity, or on pressure)."[45]

As a result, the WDL has by unwritten consent become the chief referral channel through which virtually all minority applicants must pass if they seek entry into an apprenticeship program in the city. Indicative of this accord is the fact that most of the major unions, which are under no legal compulsion to do so, now notify the WDL in advance of the dates on which entrance tests are to be given so that minority applicants can be assured of an opportunity to apply. It is apparent from our interviews with various union officials that the WDL representatives have worked hard to develop this rapport and hope to strengthen it in the future. Evidence of a feeling of relative achievement can be found in a 1966 report of the WDL activities for the preceding year. The report stated: "It is our impression that some trade unionists who now realize that their unions must be integrated are relieved to discover a responsible and reliable source with which to work."[46]

Unlike most of the recruiting efforts conducted by human relations boards or civil rights groups in other cities, the task of the WDL does not simply end with the provision of people to union examination sessions. The WDL goes much farther. Once notice of a forthcoming examination is received, a group of applicants is picked for special preparatory classes. The selected group—who are ideally "above average high school graduates . . . who can most easily obtain other work, or who think of higher education as an alternative"[47]—have all been interviewed and given a thirty-minute aptitude test (the Otis Quick Scoring Test of Mental Ability— Gamma C) by the WDL staff. The WDL defends its practice of concentrating—but not relying solely—on the cream of the crop of minority people because of its experience with the "time-lag problem" that has frequently been the pitfall of similar efforts in other cities. That is, there is frequently a long waiting period between

45 Workers Defense League, "Report of the Committee on Minority Employment Rights: Report of the Apprenticeship Program" (undated mimeographed material), p. 4.
46 Report to the Taconic Foundation from the Workers Defense League for the period June, 1965, through December, 1965, dated January 4, 1966, p. 3.
47 Ibid.

the time when an applicant initially expresses an interest in apprenticeship and the time when a class is officially formed. The WDL's experience (which agrees with the findings of our study in the other nine cities), is that "persistence—and without any assurance of eventual success—is rare among applicants."[48] With the advent of its full-scale tutoring program, however, the WDL reports that it has been able to lower its initial acceptance criteria. An enlarged staff and better instructional materials have enabled the WDL to broaden its tutorial program and to adjust to individual needs and abilities.

In addition to tutoring, the WDL provides a host of other vital services to its applicants which has added significantly to its successful placement experiences. Medical examinations are given without charge to the applicants through an arrangement made with the Medical Committee for Human Rights; loans are provided to needy applicants to pay application fees, initiation dues, and tools; donations are given to those who need financial assistance to pay for notary fees, photostat records of transcripts, transportation costs (to union halls, job sites, or to employer's offices); applications are processed for applicants which include such services as sending the materials by certified mail, writing to high schools for transcripts; or personal assistance in completing application forms (the Sheet Metal Workers' application form, for example, was nine pages in length); appeal cases are prepared by the WDL before union appeal boards and, if necessary, before public antidiscrimination authorities; and temporary jobs are found for needy applicants who must await the often lengthy union screening process (in this regard, many of these jobs have been secured through special arrangements made between the WDL and the New York Employment Service and with other unions such as the International Ladies Garment Workers Local 99, the Hospital Workers Union Local 1199, and the Drug and Retail Clerks Union, District 65).

A review of some of the WDL's specific experiences would be useful. As noted previously, when, early in 1965, Sheet Metal Workers Local 28 was ordered by the State Supreme Court to give its first entrance examination, there were 340 applicants for 65 positions (50 of whom were Negroes and Puerto Ricans). The WDL had recruited 28 of the Negro applicants. Dr. Kenneth Clark, director of the City College of New York Social Dynamics Institute, began a tutoring class on vocabulary and algebraic equations. The ex-

48 *Ibid.*, p. 3.

amination was given by the New York University Testing and Advisement Center on February 13, 1965. Scott Green, the brother of WDL's assistant director and one of the Negroes recruited by WDL, placed sixty-eighth, which was the highest of all of the Negroes tested (the next highest Negro placed ninety-seventh). But when three whites who made higher scores than Green declined to accept the openings offered to them, Green became the sixty-fifth man on the list. He, thus, became the first Negro ever to be admitted to the union.

In November, 1965, when the next apprenticeship class was formed by Local 28, 12 of 25 applicants sent by the WDL—all of whom had been recruited and given special preparatory work—placed among the top thirty taking the examination. One Negro dropped out, which left eleven who were accepted into the program. (Under another court order, Local 28 was directed to admit an additional 35 *applicants*. Two WDL applicants were among the next 35 but, since both of them dropped out, all of the additional 35 were white.) The results of the WDL program are indicated by the fact that of the first Local 28 class, 22 per cent of the whites and none of the Negroes placed among the top 65; but in the class that had been tutored intensively by the WDL, 56 per cent of the nonwhites (14 of 25) and 38 per cent (51 of 135) of the whites placed among the top 65. The WDL had far more notice prior to the November, 1965, examination than it had had for the preceding one. As a result, all of those who passed had attended the special classes conducted by a WDL staff member for two and a half hours every Tuesday, Thursday, and Saturday for two months prior to the examination. The tutoring sessions were geared to passing a specific test rather than toward providing a general education. Those who passed the written test were then briefed on what to expect from the oral interview.

Another Sheet Metal Workers class was formed in the Fall of 1966. Again the WDL sought to recruit and to prepare a group of Negro applicants. The group was tested in November, 1966. Of the 147 applicants who were actually examined, 32 were Negroes, 24 of whom passed the test. Thus, 75 per cent of the Negroes passed the test as compared with only 31 per cent of the whites. Moreover, of the top 10 scores, 9 were achieved by Negroes—one of whom had a perfect score. Indeed, the WDL applicants were so successful that Local 28's leadership suspected that the scores might have been obtained by "some nefarious means." The Local therefore proposed to re-test the group tested in November but were prohibited from doing so by the State Commission for Human Rights, which obtained an injunction against the union from the State Supreme Court.

Recently, with respect to its efforts to perform a similar miracle in placing Negroes into Plumbers Local 1, a new twist has been added to the Defense League's remedial program. Besides the WDL staff tutoring for the written examinations, several "volunteers" from Western Electric joined the program. In addition to attending tutorial sessions on test taking, basic mathematics, algebra, spatial relations, and mechanical reasoning, those who passed the written examination were invited to attend additional sessions after the written test. These sessions were mock oral interviews, with the Western Electric volunteers serving as make-believe members of the Joint Apprenticeship Committee.

The WDL's experience in recruiting for the Plumbers Local 1 examination given in July, 1966, is also revealing. Local 1 had notified the WDL on April 1, 1966, that it would accept applications until May 31, 1966, for its examination. The union stated that it would allow Murphy and Green to be co-sponsors for all applicants to the union from their office. Immediately, the WDL set out through all of its channels to locate interested applicants. Ultimately, fifty-one Negroes and Puerto Ricans were interviewed and pretested by WDL. The sources of the applicants are shown in Table 4-6. The city's academic schools, rather than the city's vocational schools, proved to be by far the more fruitful source of applicants to the skilled trades for minority youngsters. In most other

Table 4-6

Sources of Application to Workers Defense League for
Plumbers Local 1 Examination, Summer, 1966

Academic high schools	17
Antipoverty organizations	17
Sign in WDL office	6
Ad in *Amsterdam News*	4
Vocational schools	3
N.Y. State Employment Service	2
Churches	2
Community center	2
Civil rights organizations	1
Community college	1
Another apprentice	1
Total applicants	51

Based on data in Workers Defense League, "Memorandum" (May 9, 1966).

cities surveyed by the study, similar recruitment efforts have usually centered on vocational schools for candidates—usually with the same results. The experience of the WDL in this recent recruiting venture and in earlier attempts for other apprenticeship programs has proven to the WDL personnel that the academic schools are a rich source of talent—both with respect to numbers who apply and with respect to numbers who pass. The WDL's experience probably also supports the common assertion that vocational school youths are poorly educated.

Yet, lest one should conclude that the WDL's efforts never fail, its experiences with the 1966 class of apprentices for Plumbers Local 1 should be reviewed. Giving an admission test for the first time in two years, the union announced that a class of twenty apprentices would be formed. The WDL had fourteen applicants file through its offices to take the examination. Ultimately, only three WDL recruitees took the test in July, 1966. The Local announced that one of the criteria to be used to qualify to take the written examination was a 75 per cent average in the senior year of high school. Since none of the eight WDL recruitees who had originally intended to take the test had such averages, the WDL appealed unsuccessfully to the union that the average of 75 per cent was arbitrary and that in a competitive examination prior grades take care of themselves. The union replied that the requirement had been approved by the state and refused to allow the recruitees to take the test. The WDL then enlisted the support of the United Federation of Teachers, who were able to have grades changed for three of the applicants so that they would have a 75 per cent average. The three took the written test and placed third, fourth, and nineteenth out of a total of fifty people taking the exam. Plumbers Local 1, however, was at the time of this writing refusing to appoint them to the class because (1) they did not score in the thirtieth percentile in each of the five sections of the test, and (2) the union claims that it did not receive official notification that the high school records of the three applicants had been changed. The WDL replied that the first requirement was arbitrary and that the over-all ranking should be the determining factor, and, as for the second contention, it reported it had written each high school principal involved asking that such appropriate notification be given.[49]

[49] The data used in this paragraph are drawn from the testimony of the Workers Defense League before the City Commission on Human Rights on September 26, 1966 (mimeographed material).

In addition to work with the recruitment and the preparation of applicants, WDL has done a limited amount of research into the background of the whites who successfully enter these programs. One of their most detailed studies was of the spring, 1965, Sheet Metal Workers apprenticeship class. The backgrounds of the sixty-five entrants who were accepted into the class were reviewed. With respect to high school diplomas, the following results were gathered:

Type of Diploma Received	No. of Recipients
Academic	21
General	21
Commercial	7
Vocational	4
No diploma	4
High school equivalency	2
Mechanical	1
Technical	4
Other	1

Of the ten who scored highest on the examination, eight had academic diplomas, one had a technical diploma, and one had a general diploma. Moreover, twenty-five of the sixty-four white entrants had spent between one semester and two and one-half years in college. In other words, the conclusion is inescapable that the recruits gathered by the WDL were in competition with many students who had received academic preparation in high school and, in many cases, in college.[50]

Similar research should be undertaken by other groups who are interested in the placement of minority youths into apprenticeship classes. Such studies, it would seem, are prerequsites for successful preparatory programs. The WDL, now recognizing the scope of the competition, has continued to require a high school diploma for all of its recruits, even though the sheet metal workers' and the ironworkers' standards required applicants to have only a tenth-grade education. In view of a 1966 study of the U.S. Office of Education, which found that at Grade 12 nonwhites in the Northeastern cities were over three years behind whites on the average, the WDL's standards seem well founded.

In order to implement its informational program, the WDL also distributes a periodic apprenticeship bulletin and newsletter to

[50] The data contained in this paragraph were derived from materials supplied by the WDL.

agencies and individuals concerned with apprenticeship as well as to applicants for apprenticeship programs.

CONCLUSIONS

As the nation's largest city, New York has had some of the most chronic cases of municipal problems. In the past, the apprenticeship question has been more volatile here than elsewhere. Yet, as is also typical of events in this unpredictable city, the remedial developments have been far more extensive and unusual than in any of our other study cities.

Significantly, however, although the issue has been in the public spotlight and frequently has involved public agencies, the greatest strides toward resolution have come from private activities. The Workers Defense League has no legal status. Its role has been to accomplish the task of promoting apprenticeship in general, of dispensing detailed information about specific programs, of recruiting individuals interested in applying, of tutoring applicants to pass the written examination, and of conducting follow-up research studies of the experiences of the successful white and nonwhite entrants into the programs in order to improve their procedures for the future. We are persuaded that such comprehensive efforts are required to produce meaningful progress in the construction trades.

Similarly, the program in the printing industry was instituted by private initiative. Access to the pool of "helpers" from which all typographical apprentices are to be drawn in the future has proven no obstacle to nonwhites in the past. The opportunity to be considered for an apprenticeship program, a voluntary program of tutoring, and an impartially administered and graded examination procedure affords nonwhites a chance to qualify for admission that is absent in all other survey cities.

Yet, before all the accolades are given to private initiative, it is important to recall the events that paved the way for such action. Had it not been for the prodding of the state and city human relations commissions and the 1963 demonstrations, it is questionable that either private program would have been instigated in the present thorough form. The demonstrations served to focus public attention on this problem; the public reports acted to document the pattern of exclusion; the legal proceedings worked to eliminate some of the anachronisms of the past. In other words, the activities of the public bodies have been to set the stage whereby private, long-term programs can be established on the basis of principles of equal opportunity. The public agencies, with the lone exception of the CCHR in the 1964 Plumbers case, have stayed out of the vital recruitment area. In most other cities where any progress has been made in this area, the public agencies have been in the vanguard of recruiting activities. When these public agencies enter into the labyrinth of apprenticeship, they are forced to consider the issue as but one of the many social problems they are called upon to resolve. Accordingly, their activities are typically short range and designed to meet an immediate need. In most cases, city human relations agencies lack the staff and the facilities to perform all of the needed tasks to accomplish meaningful long-run results. New York, therefore, is fortunate to have the establishment of such an organization as the WDL which can provide the specialized expertise needed to understand apprenticeship and the continuing relationship required to maintain channels of communications between the community as a source of supply of applicants and the JACs as a source of demand for apprentices.

The WDL approach also has another unique advantage over public agencies. The WDL has no punitive measures at hand to threaten recalcitrant unions. It cannot convene public hearings, revoke contracts, shut down projects, or require head counts. Its success is premised upon the existence of a climate of mutual respect for all parties concerned. While the WDL operation can benefit by the removal of artificial obstacles to Negro entry into the trades by the public agencies, it cannot be associated with the direct use of punitive powers by these public authorities.

A number of factors probably accounts for IBEW Local 3's sharp reversal in 1962. Local 3's action was a tactical maneuver to obtain the twenty-five-hour work week, as well as the response of enlightened union leadership to a chronic social problem, but it is clearly without parallel anywhere in the United States. Since 1962, the continued accessibility to entry by Negroes to the local has come through the efforts of the WDL and the co-operative attitude of the union's leadership.

Thus, New York represents a ray of light in an otherwise foggy area of national concern. Each city has its unique characteristics and personalities, but in no other city have the divergent forces worked together so successfully as here. While the experiences of no single city can be transferred in their entirety to another differing locality, there still remains much that can be learned from the experiences of New York by all parties to this issue in every sector of the nation.

CHAPTER V

PHILADELPHIA

INTRODUCTION

With a population of slightly over two million, Philadelphia ranks as the nation's fourth largest city. In 1960, the nonwhite population was approximately 27 per cent of the total. As is true of many other Northern cities, whites are migrating to the suburbs and Negroes are moving into the central city. During the decade from 1950 to 1960, for example, the over-all population declined by about 70,000 (the net decline in the white population was 225,000, while the net increase in nonwhites was 156,000).

With respect to education, approximately 53 per cent of the children in the public schools in 1964 were nonwhites. About one-half of Philadelphia's white children attend private schools, while only 10 per cent of nonwhites attend such institutions. Approximately 49 per cent of the students in vocational high schools in 1964 were Negroes. Furthermore, it is reported that the city has one of the worst dropout problems of any large city in the nation. In 1963 only 53.4 per cent of the tenth-graders in the school system completed their high school studies.[1]

The area co-ordinator for the now-defunct President's Committee on Equal Employment Opportunity described the city as a "strong union town with strong union traditions." It was estimated in 1965 that there were about 200,000 union members in the city, of which 25,000 were nonwhites.[2] The apprenticeship programs in pipefitting, masonry, and electrical work have often won national awards. During the period of this survey, however, the former AFL and CIO elements in Philadelphia split into separate camps. There are

[1] The figures in this paragraph are drawn from Leonard Rico, "The Negro Worker in Philadelphia," in Herbert R. Northrup and Richard L. Rowan (eds.), *The Negro and Employment Opportunity* (Ann Arbor: University of Michigan Press, 1965), pp. 349–75.

[2] *Ibid.*, p. 368.

some indications that one of the differences between the two union groups is the issue of Negro participation in apprenticeship programs. The former CIO unions advocate a more aggressive non-discrimination policy while the former AFL affiliates are dominated by the building crafts and represent a more cautious approach.

Table 5-1 shows that in 1960 Negroes comprised over 16 per cent of those employed in the construction industry. Compared to other cities in this study, the participation rate ranks fifth highest. While it is true that the bulk of the Negroes were concentrated in the laborer classification, the dispersion into other trades (such as sheet metal workers, electricians, and plumbers) shows a substantial number of Negro workers. Many of the Negroes in the building industry find employment in the nonunion residential field.

Pennsylvania has its own apprenticeship council and program. The state has had a nondiscriminatory pledge requirement for all certified apprenticeship programs since 1961. All JAC programs and selection procedures must be approved in advance by the state. The state regulations on nondiscrimination were circulated in January, 1965, after they had been approved by BAT. While there are some similarities between the state law and 29 CFR, they differ in a meaningful and significant manner over the crucial issue of selection of apprentices for programs adopted before January 17, 1964. Title 29 permits approval by either of three means: (1) selection by qualifications alone; (2) a demonstration of an acceptable degree of minority participation, or (3) selection from existing employees.[3] The Pennsylvania statute, on the other hand, extends approval of selection procedures either (1) on the basis of qualifications alone or (2) on the basis of selection from existing employees who were admitted to an employee pool in a nondiscriminatory manner,[4] but it does not permit compliance by demonstrating nondiscrimination.

NEGRO PARTICIPATION IN SELECTED UNIONS AND APPRENTICESHIP PROGRAMS

Tables 5-2, 5-3, and 5-4 indicate the degree of Negro participation in unions and apprenticeship programs in Philadelphia. Table 5-2 presents the findings of the Commission on Human Relations (CHR) through 1965. The CHR found these six building trades unions to be "discriminatory" in their admission practices. From our interview work, we know that at least one more Negro had been

[3] 29 CFR 30.4.
[4] P. L. 604, Act 304, sec. 4.

Table 5-1

Employment in Selected Occupations by Race, 1960—Philadelphia Metropolitan Area

	Number Employed				Percentage Distribution			
Occupation	Total	White	Negro	Other nonwhite	Total	White	Negro	Other nonwhite
Selected occupations								
Carpenters	14,636	13,655	969	12	100.0	93.3	6.6	0.1
Plasterers and cement finishers	2,444	1,739	705	—	100.0	71.2	28.8	—
Structural metal workers	2,967	2,654	313	—	100.0	89.5	10.5	—
Electricians	9,827	9,370	453	4	100.0	95.3	4.6	0.1
Plumbers and pipefitters	10,933	10,384	549	—	100.0	94.2	5.8	—
Construction laborers	13,302	6,585	6,717	—	100.0	49.5	50.5	—
Total employed	1,092,806	951,806	138,775	2,255	100.0	87.1	12.7	0.2
Total construction industry	79,350	66,317	12,986	47	100.0	83.6	16.4	<0.05

Note: Percentages may not add to total because of rounding.   Based on data obtained from U.S. Bureau of the Census.

Table 5-2

Progress Report on Nonwhite Participation in Six "Discriminatory"
Unions, April, 1965—Philadelphia

Union	Total Membership 1965	Admitted in 1963	Admitted in 1964	Admitted in 1965
Plumbers 690	1,500	2 apprentices 1 journeyman	0	0
Steamfitters 420	2,000	0	1 apprentice	0
IBEW 98	1,200	? apprentices	2 journeymen 1 apprentice	N.A.
Sheet Metal Workers 19	1,800	0	1 apprentice	
Roofers 30	250	0	0	0
IBEW 126	N.A.		3 journeymen "several" apprentices	

N.A., not available.
Based on data obtained from Commission on Human Relations, City of Philadelphia.

Table 5-3

Status of Negro Participation in Construction Trades (Other Than Those
Held To Be Discriminatory), April, 1965—Philadelphia

Union	Total Membership	Nonwhite Membership
Bricklayers 1	1,050	100 (approximately)
Carpenters District Council (several locals)	5,000	All locals integrated to varying degrees
Cement Masons 592	600	200 (no formal apprenticeship program)
Operating Engineers 542	5,000	500
Ironworkers 401	500	0
Painters District Council (three locals)	1,000	50 (no formal apprenticeship program)
Painters, Cleaners, and Caulkers 35	120	4 journeymen 2 apprentices
Reinforced Rodsetters 405	300	100 (1/3 of apprenticeship class is nonwhite)
Sheet Metal Workers 194 (industrial work)	670	160 Negroes 25 Puerto Ricans
Stone Masons 32	485	0
Roofers 113	65	20
Elevator Constructors 5	420	0

Based on data obtained from Commission on Human Relations, City of Philadelphia.

admitted to the Sheet Metal Workers program. Table 5-3 shows the broader picture of Negro participation in Philadelphia apprenticeship programs. Table 5-4 shows the degree of nonwhite participation in the printing trades in Philadelphia. These tables reveal the familiar pattern of nonwhite concentration in the trowel trades or the industrial sections of building trades unions. Over 70 per cent of all nonwhites in the Philadelphia printing industry were concentrated in the bookbinders, though the lithographers had over 20 per cent of the industry's nonwhite employment. The other four printing unions combined had only about 7 per cent of the industry's nonwhites. As we shall explain in the following sections, considerable effort has been exerted to get Negroes into those unions and apprenticeship programs where few nonwhites were employed.

Table 5-4

Nonwhite Members of Printing Trades Unions in Philadelphia, June, 1965

Union	Total Membership in Union	Total Nonwhite Members
Lithographers	1,583	88
Electrotypers	175	9
Bookbinders	1,825	300
Pressmen	1,080	1
Typographers	1,097	19
Stereotypers	32	0

Based on data obtained from Graphic Arts Employment Committee, Philadelphia, Pa.

ACTIVITIES OF THE PHILADELPHIA
COMMISSION ON HUMAN RELATIONS

The pent-up frustrations and resentment of many of the nation's Negro communities erupted into demonstrations and violence during the 1950's and the 1960's. Beginning in Philadelphia and spreading to several Northern cities, a wave of 1963 demonstrations centered upon the lack of Negroes in the building trades. In early May, 1963, sit-ins, sleep-ins, and picketing occurred at the construction site of the Philadelphia Municipal Services Building across from City Hall. The demonstrations, however, soon turned into violence when police sought to escort workmen through the picket lines. Shortly afterward, Mayor James H. J. Tate ordered the $18 million project shut down. It remained closed for two weeks until an agreement was achieved by which nonwhites would be employed as the work on the project progressed.

Against this backdrop, the CHR began an investigation into the employment practices of the city's construction industry. While it started as a study of the charges made against four unions (the Sheet Metal Workers, Steamfitters, Plumbers, and the IBEW) working on the Municipal Services Building, the ensuing investigation was broadened into a study of general racial employment practices of city contractors.[5]

The Commission concluded that "Substantial evidence had been produced which tends to show that certain local unions covering skilled trades have followed customs and practices in the selection of apprentices and in admission to the unions which have inevitably resulted in the exclusion of nonwhites from the particular trades."[6] In the report, five local unions were specifically found to be fostering "conditions resulting in a pattern of discrimination against qualified Negroes."[7] They were:

Plumbers Local 690	0 Nonwhites
Steamfitters Local 420	0 Nonwhites
Sheet Metal Workers Local 19	0 Nonwhites
Composition Roofers Local 30	0 Nonwhites
IBEW Local 98	2 Nonwhites
	(850 whites)

Additionally, three employers were cited as having contracts exclusively with labor unions that had no "nonwhite members or [where] the number of nonwhite members comprise[d] no more than a token." Under city contract procedures, the contractor not only was required to abstain from the practice of discriminatory action himself but also agreed not to permit discrimination. These contractors also were cited for not taking affirmative action to prevent discrimination.

Shortly after the May, 1963, report, another union—IBEW Local 126 (outside electricians)—was added to the list of violators. It, too, had never had a nonwhite member.

About a year later, in April, 1964, the Commission published a progress report which showed that of 300 applicants for journey-

---

[5] The findings of the Commission made it clear that the contractor, McShain & Co., "has not engaged in any discriminatory hiring. Indeed the testimony indicates that of the workers employed by McShain, namely laborers, carpenters, cement finishers, dock builders, and rod setters, approximately 65 per cent are nonwhite and 35 per cent white."

[6] "Conclusions and Recommendations Pertaining to Employment Discrimination on Certain City Work Contracts and for the Construction Trades," Commission on Human Relations, *Report to Mayor James H. J. Tate, City of Philadelphia* (May 20, 1963), p. 1.

[7] *Ibid.*, p. 3.

men and apprenticeship registered and tested, during the intervening year, "fewer than 10 per cent were able to qualify."[8] The registrants were obtained through extensive public information efforts—such as press, radio, and television announcements as well as personal contacts with interested persons and agencies. During this period, 200 local contractors asserted that they would hire without regard to race, religion, or national origin. "In many instances where openings have occurred, employers have requested qualified nonwhite journeymen, but the Commission has not been able to make referrals because of the scarcity of properly qualified applicants."[9] Furthermore, during this period the six unions cited in the initial report "promised" to avoid discrimination in their admission practices.

The three contractors cited in the 1963 report were told that their contracts would be revoked if they did not come into compliance at once. All three did so "immediately" by adding nonwhite journeymen and by promising to work with the objectives of the CHR in the future.

The causes for the lack of substantial increases in Negro participation were listed in the report as follows: (1) employment opportunities declined during the year (there were 13,000 fewer construction jobs in 1963 than eight years earlier); (2) the number of qualified nonwhite craftsmen is small; (3) the unemployment rate in the building trades was high; (4) union membership policies restrict sharply the number of new members of any race admitted.

During 1963, the CHR sought referrals for each of the six cited unions. With respect to the steamfitters, two nonwhite journeymen were tested; they both failed. A third failed a journeyman's test given by the city. There was one nonwhite applicant to the steamfitters' apprenticeship class. He was sent a registered letter to take the test, but he did not show up. Five qualified nonwhite plumbers did work intermittently and one nonwhite journeyman was admitted to the union. None of the nonwhite tradesmen referred by the Commission to the sheet metal workers passed the test. The union had agreed to admit them if they could pass the examination given to the white applicants at the same time. "At least a dozen" nonwhite electricians secured intermittent employment as a result of the CHR efforts. One nonwhite electrician passed the admission test for IBEW Local 98 (along with another white). *Both* were re-

[8] "City Contract Compliance: Progress in 1963," in Commission on Human Relations, *A Special Report* (April, 1964), p. 1.
[9] *Ibid.*

jected for membership by a vote of the union on the grounds that "no journeyman, white or nonwhite has been admitted since 1937 as a 'walk-in.' " (Admission was granted only by way of the apprenticeship route.) The nonwhite, however, did continue to work without any interference from the union. As for IBEW Local 126, one nonwhite journeyman was accepted into the union. All efforts to recruit and refer applicants to the roofers' union failed. It should be noted, however, that the roofers do not have a formal apprenticeship class. Thus, only two qualified journeymen were placed in these unions during the year.

The third progress report was issued in April, 1965. The CHR's findings with respect to the six unions held "to be discriminatory," are set forth in Table 5-2 (p. 86). The Commission stated that the main obstacles to placing two more apprentice plumbers was the Negroes' inability to pay a $500 joining fee. With regard to the steamfitters, only one Negro youth passed the test. The reason no journeymen steamfitters were placed was that "there are no nonwhite journeymen because none seem to be around."[10] IBEW Local 98 admitted one nonwhite apprentice in 1964. The apprentice was the son of a journeyman member.[11] The two nonwhite journeymen were taken in as the result of an organizing drive. The Commission reported that the local would continue to conduct strong organization drives and hoped in this way to provide entry for more nonwhite journeymen and their relatives. Of the nonwhites who took journeyman and apprentice tests for Sheet Metal Workers Local 19, only one nonwhite apprentice applicant passed. Roofers Local 30 had no nonwhite members or applicants. IBEW Local 126 took in three nonwhite journeymen hired by a contractor. "Several" nonwhites were taken into apprenticeship classes, but, since virtually all of the union's work is done outside the city, at least two of these quit rather than commute to distant job sites. Operating Engineers Local 542 had a sizable number of nonwhite members, but almost all of them were concentrated in the unskilled job classifications. Complaints have been made against the engineers, but no progress was made because "the union officials and their attorney have absolutely refused to cooperate."[12]

Nonetheless, in summarizing its April, 1965, report, the CHR

[10] "Construction Trades," in Paul Dandridge, *Memorandum to Commission on Human Relations* (April 28, 1966), p. 2.

[11] Of the thirty-two apprentices admitted during the year, twenty-seven were sons of journeymen and five were nephews (*ibid.*, p. 2).

[12] *Ibid.*, p. 4.

said optimistically that a "new enlightened attitude" could be seen in all of the hitherto all-white unions. The Commission also noted that "in no instance have we had reports of these pioneer nonwhites being treated in a discriminatory manner."[13]

By November, 1965, however, conditions seemed to have deteriorated. The CHR was forced to request that nine apprenticeship classes be denied the use of the public school facilities, and in January, 1966, the Commission notified the Governor of Pennsylvania that it was having difficulties with Steamfitters Local 420, Plumbers Local 690, IBEW Local 98, Roofers Local 30, and Sheet Metal Workers Local 19.[14] The Commission objected to the "unrealistic, objective criteria" established and to the "dilatory tactics" of some of these unions in complying with the Commission's directives. Furthermore, the CHR expressed fears that demonstrations were likely to break out again unless a settlement was reached.

The Philadelphia local AFL-CIO Human Relations Committee initiated its own study of minority participation in the apprenticeable trades prior to the 1963 demonstrations. The Committee had sought the voluntary co-operation of the unions in submitting information, but after a delay of almost a year, the Committee personally visited every apprenticeship class and made its own head count. The report, made public in 1964, found virtually no Negro apprentices in any of the building trades classes, and therefore recommended to the Board of Education that public school facilities be denied classes conducted on a discriminatory basis. As might be expected, the Building Trades Council roundly attacked the findings and the recommendations of this committee.

The AFL-CIO Human Relations Committee's support for the denial of school facilities to what appeared to be discriminatory apprenticeship classes reinforced an earlier recommendation made by the CHR in 1963. Complying with the CHR recommendation, the Philadelphia Board of Education ruled in August, 1963, that public school facilities would not be available for apprenticeship training which did not accept qualified nonwhite applicants. Eleven apprenticeship programs were reviewed on the basis of:

1. Enrollment of an appreciable number of nonwhites
2. Affirmative action taken to enroll nonwhites
3. A nondiscriminatory admission system with wide dissemination of information.

13 *Ibid.*, p. 5.
14 [Confidential Memorandum].

91

If any one of these criteria were met, the program would be admitted. After the Board's inquiry and at the specific recommendation of the CHR, Ironworkers Local 401 was denied the use of the public schools late in 1963. Within a year, however, the Local was found in compliance and re-admitted when its admission standards were amended and when it promised to undertake affirmative recruiting policies. The Local notified the CHR and two Negro trade union leaders (Jimmie Jones and William Foster) in advance of the details concerning its fall, 1964, class. The response by the Negroes to these new efforts was, according to the CHR, "very poor." Several Negroes were tested by the Local but they all failed. The Bricklayers withdrew their classes from the public school over a "misunderstanding" during the public hearings in 1963 and they have stayed out. In November, 1965, the CHR recommended that a number of programs be denied the use of the public school facilities. The specific unions involved were: the Carpenters, IBEW Local 98, Glaziers Local 252, Bricklayers Local 64, Plumbers Local 690, Roofers Local 30, Sheet Metal Workers Local 19, and Steamfitters Local 420. Each of these programs was charged to be "not in reasonable compliance with [the] non-discriminatory requirements."[15] By January 1, 1966, however, each of these unions submitted their selection procedures for review by the state apprenticeship officials. As a result, and even though final approval was not given to several of the programs, the request to deny the use of facilities was dropped. The CHR felt that, other than causing the unions some measure of inconvenience, little would actually be accomplished by denying them the use of public schools.

DEVELOPMENTS IN THE PRINTING INDUSTRY

The publicity given alleged discrimination in building trades apprenticeship programs focused public attention on all apprenticeship programs. In order to forestall racial difficulties in their industry, the unionized and nonunionized employers in the printing industry, through their single association, Printing Industries for Philadelphia (PIP), decided to seize the initiative by adopting a written, nondiscriminatory policy. PIP adopted the program and then notified the printing unions and the local AFL-CIO Human Rights Committee of its implementation.

15 Letter from the Commission to the Philadelphia Board of Education, November 23, 1965.

92

On August 19, 1963, a committee consisting of the Graphic Arts Unions,[16] representative employers, representatives of the Negro Trade Union Leadership Council, the AFL-CIO Human Rights Committee, and PIP unanimously adopted the program, which provided for a nondiscrimination pledge in all negotiated contracts and set up a special committee, the Graphic Arts Employment Committee, to receive quarterly reports from employers and unions concerning referrals, hiring, and apprentice placements. A semi-annual report, containing a list of the noncomplying participants, is sent to the city's Commission on Human Relations. The Committee also receives individual complaints of discrimination. (Only one such complaint had been filed by the summer of 1966 and it was quickly resolved to the satisfaction of all parties concerned.)

According to officials connected with the program, nonwhite recruitment efforts have been very difficult. The Pennsylvania Bureau of Employment Security "has not supplied one person to our program." Most nonwhites have come from private employment services in Negro communities, "walk-ins" to the PIP office in central Philadelphia, the Opportunities Industrialization Center run by the Reverend Leon Sullivan, and personal recommendations from Jimmie Jones (of the Steelworkers) and Paul Dandridge (formerly with the Human Relations Commission).

The obstacles to greater participation as seen by PIP representatives are: (1) the scarcity of qualified Negro applicants (the work has become more technical and the job requirements have risen accordingly), and (2) the fact that many of the firms are small family enterprises which are set in their ways. Small family enterprises, however, are declining sharply in number as the result of mergers dictated by rising costs and limited capital. As these larger enterprises increase, it is likely that personal resistance to Negroes will diminish.

A compilation of the reports of the Committee to the city's Human Relations Commission was given in Table 5-4 (p. 87). As of June 30, 1965, there were 417 nonwhites in the printing unions out of 5,792 listed in the union reports. While the data on nonwhite apprentices are not broken down by individual union programs, the semi-annual reports show that between July 1, 1963, and June 30, 1965, twenty-one nonwhite apprentices were accepted.[17]

[16] The signatory local unions were Typographical Local 2, Lithographers Local 14, Pressmen's Local 11, Bookbinders Local 2, Electrotypers Local 72, and Stereotypers Local 7.

[17] Report to the Graphic Arts Employment Committee (June, 1965).

APPRENTICESHIP INFORMATION CENTER

At the time of our survey, Philadelphia did *not* have an Apprenticeship Information Center. The topic has been a controversial one. In the agreement reached in 1963 between the city Human Relations Commission and six unions found to be "discriminatory," it was agreed that such an agency should be established, but efforts to create such a center soon foundered. Exactly who is to blame for its demise is not clear According to the man picked to head the AIC, Mr. Warren Mulveany, a staff was actually appointed in April, 1963, only one month after the federal directive providing for AICs was issued. The BAT was supposed to set up the Philadelphia co-ordinating group that is the first step to actually obtaining a federally funded Center, but, since BAT never acted, the Center was not opened.

A simultaneous development complicating the establishment of an AIC in Philadelphia was a major controversy between organized labor and Governor Scranton concerning an overhaul and tightening of the state's unemployment compensation program. Organized labor had opposed the revisions but was unsuccessful. Mulveany unfortunately had the difficult dual job of simultaneously explaining the unpopular new unemployment compensation system to the unions while trying to enlist their co-operation in setting up the AIC machinery. In November, 1964, after months of futile efforts, the AIC idea was abandoned but efforts to establish such a center were being revived in late 1966.

There have been other efforts to bridge the information gap, most of which failed. Prior to the fiasco described above, the Urban League suggested a program to establish information centers in the Negro community. When it sought financial assistance from the city government, the project died in the municipal bureaucracy. It was known, however, that the Pennsylvania Bureau of Employment Security opposed the project on the grounds that it felt such an undertaking would be an enfringement on its functions. Later, after the employment services' own project failed and after serious rioting in the summer of 1964 in North Philadelphia (the Negro ghetto), the AFL-CIO Human Relations Council (chaired by Jimmie Jones of the Steelworkers) and the Negro Trade Union Leadership Conference (NTULC) jointly established the Philadelphia Council on Community Advancement. The project centered its work in North Philadelphia, where it sought to explain unions to Negroes, to teach remedial classes, and to dispense information on apprenticeship. The project was concerned with acquainting Negroes with unionism in general and did not concentrate solely on the apprenticeable trades. However, the project was short-lived and slipped into oblivion when the federal Economic Opportunity Act was passed. It was felt that the functions of this special project would be absorbed by this omnibus legislation.

Mention should also be made of the fact that a leaflet on the topic of apprenticeship was distributed throughout the Negro community by the NTULC but had little impact in arousing interest. The NTULC attributes this to the fact that most Negro youths simply feel it is futile even to try.

OPPORTUNITIES INDUSTRIALIZATION CENTERS

Funded originally as an experimental and demonstration project under the Manpower Development and Training Act, a special training program has been created in the city. Known as Opportunities Industrialization Centers, Inc., the project is led by the Reverend Leon Sullivan. With funding taken over in 1966 by a $1 million grant from the Office of Economic Opportunity and with the Philadelphia Chamber of Commerce donating many facilities to the program, the project has been able to assemble a competent staff with good facilities to train disadvantaged youth. Much of the orientation of the program is toward the development of good work habits. Hopefully, as the project progresses, some of its trainees may prove to be successful applicants to apprenticeship programs.

CONCLUSION

Philadelphia was the first city to experience demonstrations over Negro participation in building trades unions and apprenticeship programs. While the issue was not new, the topic had seldom generated enough concern to be the primary target for demonstrations. When they did occur and violence broke out, the cause received nationwide attention. Like ripples in a pond, the events in Philadelphia spread interest in the issue elsewhere. Apprenticeship became a rallying cry for civil rights advocates in many northern cities. Demonstrations started within days in New York, and shortly afterward in Cleveland. Other cities, in an effort to avert similar occurrences, sought to find preventive cures. In Cincinnati, where street demonstrations were threatened, the Building Trades Council signed its now well-known pledge for equal opportunity. In Detroit, the Board of Education later in the year ousted the IBEW program from its facilities. Thus, the long-smoldering discontent over the lack of Negroes in the skilled trades burst into an open flame.

Philadelphia, however, was more fortunate than many of the other cities in that it had an experienced Commission on Human Relations already in existence. In fact, the Philadelphia CHR had one of the best reputations in the country with respect to effectiveness of action. Its efforts regarding apprenticeship have been constant and thorough even though limited in short-run results.

The CHR's immediate intervention in the building trades dispute and its subsequent efforts have been insightful in illustrating the full dimensions of the problem. Its annual reports dramatize the difficulties in overcoming recalcitrant unions on one hand and in recruiting interested Negro youth on the other.

The CHR has experienced difficulties in working with this problem. For example, some unions, like IBEW Local 98, have refused to co-operate with the CHR and have clung tenaciously to the "father-son" tradition. Local 98 has declared that Negro participation in their apprenticeship program can best be increased through the organization of nonunion Negro tradesmen who can then bring in their sons and nephews. Moreover, the CHR has had great difficulty in persuading many of the building craft unions to give it details on the formation of new classes. Thus, despite an earlier agreement to supply such information, made at the public hearings following the 1963 demonstrations, most unions have failed to keep their word.

The CHR also has experienced recruitment problems. Despite its valiant efforts, it has not been able to supply an adequate number of Negro youths to the programs when opportunities opened up. With its small staff and diverse responsibilities, such an agency cannot handle the entire task of recruitment. The CHR can assist in promotion, help to compile lists, gather application data, and supervise tests, but it cannot do it alone—especially if remedial or tutorial work is involved.

Furthermore, the CHR, like similar agencies elsewhere, has been plagued by personnel problems. The loss of those who have developed an understanding of the many facets of this complex issue can be devastating to progressive efforts.

Lastly, the policy quandary confronting the CHR is typical of that which has perplexed similar groups in other cities. The Philadelphia Commission has used or recommended virtually every type of remedial action available to city officials: denial of the use of school facilities to one program; the closing of city construction projects; and the use of threats of contract revocation against employers. The results of these efforts have varied and it is difficult to generalize about their effectiveness. It seems clear, however, that the initiative to use any of these remedies resides with the CHR. But here the CHR faces a dilemma, because it is quite difficult for the Commission to try on the one hand to develop an amicable relationship with the unions when it also has the task of punishing the same groups when it believes them to be dilatory in their actions. Under such circumstances, it is very hard to build the foundations needed for a satisfactory long-term accord.

It has been rumored that Philadelphia is in line for the establishment of an AIC. Unless its operations in Philadelphia are more effective than they have been in most of our other study cities, the advent of such a center would not provide much assistance to the beleaguered CHR. The Pennsylvania Bureau of Employment Security, which would probably administer the center, was lambasted throughout our interview work. The criticisms have come as a single chorus from civil rights, academic, union, city, BAT, and employer spokesmen. Furthermore, it is apparent that the Negro community has no confidence in the agency. To make matters worse, it was manifestly clear that much of the personnel of the employment service in the city has little awareness of apprenticeship. In interviews with officials in its central office, we were told that the answer to the entire problem rests in the abolition of union entrance tests and that the city swarms with qualified Negro youth who are eager to snap at any opportunity to enter the trades once the tests are done away with. It is therefore clear that, to be effective in this area, the employment service would need to become more informed on the topic of apprenticeship and to change its image among civil rights groups.

Thus, in summary, there now is token Negro participation in programs where hitherto there had been none. The controversy, however, is by no means settled. In fact, the events of late 1965 and early 1966 seem to indicate that the entire issue has lost any momentum for change that it might have had. There is every indication that the viewpoints have ceased to converge and are beginning to diverge to their earlier poles.

CHAPTER VI

CLEVELAND

GENERAL BACKGROUND

Cleveland, the nation's eighth largest city, had a population of 876,050 in 1960, 253,108 (or 28.9 per cent) nonwhites. The city is heavily ghettoized but not simply on the basis of race. In the words of one city spokesman, "There are walls between groups everywhere. People in the city of Cleveland stay in minority ghettos—not only on the basis of race but also on the basis of national origin and of religion." The Negro community is clustered in the east side of town. The Cuyahoga River is the "Mason-Dixon Line."

Although Table 6-1 reveals that Negroes comprised 12.1 per cent of Cleveland's construction employment, they were concentrated in the trowel, carpentry, and laborer classifications. Since residential —as well as commercial and industrial—construction is relatively well organized, Negroes have few opportunities in nonunion construction work. Although there are a number of small nonunion Negro contractors who perform remodeling and "patch" work in the Negro community, Negroes have, in spite of concerted efforts over a long period, not had equal employment opportunities in some of the unionized construction crafts.

Inequality has not been limited to employment, however, because Cleveland Negroes have had unequal educational opportunities. There are two main vocational schools in the city, Max Hayes in the West Side (where the white population is concentrated) and East Side Tech (which is predominantly Negro). All of the apprenticeship classes are conducted in Max Hayes School. Several interviewees representing differing points of view agreed that Max Hayes is by far the superior school. There seems to be the feeling that East Side Tech does little to prepare a youth interested in the apprenticeable trades to qualify for such opportunities.

In support of the contention that the school system is not properly preparing Negro youths to qualify for apprenticeship training, a counselor for one of Cleveland's Negro high schools reported that

Table 6-1

Employment in Selected Occupations by Race, 1960—Cleveland Metropolitan Area

Occupation	Number Employed				Percentage Distribution			
	Total	White	Negro	Other nonwhite	Total	White	Negro	Other nonwhite
Selected occupations								
Carpenters	4,933	4,691	233	4	100.0	95.1	4.8	0.1
Plasterers and cement finishers	827	625	202	—	100.0	75.6	24.4	—
Structural metal workers	542	521	21	—	10C.0	96.1	3.9	—
Electricians	4,031	3,966	64	—	10C.0	98.4	1.6	—
Plumbers and pipefitters	3,082	2,946	136	—	100.0	95.6	4.4	—
Construction laborers	4,084	2,471	1,613	—	100.0	60.5	39.5	—
Total employed	467,481	412,173	54,261	1,047	100.0	88.2	11.6	0.2
Total construction industry	28,340	24,885	3,438	17	100.0	87.8	12.1	0.1

Note: Percentages may not add to total because of rounding.   Based on data obtained from U.S. Bureau of the Census.

prior to the 1965–66 academic year there was only one school on the East Side which taught first-year algebra and then only to those who could pass an algebra aptitude test. Since many apprenticeship examinations involve a section on mathematics, it is small wonder that many Negro applicants fail to qualify. Accordingly, our findings support the conclusions drawn by OMAT's Division of Special Programs which investigated the apprenticeship issue in Cleveland and concluded: "Evaluations of the problem showed considerable actual education gap between Cleveland school products and the implied expectations in apprenticeship qualification standards."[1]

Cleveland's apprenticeship program is financed by employers and by public funds. Contractors are required to pay the apprentices full wages during the days they are in school and away from their work. The unions do not contribute any direct sums to the training of the apprentices in the city.

Students who attend the apprenticeship classes at Max Hayes School are selected by the various JACs except for a few who are sent by independent contractors. The school system does not have any control over the selection of students.

EXTENT OF NEGRO PARTICIPATION IN APPRENTICESHIP PROGRAMS AND TRADE UNIONS

Table 6-2 shows the extent of Negro participation in seven programs which have been under heavy attack from civil rights

Table 6-2
Negro Apprentices in Selected Unions in Cleveland, Fall, 1966

Union	Negro Apprentices
Pipefitters 120	0
Sheet Metal Workers 65	1
Plumbers 55	1
Ironworkers 17	3
IBEW 38	2
Elevator Constructors 17	0
Tilesetter Helpers 17	0[a]
Total	7

Based on data obtained from the Cleveland Community Relations Board.
[a] The union reported that three Negro "helpers" would be initiated into the union in late 1965.

[1] Minutes of the Advisory Committee on Equal Opportunity in Apprenticeship and Training, Meeting of June 29, 1965; comments by Mr. Charles Gilmore of OMAT, p. 8.

groups. Although these results are very meager, they represent concerted efforts by a variety of groups over a long period of time.

SPECIFIC DEVELOPMENTS

Attempts by Negroes to enter the building craft unions in Cleveland have a long history. Efforts to enter IBEW Local 38 date back to 1917. Following World War II, a special club of Negro electricians was formed for the express purpose of soliciting the officers of the international union to intercede against the local. But when a business agent of the local who was sympathetic to the idea drowned in Lake Erie, the drive was scuttled and the civil rights groups turned to legal action.

In 1955 the Community Relations Board (CRB) found Local 38 guilty of racial discrimination. Despite the intervention of Mayor Anthony Celebrezze in support of the CRB, no Negroes were admitted. Local 38 accepted three Negroes in 1957, but only after the case was turned over to the AFL-CIO Civil Rights Committee and AFL-CIO President George Meany instructed the local to admit Negroes by July 1, 1957, or lose its charter. The man who had originated the CRB complaint, Theodore Pinkston, was not one of the three admitted. According to Local 38's leaders, these were the first journeymen admitted to the local since 1950 who had not already served apprenticeships. No Negroes were accepted by Local 38 between 1957 and 1963, when threatened demonstrations against construction projects caused the union to admit two Negro apprentices.

The record of the Cleveland Plumbers' union has paralleled that of the electricians. An organized drive by Negroes to enter Plumbers Local 55 began in 1933, but the Local's officers refused to open the letter the Negroes brought to the union meeting at which their admission was discussed. As late as 1944 there were as few as six Negro plumbers in Cleveland. On March 15, 1960, eight Negro journeymen, all of whom possessed licenses issued by the city, again were denied membership in Local 55. These eight journeymen were aided by the Urban League and had been trained in a special school started by a group of Negro plumbers in 1950. By 1962, the school had turned out fifty Negro journeymen who had passed the city's test. During the 1963 showdown on Negro participation in Cleveland building trades unions, Local 55 admitted the Negro plumbing contractor who had established the school and who had been instrumental in the efforts to get Negro journeymen admitted to the union. As a condition of entry, however, the contractor had to close the plumbing school. When organized, the Negro contractor had one Negro apprentice who was taken into the union after being given a brief aptitude test. Since his admission, though, the Negro apprentice has worked exclusively for the Negro contractor.

In 1963, demonstrations over minority participation in the construction trades erupted in Philadelphia, New York, Cleveland, and other cities. The various civil rights groups in Cleveland combined their forces into the United Freedom Movement (UFM), and were far better organized and more specific in their target objectives than were the civil rights forces in most other cities. In July, 1963, the UFM announced that it would begin public demonstrations at a city building project surrounding the City Mall unless three Negro electricians and two Negro plumbers were hired. On July 20, 1963, after a series of negotiation sessions between city, union, civil rights, federal, and AFL-CIO officials, an accord was reached. It was agreed that two Negro apprentices would be taken into the IBEW and the plumbers agreed to admit two nonunion Negro journeymen (whose applications were being processed) to work on the project. The union spokesmen, however, underestimated the recalcitrance of the membership. When the two Negro plumbers showed up for work, the union plumbers, pipefitters, and asbestos workers walked out— allegedly because the two Negroes were not members of the union. An international officer of the union was called in, and the next day work resumed. Later in the week, however, union members met and voted a "holiday" for Monday, July 29, 1963. The international's representative hinted that such an action could result in the local being placed into trusteeship. Nonetheless, on that day about 700 of the 1,400 members of the local did not go to work in the city. The next day, about 1,200 plumbers worked. The 200 who did not were those employed on the jobs of the plumbing subcontractor on the Mall project. All of that company's jobs were boycotted in defiance of the pronouncements by the local and international officers of the union against such action. The evening of the third day of the protest, it was announced that an accord had been reached whereby the two Negroes would be fired as journeymen and asked to take an examination for the apprenticeship class. If they passed, they could be hired as apprentices. The UFM was infuriated and renewed its threat of demonstrations. Hastily, another series of high-level meetings were convened with city, federal, local union, AFL-CIO, and UFM representatives. Out of their talks came a new agreement on August 4, 1963. Local 55 agreed to sign contracts with Negro plumbing contractors and admit their Negro journeymen to the union if they passed the test. A review procedure was established for any who felt unfairly treated. In addition, the plumbing contractor would sublet part of his contract to a Negro contractor who would hire the two Negro journeymen working on the project. Furthermore, it was agreed that all future apprentice classes would be open for all to apply. On August 15, the Negro contractor and his journeymen and apprentice were admitted to the union.

With one crisis ended, another loomed in its place. On August 6, 1963, fourteen white sheet metal workers walked off their jobs when a Negro sheet metal worker was hired. The application of the Negro to the union was being processed. They were ordered back to work by their officers and they complied with the directive but only after the Negro was assigned to the contractor's trailer while he was "familiarizing himself with the job."[2] After being on the job for seven days, in compliance with standard procedures, he attempted to secure an application form from the union office for "a temporary card" until his formal application could be acted upon. There were no union officials in the building the day he applied. The UFM again threatened to picket the construction project, but it was decided instead to await the union's action on the application. When the Negro's application was processed in September, the sheet metal workers announced that he and a white applicant had both failed to pass the written examination. The UFM did not protest the result.

The same day that the sheet metal workers walked out, it went almost unnoticed that the first Negro electrician apprentice started to work on the Mall project. Neither his appearance, or that of a second Negro apprentice who started a week later, caused any incidents. However, the UFM had charged Local 38 with "bad faith" for its delay in placing the Negroes on the job.

REMEDIAL PROGRAMS

The Cleveland Community Relations Board

The Cleveland Community Relations Board has been in existence for over twenty years and has been in the center of the controversy over apprenticeship since the issue erupted. The CRB has actively recruited Negro youths since the summer of 1963. Particularly active in these efforts until his resignation in 1965 was Mr.

2 *The Plain Dealer,* August 8, 1963.

Ellsworth H. Harpole, the director of the CRB. He and his staff deserve special mention for the detailed work that they have done in laying the groundwork for all attempts to resolve this issue. Harpole, who had held the post for two and one-half years, was the third director to hold the thankless post since 1962.

Against the backdrop of the 1963 demonstrations, the CRB redoubled its efforts to find qualified Negroes for the building crafts. Working with the Cleveland Board of Education and the high school counselors in the predominantly Negro schools, efforts were made to identify prospective applicants. Once discovered, each prospect was sent a letter from the CRB inquiring as to his interest in apprenticeship. Each was instructed to go to the Ohio State Employment Service for testing, counseling, and screening. During the period covering June, 1963, through December, 1964, 136 Negroes were contacted. Forty-four responded to the CRB's letters, were screened by the State Employment Service, and applied to union programs.[3] During the first ten months of 1965, of an additional forty-five graduating seniors who were contacted in a similar fashion, twenty-eight were processed and subsequently made application to union programs.

Seven unions were the targets of these efforts. They were Plumbers Local 55, Sheet Metal Workers Local 65, Ironworkers Local 17,

Table 6-3

Results of Efforts by the Cleveland Community Relations Board To Place Negro Youths in Seven Apprenticeship Programs, June, 1963, to October, 1965

	Number of Negro Youths				
Union	Recruited for union program	Recruited but did not apply	Recruited, applied, but were NOT tested	Recruited, applied, and were tested	Accepted in the union
Pipefitters 120	9	0	6	3	0
Sheet Metal Workers 65	30	7	16	7	0
Plumbers 55	23	5	11	7	(1)[a]
Ironworkers 17	8	0	0	8	1
IBEW 38	49	3	29	17	2
Elevator Constructors 17	7	0	7	0	0
Tilesetter Helpers 17	2	0	2	0	0

Based on data obtained from the Cleveland Community Relations Board.
[a] Applicant passed union test but was drafted into the armed forces.

[3] Cleveland Community Relations Board, "Recruitment by the Community Relations Board of Minority Youth for Entry into Seven of the Construction Trades' Apprenticeship Programs," report for the period of June 27, 1963, to October 1, 1965 (1965), p. 1.

IBEW Local 38, Pipefitters Local 120, Elevator Constructors Local 17, and Tilesetter Helpers Local 17. The results of these activities are presented in Table 6-3.[4]

Out of the seventy-two applicants (it is apparent that many applicants applied to more than one program), only four youths were actually accepted into formal programs. The one who is said to have passed the plumbers' test, William Pope, claims that he did not hear a word from the union during the eleven days that passed from the time he took the exam and the time he was drafted into the army. Moreover, he claims that neither he nor his relatives have ever subsequently received notice of any kind from the union. When he returned from the service in January, 1966, Pope reapplied to Local 55 but was informed by union officials that he would have to be retested. When he told the union officials that he had passed the earlier test, Pope was informed that, since he was now 24 years old, he was too old to be admitted to the apprenticeship program, but that his case would be sent to the JAC for consideration. As of September, 1966, his plea has been unanswered and he has a job as a postal employee.

Table 6-4 presents in tabular form the CRB's findings on why many of those who were recruited for the respective unions failed

Table 6-4

Reasons Given by Negroes Who Were Recruited, Who Applied, but Who Failed To Show Up for the Test at the Appointed Time—Cleveland

Reason	No.
Enrolled in college	13
Could not get off from work	9
Military service	9
Found another job	6
Lost interest	6
Lost contact	4
Family obligations interfered	2
Arrived late for test, denied access to test	2
Felt testing center was too crowded	1
Forgot admittance letter, denied access to test	1
No excuse	1
Went fishing that day	1
Had to attend a Reserve meeting on that day	1
Did not obtain money order for test fee, denied access to test	1

Based on data obtained from the Cleveland Community Relations Board.

---

[4] The information found in this table is taken from *ibid.*, pp. 1–14.

to show up to take the tests for admission. The fact that elapsed time between initial contact for interest and the time the qualification test is actually given varies widely means that the success of a recruiting drive which depends upon those recruited being available at a later date diminishes with the passage of time. If the relevant dates are known when recruiting is done for specific programs, efforts to supply applicants can be tailored to that specific program. On the other hand, when a roster of Negro youths is gathered for apprenticeship in general, it is likely that the time lags and diversity in examination schedules will markedly increase the fail-to-show rate.

The Apprenticeship Information Center

Cleveland's Apprenticeship Information Center has been embroiled in disputes since its inception in December, 1964. Its director, Mr. William Mengerink, was the only candidate offered to those in Cleveland who sought the establishment of an AIC. His choice—which apparently was the "unofficial" decision of the regional BAT office—was not welcomed by any of Cleveland's civil rights leaders. Subsequent action—or inaction—by this Center seems to bear out the hesitancy surrounding his selection. One BAT official interviewed in August, 1965, summed up the work of the Center with the statement that "the staff has not been distinguished by its brilliance." Other interviewees had far more derogatory comments to make. In November, 1965, when an evaluation team from Washington visited the AIC, the director stated that after eleven months of operation he had placed five Negroes into apprenticeship programs—three in a single automobile mechanic program, one in an industrial tool-and-die program, and one in another unidentified nonunion program. In other words, there had not been a single placement in any of the building crafts apprenticeship programs. The director admitted that he had visited only four schools in the city to discuss the operation of the AIC: two of these high schools were 100 per cent white; one high school had two Negro students; and one was a Negro junior high school. There is small wonder that Negroes interviewed for this study expressed a complete unawareness of the existence of the Center. At the time of the evaluation, the NAACP and the Urban League representatives had ceased attending the meeting of the AIC Advisory Committee. Noting that the building crafts representatives had a perfect attendance record and that the AIC had accomplished so little, one of the members of the evaluation team quipped that "it looks as though these unions have been attending the meetings for 'watchdog' purposes rather than for constructive purposes." The team rebuked the director for his failure to develop "outreach programs" to inform the public of its services.

Urban League-NAACP Project

In May, 1965, the Urban League and the NAACP branch in Cleveland were the joint recipients of an MDTA grant of $380,000. The first paragraph of the contract provided: "This experimental and demonstration project, jointly sponsored by the Urban League of Cleveland and the Cleveland branch of the NAACP, is designed to identify, recruit, test, give in-depth counselling and remedial assistance to 1250 greater Cleveland youth to enable them to qualify for opportunities in today's world of work, including apprenticeship and other training opportunities. Referrals to suitable training and placement in jobs will be made." At the time of its announcement, the newspaper accounts gave the impression to many union and BAT officials that the sole purpose of the project was to train Negro youths to qualify for apprenticeship. Many feared that they would be inundated with applicants. Actually, as is apparent from reading the declaration of the proposal, apprenticeship preparation is only a part of the ambitious project. Its objective is a very broad program to help Negroes qualify for jobs in a variety of occupations. The specific mention of apprenticeship was unfortunate since it gave the entire project a bad name in Cleveland labor circles. It is apparent from our interviews with union officials that many of them still believe apprenticeship to be the goal of the entire project. On more than one occasion, union leaders asked during interview sessions how the limited number of apprenticeship openings (about 170 each year) could accommodate 1,250 Negroes (one claimed the figure to be 3,000 Negroes) who were completing the Urban League-NAACP program.

Known as the Manpower Advancement Program (MAP), the Urban League-NAACP project commenced in the early fall of 1965. After experiencing some early administrative difficulties, the program began to show the results of its efforts during the summer of 1966. With respect to the preapprenticeship phase of the project, four of its trainees were tested by the ironworkers and two passed the examinations; eleven took the sheet metal workers test and six passed; and thirty-one took the electricians' written test and thirty passed. When it came to the oral, however, all of the MAP trainees failed the electricians' oral examination. It is reported that a charge of discrimination will be filed, but such action is pending as of this writing.

The trainees had taken a prevocational curriculum which consisted of instruction in mathematics, blueprint reading, structural problems, English, and job readiness. The MAP trainees, as opposed to the WDL recruitees, who did not receive any financial incentives to attend the preparatory sessions, were paid a benefit allowance for each class they attended. In addition to the institutional instruction, the trainees, as a part of the job-readiness aspect of the program, spent several days on construction jobs where they could become acquainted with the different tools of the job and with their uses. Despite the setback with the electricians, the preliminary results of MAP's work seem promising and its activities should be followed very carefully.

GENERAL CONCLUSIONS

In Cleveland, the squirrel wheel had spun around many times over Negro entry into the building crafts before the summer of 1966. Little progress had been made and frustrations were mounting. The CRB had sought continually to bridge the gap between the craft unions and the Negro community. Its efforts had been extensive, yet its placement results were disappointing. Consequently, its staff and its operations have been attacked by both sides, by the unions for aggressiveness, by the civil rights groups for timidity. With many quarters arguing the issue but few offering remedies, the CRB should be congratulated for its limited accomplishments. It has not had much assistance from any group, not even the city government.

The year 1963 was thought by many to be the year in which—after all the agreements that were made—the door to greater minority participation would be opened, but 1964 saw little accomplished and marked the beginning of disillusionment with the preparation being given to youth by the school system. In 1965 there were municipal elections, during which all parties sought to avoid any public disorders which might assist the opposition (the incumbent mayor was seeking re-election against a strong conservative and a Negro independent), while 1966 appears to be one of renewed interest in the issue of integration in all facets of city life. Apprenticeship will certainly be included. Accordingly, it is unlikely that the city government can continue to placate civil rights groups with its past reliance upon mediatory settlements alone. Far greater public support must be given to the CRB by the city government if the agency is going to be able to maintain any semblance of confidence among minority groups.

By the same token, some other civil rights agency, preferably a private group like the NAACP and the Urban League, should supplement the CRB's recruiting efforts. More attention needs to be placed upon qualitative selection and less upon quantitative supply of applicants. In the past, it seems, the CRB has spent too much time and effort in trying to place almost anyone who expressed the slightest interest in apprenticeship. There is little indication of any type of prescreening. Given the fact that the AIC in the city has been so inept, however, one cannot blame the CRB for being somewhat lax in its screening of applicants. This is a job that the AIC should be doing. The CRB staff has only limited capabilities to make judgments concerning aptitudes and vocational interests. Yet the complete failure of the AIC has meant that the CRB has had to fill the vacuum. As a result, it is clear from the records presented of its own activities (see Table 6-4) and from many of our interviews that too many of the CRB's recruits lacked awareness, motivation, or interest in apprenticeship. Placement results are correlated with the quality of the applicants. It would seem more appropriate for the CRB to concentrate on bringing the city's resources to bear on getting qualified Negroes into apprenticeship programs and let other civil rights agencies or organizations recruit, screen, tutor, and refer applicants. The MAP project may represent a beginning step in this direction. Its experience with IBEW Local 38 could prove to be of special significance. Local 38 had become a symbol of past intransigency to civil rights groups, but its business manager, George Chapple, told us: "Our problems are over with discrimination. This is not going to be a problem with us. All we demand is that the individual be qualified." In addition, William Hirsch, business agent for Local 38, stated during an interview that he considers his local to be "one of the most progressive locals in the IBEW" and that "we consider ourselves second only to Local 3 in New York." It appears that the early results from MAP's efforts to upgrade the caliber of the Negro applicants may provide the opportunity to prove the validity of these opinions by the Local's officials.

Lastly, some mention needs to be made concerning the role of BAT and of the AIC in the city. In no other city studied by this project did these agencies make a poorer impression in the search for resolution of the civil rights controversy. From BAT little cooperation was expected and less was received. The AIC, by the same token, was visualized by the Negro leaders in the community to be an agency to supply the information needed on how, when, and where to apply for apprenticeship. Without this minimal data, it is impossible even to begin to make progress. The AIC, however, has not been able to gain support from the unions, nor has it attempted to co-operate with the CRB. Indeed, it is difficult to ascertain just what it is doing to justify its existence.

CHAPTER VII

PITTSBURGH

INTRODUCTION

Although the 1960 census reported Pittsburgh's population of 604,332 to be 16.8 per cent Negro, it also reported that Negroes constituted only 4.7 per cent of those employed in the city's construction industry (see Table 7-1), which was the lowest of any of our study cities. The slight degree of Negro participation is further indicated by the fact that, while 65 per cent of the Negroes employed in the industry were in the laborer and plasterer and cement occupations, Negroes accounted for only 13.6 per cent of all laborers and only 10.7 per cent of all plasterers and cement masons in the area. In no other city have these figures been so small. Thus, neither the union (commercial and industrial construction) or nonunion (residential) sector of the industry has afforded opportunities for Negroes to find any meaningful amount of employment.

STATISTICS ON THE DEGREE OF NEGRO PARTICIPATION

Table 7-2 presents the data that is available through 1964 for both nonwhite journeymen and apprentices. The figures show virtually no Negro apprentices. The only known Negro apprentices admitted since 1964 are one Negro in the operating engineers' program, two in the sheet metal workers, one in the lathers, four in the carpenters, one in the bricklayers, and three in the painters. As elsewhere, moreover, it took considerable governmental and civil rights activity to produce even these meager results. As of October, 1966, there are no Negro apprentices in the plumbers, electricians, pipefitters, or ironworkers.

SPECIAL ACTIVITIES

On June 17, 1963, a special meeting was called by Pittsburgh's Mayor Joseph M. Barr of the City Commission on Human Rela-

Table 7-1

Employment in Selected Occupations by Race, 1960—Pittsburgh Metropolitan Area

Occupation	Number Employed				Percentage Distribution			
	Total	White	Negro	Other nonwhite	Total	White	Negro	Other nonwhite
Selected occupations								
Carpenters	7,220	7,126	94	—	100.0	98.7	1.3	—
Plasterers and cement finishers	1,303	1,164	139	—	100.0	89.3	10.7	—
Structural metal workers	1,188	1,185	3	—	100.0	99.7	0.3	—
Electricians	4,522	4,490	32	—	100.0	99.3	0.7	—
Plumbers and pipefitters	5,336	5,291	45	—	100.0	99.2	0.8	—
Construction laborers	7,954	6,869	1,085	—	100.0	86.4	13.6	—
Total employed	592,335	560,686	31,079	570	100.0	94.7	5.2	0.1
Total construction industry	40,230	38,336	1,877	17	100.0	95.3	4.7	<0.005

Note: Percentages may not add to total because of rounding.   Based on data obtained from U.S. Bureau of the Census.

Table 7-2

Nonwhite Participation in Selected Building Trades Unions, July 8, 1963, to December 31, 1964—Pittsburgh

Local Union	Total Membership	Total Nonwhites	Nonwhite Journeymen Applications	Nonwhite Journeymen Admissions	Number of Apprentices	Nonwhite Apprentice Applications	Nonwhite Apprentice Admissions
Asbestos Workers 2	212	0	0	0	27	1	0
Carpenters District Council	7,500ᵃ	50ᵃ	1	0	115	42	3
IBEW 5	1,000ᵃ	1	4	0	18ᵃ	6	0
Operating Engineers 66	5,880	120ᵃ	N.A.	N.A.	19	0	0
Ironworkers 3	1,937	2	0	0	1	0	0
Painters 6	800	22	8	3 or 4	22	1	1
Sheet Metal 12	1,200	20ᵃ	0	0	50ᵃ	0	0
Steamfitters 449	1,400	0	2	0	50ᵃ	0	0
Elevator Constructors 6	227	0	0	0	0	0	0

Based on data obtained from the Commission on Human Relations, City of Pittsburgh.

ᵃ Estimated.

N.A., not available.

Note: Plumbers 27 was not surveyed due to court litigation proceedings. It was estimated that the total membership in the local was 886 in 1964. The local did not conduct an apprenticeship class between 1960 and 1966.

tions, the Human Relations Committee of the Building Trades Council, and representatives of the Master Builders' Association. At the meeting, a resolution was presented that had been unanimously adopted at a June 12, 1963, meeting of the Building Trades Council. The resolution stated the intention of the council to cooperate with the Commission "in the Commission's primary objective of eliminating discrimination in the employment of persons in the building and construction industry where it exists."[1] A special subcommittee was appointed to implement the declaration. An interim report was released by the subcommittee on July 8, 1963, which stated that meetings had been held with all the major unions within the Building Trades Council (with the exception of IBEW Local 5). All of those except IBEW Local 5 gave their assurance of intention to comply with the resolution. On July 23, 1963, Local 5 concluded a similar agreement with the committee. The subcommittee viewed the participation of the major craft unions "as evidence of their desire to cooperate and to implement a positive program." It was felt, however, that the ultimate resolution of the problem rested with an improvement in the extensive unemployment problem in the Pittsburgh construction industry.

On July 15, 1963, the Pennsylvania Human Relations Commission ordered "seven all white local craft unions in the Pittsburgh area . . . to begin admitting Negroes to membership and to apprenticeship training programs."[2] The seven unions were IBEW Local 5, Ironworkers Local 3, Asbestos Workers Local 2, Elevator Constructors Local 6, Painters Local 751, Plumbers Local 27, and Steamfitters Local 449. Of the twenty-two witnesses appearing the first day of the Commission's proposed three-day hearings on discrimination by the unions, five were Negro electricians and two were Negro plumbers who claimed that they had been denied membership because of their race. On the second day of hearings, the seven unions decided not to contest their cases any further and to allow the Commission to enter an order against them. Charges against Roofers Local 37 and Sheet Metal Workers Local 12 were dismissed earlier "when it was established that their membership [was] integrated."[3] The Commission ordered the unions to accept qualified journeymen immediately; to permit neutral observers

[1] Resolution adopted June 12, 1963, by the Building Trades Council of Pittsburgh and Vicinity (mimeographed).

[2] News release issued by the Pennsylvania Human Relations Commission, Harrisburg, Pa., July 15, 1963, p. 1.

[3] Ibid., p. 3.

appointed by the Commission to be present at written, oral, and/or performance examinations; to admit on a nondiscriminatory basis qualified applicants to apprenticeship programs; to accept "an appropriate number" of nonwhite applicants in all future apprenticeship classes; and to present on request written statements of the nonwhite applicants, rejectees, and acceptees into apprenticeship classes for the next two years.

Late in 1963, demonstrations were conducted by civil rights groups against the Carpenters' District Council and the Master Builders' Association. It was alleged that Negro members of the Council were unable to secure work with contractors who had agreements with the union. In early spring, 1964, a meeting was held between the parties, out of which came an agreement by the Master Builders' Association to place all "card-carrying Negro carpenters" referred to the Association.

In 1965, the Commission on Human Relations (CHR) issued a report, entitled *Status of Negroes in Craft Unions . . . Pittsburgh Labor Market,* which sought to portray developments in this industry since the 1965 agreement. A summary of the CHR's findings was presented earlier in Table 7-2 (p. 115). The Commission was hopeful that Negroes could enter apprenticeship because (1) it offered training in all aspects of a trade, (2) it had an escalating wage scale that provided an incentive for the trainee to continue, and (3) the programs are supervised by state and federal Bureaus of Apprenticeship and Training. It concluded from its survey, however, that "generally the unions which have desegregated their apprentice programs represent the 'trowel trades.' "[4] The report attributed the low number of Negro applicants to be the results of (1) a lack of motivation by Negro youth as a result of the past practices of these unions, and (2) an unawareness, due to their low participation in the programs, of the opportunities to be realized. With respect to journeymen, the report concluded that the pattern paralleled that of the intake of Negro apprentices.

The second significant development in 1965 was a court ruling upholding the legality of the city's Fair Employment Ordinance. The specific case, *City of Pittsburgh* vs. *Plumbers Local Union No. 27,* found the union guilty of discriminating against two Negro nonunion journeymen who sought admission to the local. Local 27, which was fined $400, announced plans to appeal the verdict to a higher court, but later relented and gave an examination to the two

---

[4] *Status of Negroes in Craft Unions . . . Pittsburgh Labor Market,* Special Report of the Commission on Human Relations (1965), p. 10.

applicants with CHR observers present. Out of a possible 100 points, one applicant scored 19 and the other 14. The fact that both had failed was recognized by all observers and there was no charge of unfairness. In the summer of 1966, Plumbers Local 27 announced that it would form its first apprenticeship class in over five years. Applications were accepted until August 15, 1966, and selection proceedings began shortly afterward.

The Master Builders' Association has adopted several resolutions pertaining to equal opportunity for minorities. It is not clear, however, just what power the association has over the practices of the individual contractors. Very little, it seems. Morever, the Association seems not to feel that it has any obligation to undertake affirmative recruiting efforts.

In August, 1965, civil rights groups staged demonstrations at the office of IBEW Local 5 and the Pittsburgh Public Housing Authority in an effort to obtain access for Negro electricians. During the summer of 1966, Local 5 gave its qualification examination to about 200 applicants, of which about fifteen were Negroes. The results are yet to be released.

REMEDIAL PROGRAMS

Prior to October, 1966, Pittsburgh did not have an AIC. As of that date a federally funded and state-administered AIC was established. Only the future can tell whether or not it will be of any assistance. There was not much interest expressed about such an agency during our interview work. In fact, Mr. Edward E. Smith, Director of Job Development for the local Urban League, said that "an AIC is not an answer because it only goes through the motions."

The CHR has been at the center of activities to get Negroes into apprenticeship programs. Most unions inform the CHR when they are planning to conduct classes, the qualifications needed, and the places to apply. Moreover, the CHR has actively recruited Negro applicants for these classes. The Commission has had an observer present at all written tests and has a follow-up procedure to find out such things as why some applicants fail to show up for exams or drop out of classes.

The CHR has done an excellent job in documenting its work. Unfortunately, despite an aggressive attempt to seek out recruits and to chaperone potential applicants, the Commission has had little success in obtaining applicants for the building trades. In 1965, for example, the CHR attempted to recruit applicants for the operating engineers by writing letters to sixty recent graduates of four predominantly Negro high schools. None of the sixty, whose names were obtained from the schools' head counselors, planned to go on to college. Thirty-seven of these high school graduates responded to the CHR and were given detailed instructions on application procedures for the operating engineers program. All thirty-seven promised to apply; only five did. Of the five, only four showed up to take the written examination. Two of these failed, two passed and were admitted, but one of these has subsequently dropped out of the program. The CHR staff then went back to find out what happened to those who said they would take the test but didn't; twenty-nine were located. A staff official said he was "flabbergasted" at the excuses he received—"they were absurd": "they forgot," "they overslept," "they got another job," and "many just didn't have an excuse."

Similar experiences can be related with almost every program in Pittsburgh. For example, IBEW Local 5—the target of demonstrations in 1965—has had similar experiences. In 1963, IBEW Local 5 extended by three months its period for accepting applications after it had been pressured to open up its program. Three Negroes applied. Of the three, one failed to appear, one failed the test, one passed the test and was offered a position in the class only to turn it down to accept a job as a messenger at a utility company. In 1964, three more applied. Two failed the test, one did not appear. In 1965, none applied.

It seems that, except for the CHR, no other group has had an inclination to undertake the difficult task of recruitment. Many are concerned with the issue, but it seems that they are doing little to supply names for positions in the building trades. It may be that their implicit withdrawal is indicative of a feeling of futility. The Urban League, for example, has abandoned the building crafts and has been supplying applicants only to the industrial apprenticeship programs—especially at Westinghouse—in the area. While it had no precise figures to support its claims, the Urban League attributed its success at Westinghouse to the fact that a Negro who had succeeded in the program came and spoke personally in some of the high schools.

GENERAL CONCLUSIONS

With the incredibly small degree of participation by Negroes in the construction industry, the problem of entry into the trades is made more acute in Pittsburgh than elsewhere. In other cities, there is often an opportunity in the nonunion sector for Negroes to become acquainted with building trades occupations. Such is clearly not the case in Pittsburgh. Until October, 1966, the responsibility for spreading information concerning apprenticeship has fallen upon the CHR. As is usual, the Commission has a multitude of duties and responsibilities to perform, but it has, nonetheless, devoted a good part of its attention to this area. Prior to the coming of the AIC, the CHR has had to perform the tasks of promoting apprenticeship, gathering and disseminating pertinent data on entrance requirements and testing dates, recruiting applicants, counseling applicants, supervising tests, following up on fail-to-shows, rejectees, and placements, and publishing reports on developments in the city. Given the experiences of most of the other AICs, it is likely that the CHR will have to remain active in this area. With the possible exception of Cleveland, there is no CHR in any city included in this report that has tried more thoroughly and valiantly to resolve this issue but which has received less co-operation from either unions or civil rights groups. The city is fortunate to have such a dedicated body in its midst; it is a shame it does not receive greater support.

CHAPTER VIII

CINCINNATI

INTRODUCTION

Located in the southwestern tip of Ohio, the city of Cincinnati has a metropolitan population of about a million people, about one-half of whom live in the central city itself. The Negro population is about 125,000, with approximately 85 per cent of this number residing in the central city.

Cincinnati advertises itself as the "gateway to the South." Conversely, it could as well be named "the gateway to the North." It has long been a stopping-off place for Negroes migrating to the North from the deep South. Many moved no farther. The same pattern can be noted for numerous Appalachian whites who have similarly migrated into the city. The negative attitudes on integration held by many of these whites, who comprise a substantial portion of the labor force, is felt to represent a strong crosscurrent against the advancement of equal opportunity.

It should be understood, however, that the jurisdiction included by the building trades unions is not restricted solely to the confines of the city. Their members are drawn from and their work is performed in a three-state area: southwestern Ohio, southeastern Indiana, and northern Kentucky. Within the sixteen-county area covered by the Cincinnati Building Trades Council, the Negro population is estimated to be about 7 per cent.

The Cincinnati economy was originally centered around the tanning industry. Employment in this industry—noted for its distasteful working conditions—was historically dominated by Negroes. With the disappearance of tanning and the subsequent decline of the low-wage clothing industry, many traditional job opportunities for Negroes vanished. In more recent times, the economy has been dominated by manufacturing enterprises, with over 35 per cent of the employment opportunities in the city found in this sector. Manufacturing expansion, however, has come mainly

Table 8-1

Employment in Selected Occupations by Race, 1960—Cincinnati Metropolitan Area

Occupation	Number Employed				Percentage Distribution			
	Total	White	Negro	Other nonwhite	Total	White	Negro	Other nonwhite
Selected occupations								
Carpenters	3,148	3,075	73	—	100.0	97.7	2.3	—
Plasterers and cement finishers	724	435	289	—	100.0	60.0	40.0	—
Structural metal workers	260	260	—	—	100.0	100.0	—	—
Electricians	2,012	1,982	30	—	100.0	98.5	1.5	—
Plumbers and pipefitters	1,703	1,659	44	—	100.0	97.4	2.6	—
Construction laborers	4,172	1,754	2,404	14	100.0	42.0	58.0	—
Total employed	266,275	239,868	25,988	419	100.0	90.1	9.8	0.1
Total construction industry	20,599	17,019	3,562	18	100.0	82.6	17.3	0.1

Note: Percentages may not add to total because of rounding.　　　　Based on data obtained from U.S. Bureau of the Census.

from the enlargement of existing companies rather than from the introduction of new firms or industries.

Many Negroes have found employment in the nonunion sector of the construction industry. Table 8-1 shows that about 17.3 per cent of those employed in the industry in 1960 were Negroes. Although this proportion was the fourth highest of the ten cities studied, it was the highest of the six Northern cities surveyed. Yet, as elsewhere, a closer inspection shows the familiar pattern, with Negroes concentrated in the cement masons, plasterers, and laborers. In fact, 75 per cent of the Negroes employed in the industry were in these three job classifications.

NEGRO PARTICIPATION IN SELECTED UNIONS AND APPRENTICESHIP PROGRAMS

Table 8-2 shows that in the fall of 1965, there were only twenty-one Negro apprentices out of a total of 439 in the city. While Negro figures represent 4.7 per cent of the total, it should be noted that nineteen of the Negro apprentices (or 90 per cent of their total) were members of three traditionally accessible trades: the carpen-

Table 8-2

Negro Participation in Apprenticeship Programs in Selected Building Trades Unions in Cincinnati, Fall, 1965

Union	Total Union Membership	Total Apprentices	Total Negro Apprentices
Bricklayers	550	16	0
Carpenters	2,659	58	9
Cement Masons	334	7	4
Roofers	212	39	6
IBEW	725	102	0
Elevator Constructors	110	0	0
Operating Engineers	1,100	0	0
Painters	167	15	0
Pipefitters	750	49	0
Plasterers	110	9	0
Plumbers	495	48	0
Reinforced Ironworkers	182	12	1
Sheet Metal Workers	750	56	1
Structural Ironworkers	418	28	0

Based on data obtained from the Ohio Civil Rights Commission.

ters, cement masons, and roofers. The pattern of Negro participation in Cincinnati, therefore, conforms to that of the other study cities.

UNIONISM AND APPRENTICESHIP

According to regional officials of the Bureau of Apprenticeship and Training, Cincinnati "is not a strong union town." This characteristic stems, in part, from the heritage of the German management-oriented settlers in the area. Today, with respect to the building trades, the line of demarcation in construction work is clearly drawn. Commercial and industrial construction is the domain of union work, while residential construction is for nonunion work. As indicated earlier, many Negroes have found employment in the nonunion sector, where the work is more regular but the wages lower. In recent years, according to a Cincinnati AFL-CIO spokesman, commercial construction activity in the city has failed to keep pace with the national trends in the industry. He states that "Between 1958–1964 employment in the construction trades was up 12 per cent in the U.S. but down six per cent in Cincinnati. The whole economic picture is bleak here."[1] As a result, the Cincinnati Building Trades Council stated in 1965: "It is a fact that normally the construction market would be training 1,500 to 2,000 apprentice craftsmen. Lack of construction work and automation have reduced the opportunities for apprentices and there are now less than 500 apprentices in training."[2] Thus, it seems that the mounting civil rights activities to get Negroes into apprenticeship programs came at a time of limited apprenticeship opportunities.

Apprenticeship programs in the state are administered through a state program known as the Ohio Plan. Qualifications and procedures for selection into apprenticeship must be approved by the state. Under these provisions, channels are established for appeals from selection decisions by local JACs considered to be discriminatory. To date, however, there has not been a single such complaint filed. In fact, it is unlikely that there ever will be, which only serves to demonstrate the futility of these supposed safeguards. The breakdown occurs because the appeals procedure is a lengthy and expensive process. Moreover, individual complaints of discrimination are

[1] Sidney E. Elsner, "Rights Groups Prepare To Test Labor," *The Plain Dealer*, October 11, 1965. (Statement is attributed to Mr. Al Bilick, President, Cincinnati AFL-CIO Labor Council.)

[2] Sidney E. Elsner, "Cincinnati Catholics in Vanguard of Civil Rights Fight," *The Plain Dealer*, October 12, 1965.

almost impossible to prove. Cincinnati civil rights groups consider it far more realistic to move against patterns of discrimination, which has been the tack followed in their challenges.

In January, 1952, the City Council of Cincinnati began an investigation of racial discrimination in employment in the Cincinnati metropolitan area. The Mayor's Friendly Relations Committee (MFRC) was entrusted with the responsibility of carrying out the mandate of the Council. The MFRC, in turn, requested Professor Alfred Kuhn of the Department of Economics at the University of Cincinnati to conduct the study. In his report, which was published by the MFRC, discrimination by labor unions was strongly attacked as indicated by his conclusion that "a rather clear pattern [of discrimination] exists with many AFL unions, particularly in the building trades."[3] Specifically, the report stated:

> Within the unionized construction field, Negroes are found exclusively (or with negligible exception) only on common labor jobs, skilled jobs being white only. The Hod-Carriers and Building Laborers Union has about 75 per cent Negro membership. On the other hand, the Carpenters, Bricklayers, Plasterers, Painters, Electricians, Plumbers, and Steamfitters are exclusively (or with negligible exception) white. Since there are a fair number of Negroes doing the skilled jobs for non-union contracting firms, and since many contractors accept Negroes for the common labor jobs, it seems highly unlikely that *all* union contractors adamantly refuse to hire Negroes for *any* skilled classification. It seems reasonable to conclude that these unions have consciously and systematically excluded Negroes.[4]

By 1963 it seemed clear to local civil rights groups that little progress had occurred in alleviating the situation. Thus, in part due to the enactment of a state Fair Employment Practices Act in 1959, in part due to this lack of improvement of the earlier-diagnosed problem by the Kuhn report, and in part due to the increasing momentum generated by the accelerating national civil rights movements, the issue was in the spotlight of city attention.

In late May of 1963, the NAACP chapter in the city threatened to conduct demonstrations to protest alleged discrimination by the building crafts at the site of the new Federal Building. Earlier in that same month, violence had broken out in Philadelphia over this very issue. Fearing a similar fate in Cincinnati, urgent negotiations began between MFRC, the building craft unions, the building contractors, the NAACP, and government officials (federal, state, and

---

[3] Alfred Kuhn, "Condensation of a Research Study of the Problem," in The Mayor's Friendly Relations Committee, *Report Concerning Racial Discrimination in Employment in the Cincinnati Area* (April, 1953), p. 10.

[4] *Ibid.* (emphasis contained in the original).

local). After seven weeks of negotiations by the direct participants, the formation of a special committee of volunteers (known as the Leadership Committee), and a renewed threat of demonstrations, a declaration of future equal opportunity in "jobs and training" was signed by the Building Trades Unions.[5] Contained in the pledge were such laudatory statements as "to work toward the correction of economic injustices to the members of all minority groups . . . to accept into membership any applicant who meets the required qualifications regardless of race . . . to accept apprentice applications in accordance with their qualifications and there shall be no discrimination. . . ." To supervise the implementation of these pledges, the eight-man Leadership Committee was to continue in existence.

Between July, 1963, and the spring of 1965, the major accomplishment of the Leadership Committee was the establishment in April, 1964, of an Apprenticeship Information Center in the city.

In May, 1964, the MFRC sent a questionnaire to all of the building trades unions in the Cincinnati area. The purpose of this questionnaire was to establish a benchmark from which future developments could be measured. The questionnaire sought to elicit the number of Negro journeymen and Negro apprentices in each union as of that date. The response to this request was sketchy. In fact, the files of the MFRC show only eight responses (see Table 8-3).

Beginning in 1965, the NAACP let it be known that it was extremely dissatisfied with developments since the 1963 accord. The organization asked for a re-activation and expansion of the Leadership Committee. The committee began discussions in early May.

The MFRC, which became the Cincinnati Human Relations Commission (HRC) in mid-May, 1965, at the suggestion of the Leadership Committee, again circulated a questionnaire to all unions in the area concerning the number of Negro journeymen and apprentices on their rosters. This time the data were held confidential although it is known that only nine of the twenty-five unions contacted bothered to reply.

In the meantime, two developments had occurred. Early in 1965, "The Committee of Twenty-eight" was formed. Its membership consists of fourteen whites and fourteen Negroes who presumably represent "the power structure" of the city. Their membership has not been made public and their mission is to work behind the scenes

[5] The Mayor's Friendly Relations Committee, "The Executive Director's Report for May–June and July, 1963," pp. 1–2.

Table 8-3

Summary of Data as of May 1, 1964, Concerning Racial Membership of Building Trades in Cincinnati, as Reported to the Human Relations Commission

Union	Membership Total	Total Journeymen	Nonwhite	No. of Apprentices	No. of Nonwhite Apprentices	No. of Apprentices Waiting
Ironworkers 44	456	430	0	19	0	8
Cement Masons 524	400	390	230	10	6	15
Plasterers 1	140	—	1	7	0	6
Glaziers 387	90	90	1	6	0	7
Plumbers 59	420	—	"unknown"	59	"unknown"	50
Lathers 47	75	75	"information given to the AIC" [i.e., it was not reported to HRC]			
Hod-Carriers 265	2,100	1,400	"Has no apprenticeship program"			
Roofers 42	204	185	43	25	9	43

Note: These were the only reports on file in the HRC offices.

to resolve community racial problems. Due to the Committee's anonymous nature, it is impossible to assess its impact. On the surface, it appears to have been minimal.

The second development in that year pertains to the disillusionment of the civil rights groups with the work of the AIC. Earlier hailed as a major accomplishment, the Center had become a sham. As of May 31, 1965 (after thirteen months of operation), a total of twenty Negro referrals had been made, but not a single Negro had been placed in an apprenticeable trade through the Center. The poor results occurred despite the fact that all of the local unions, except the IBEW, had by this date agreed to accept referrals from the AIC. The IBEW administered its aptitude tests in conjunction with Xavier University.

With discontent rising, the NAACP formally requested in late May, 1965, that the City Council undertake a thorough investigation. The City Council, however, demurred. Instead, it unanimously passed a resolution requesting that the Ohio Civil Rights Commission (OCRC) conduct an inquiry.

In July, 1965, meetings of the Leadership Committee broke off. Since its re-activation two months earlier, it had served as little more than a forum. The only concrete pledge that came from the ten meetings was an announcement at the meeting of May 18 by the plumbers' local that they would admit anyone to membership who applied with a city license. The Urban League and the NAACP had been asked to supply lists of potential recruits; neither did so. The plasterers and the bricklayers announced they had sought to organize Negro contractors but had not succeeded because the contractors would not agree to pay the union scale.

In early August, OCRC announced that it would conduct a full investigation of the employment practices of a hundred contractors and forty-seven local unions "to determine if there is a discriminatory pattern or practice with regard to race and color in the Cincinnati area."[6] During the week, demonstrations over the issue broke out in the city. Led by members of CORE and the NAACP, "sit-ins," "sleep-ins," and a march to the building site of a forthcoming convention center (which had been cleared by federal urban renewal funds) took place. A few weeks later, demonstrations were also conducted at a construction site at the University of Cincinnati.

As a result of the demonstrations and against the backdrop of

[6] Press Release of Ohio Civil Rights Commission, August 10, 1965, p. 1.

the Watts crisis in Los Angeles, which broke out during the same week, the HRC convened an Emergency Task Force (ETF). The ETF held its first meeting on August 13, 1965. Out of the meeting two problem areas were designated:

1. Are there competent workers available and willing to fill these jobs?
2. Were there currently any jobs for Negroes in the construction trades?

Shortly afterward two subcommittees were formed: one was called the Talent Search Committee and the other the Job Availability Committee.

The Talent Search Committee (chaired by the Negro President of the Hod-Carriers Union) began by concentrating its efforts on Negro journeymen either working for nonunion Negro contractors or journeymen in unionized construction trades (as laborers) who have familiarity with the industry and whose skills were potentially transferable to other trades. After a series of crash efforts, which included the use of door-to-door handbills in Negro communities, a series of community meetings, radio announcements on predominantly Negro-oriented radio stations, and a city-wide rally, the Committee reported in late September that it had recruited thirty-seven potential apprentice applicants and thirty-six potential journeymen. This list was later expanded to include fifty-eight potential apprentice applicants and a hundred and five potential journeymen. Out of this list of names, twelve potential apprentices were referred to JACs and five journeymen to the unions. From this number, two carpenter journeymen and two apprentice rodmen were accepted.

With respect to the Job Availability Committee, it was—according to its chairman—"not very successful." Its failure was blamed on union intransigency and employer fear of union retaliation in in the way of slowdowns.

Following the apparent failure of these subcommittees to produce tangible results and with a prediction by one civil rights spokesman that "all hell is going to break loose in the spring [of 1966]," the Cincinnati Municipal Youth Commission (whose activities are concentrated on increasing the employability of disadvantaged youths) applied to the Department of Labor for a grant to train 150 youths and adults. The specific goal of this program was to prepare the 150 to qualify for apprenticeship or journeymen status by the opening of the building season in the spring of 1966. The project, however, was scuttled after a futile attempt to obtain federal funding.

In place of the youth-training program, a new proposal was substituted. A co-operative venture, composed of union, civil rights, and local government bodies and known as the Greater Cincinnati Vocational Foundation, was formed. Primarily the program concentrated upon upgrading the job and educational skills of insufficiently trained Negro journeymen. Through such an undertaking, it was felt that the chances for the participants to qualify for journeyman status in unions would have been enhanced. The participants, interestingly, were selected by the HRC and not by the Employment Service. Funded by the Department of Labor, the first cycle of this program was completed by late 1966. However, thus far the program has been a disappointment to its sponsors because not enough partially trained Negro journeymen have been willing to participate in this kind of training. The apparent reason for the journeymen's reluctance was the reasonably good employment conditions in nonunion work. The first cycle of the program started with only thirty-five people instead of the proposed one hundred; only twenty completed the initial phase.

On October 8, 1965, the HRC released a report showing the number of Negroes who were employees of the city working in the skilled building trades. The report disclosed that there were 174 white skilled tradesmen and one Negro. The Negro was a cement finisher.

In January, 1966, all of the members of the Building Trades Council announced they would: hold open tests for journeymen; notify the HRC when apprenticeship applications would be accepted; and make public announcements concerning application dates and details.

The announcement had little impact upon civil rights spokesmen, essentially because of the imminent release of the OCRC findings. In fact, developments over the issue became even more acute as positions polarized. The breakdown occurred when a newspaper reporter was found to have sneaked into a closed meeting between the union and Department of Labor officials. After a scuffle and a second attempt by the reporter to eavesdrop on the meeting and a second scuffle, negotiations on the topic collapsed completely. All parties decided to await the OCRC report.

On February 24, 1966, the OCRC released the findings of its study. Its major conclusion was: "There is a pattern of racial discrimination in the Building Trades in Cincinnati."[7] The practices of contractors, unions, and JACs were criticized. Contractors were attacked because they had surrendered their employment decisions to the unions; unions because they "practiced discrimination by ignoring the Negro as a potential member of the building trades work force"; and JACs because they discouraged Negro applicants, limited or discontinued programs, maintained impractical standards, and failed to give adequate public promotion to recruitment of apprenticeship classes. Table 8-3 (p. 127) indicates the Commission's findings concerning the degree of Negro participation in specific apprenticeship programs. Much of the information was elicited only through the use of subpoena. With respect to the IBEW, plumbers, pipefitters, sheet metal workers, and ironworkers—whose rolls totaled 2,738 members—there was not a single Negro journeyman—and only one Negro apprentice. Accordingly, among its remedial recommendations, the report suggested: that all parties sign a statement on equal opportunity by April 1, 1966; that the City of Cincinnati establish a contract-compliance procedure for city construction; that the duties of the AIC be expanded to include journeymen; that the Cincinnati Board of Education review its policies regarding discrimination and the use of its training facilities; that the unions and JACs continue to conduct open testing with public announcements of qualifications, requirements, examination times, and dates; and, finally, that aggrieved individuals seek relief through Title VII of the Civil Rights Act and the directives of the NLRB.

The Commission's findings did not center upon any particular individual (although nine charges claiming discrimination in employment in the construction industry were filed by aggrieved individuals with the Commission during the course of its investigation), so no redress or punitive action was taken. The report was assailed by some labor spokesmen. The criticisms basically were: that the report compared union membership, which covers sixteen counties, with the Negro population figures of the Cincinnati area alone; that there were no specific individuals cited as having been discriminated against; that no mention was made of the Negro youths who have declined positions offered to them; and that all of the unions are accepting referrals from the AIC, which is open to anyone who wishes to apply.

[7] Ohio Civil Rights Commission, "Racial Discrimination in the Cincinnati Building Trades" (February 24, 1966), p. 30.

131

With respect to the recommendations of the OCRC, an unsuccessful attempt was made by the Commission to have each union sign the nondiscrimination "statement of understanding" by the April 1, 1966, deadline. After individual consultation with those who would not sign, it was agreed that in lieu of signing another pledge (the 1963 statement still being in effect), eleven trades agreed to give an open journeymen's examination within ninety days to anyone who wished to take it. Those who passed would be admitted immediately to full membership. The Commission was allowed to have an observer present at the tests. Public announcements were made through all news media of the times and places that the examination would be given.

The Negro turnout was extremely disappointing. In the words of the OCRC observer, there was "very little response" by the Negro community. None of the nine Negroes who had claimed they were discriminated against during the Commissions public hearings showed up to take the tests. Only one Negro applied for the plasterers' examination; he passed and was admitted. Likewise, only one Negro took the glaziers' examination; he failed. The carpenters agreed to give their examination to anyone at any time but, as reported, there were no takers. There is no explanation available from civil rights spokesmen for the lack of Negro response to this opportunity.

GENERAL CONCLUSIONS

The impact of the OCRC report could mark the end of an era or it could represent a Pyrrhic victory for the cause of civil rights. Prior to the decision, the Negro community and the labor movement were at polar extremes with no apparent effort being made by either side to close the gap and find accommodation. Whether the report will serve to melt or to solidify these positions remains to be seen. The most hopeful sign on the horizon is that both factions are fortunate to have enlightened leadership. What is desperately needed and what has been absent throughout these trying times is an adequate middle agent. The Leadership Committee did not fill the bill for several reasons. First, the Committee was dominated by too many of the actual participants, who had only a vested interest in presenting their side of the story. Secondly, there has been a turnover in membership and chairmanship, which has diluted the responsibility for its actions. Thirdly, and perhaps most important, is the fact that the outsiders on the Committee seem to have envisioned their roles as essentially to keep the combatants from engaging each other and to keep the channels of communication open. In other words, it seems that the neutral parties involved in the dispute have been more concerned with conciliation than with mediation. More is needed than simply a third party who arranges meeting times, finds a place to meet, and sees to it that both sides are given an opportunity to express their views. The missing link from the beginning has been the absence of any continuing body to seek out Negro youth and to press the unions with their availability. The *ad hoc* Talent Search Committee was a step in the right direction, but by its temporary nature it could not and did not develop the expertise required to get results. Much more is needed than simply an agency that rounds up random individuals during a month-long drive and then vanishes as the committee members return to their normal duties in their respective vocations. The HRC, which has long existed in the city, has apparently never exercised an affirmative role. It is clear from interviews in the city with civil rights spokesmen that they have no confidence in the agency. Moreover, it was obvious that this lack of confidence permeates the HRC itself, which is aware that it is being circumvented. The agency does not know what to do to obtain the community respect that it presently lacks. Now, it would seem, is the propitious time for the HRC to come to the center of the ring while the two parties are in their respective corners gawking at each other. In Cleveland, Philadelphia, and Pittsburgh, the city Human Relations Commissions have seized the initiative. Their role was never popular in the short run, but they did not hesitate to move into the arena. In New York and Detroit, it has been private groups who have undertaken the sometimes Herculean task of promoting, encouraging, eliciting, and tutoring Negro youth to apply to apprenticeship programs.

The HRC looms as the most appropriate body to step into the existing quagmire through a process of elimination of the other power groups in the city. First, it is obvious to all that the Cincinnati AIC is not going to do anything to rock the boat. It visualizes its mission to be the task of dispensing information to those who walk into its premises (which is in a basement with no street identification signs). In fact, it also appears that the AIC staff cannot be counted on even to promote apprenticeship programs in the city. The concept of "outreach" programs seems to apply to all agencies in the local employment service except the AIC.

Secondly, the experience in every city shows that the unions involved—no matter how sympathetic some may be—are not going to perform the task of recruitment. One might argue—as the civil rights groups in Cincinnati have—that in view of the past practices the unions have a moral duty to seek out Negro applicants. But to expect moral pressures exerted from without to move a trade union to follow a desired course of action is to deny an awareness of the development of American trade unionism. Unions in the United States have seldom responded to ideological stimuli. Rather, the movement in general and the craft unions in particular have always been extremely pragmatic in their goals and in their tactics. Apprenticeship is sacred to the craft unions, and the institution is steeped in union tradition. Asking people to join has never been a part of the code. Furthermore, equal opportunity to many union members is second to job security and family income. Cincinnati has been plagued with an inordinately high rate of unemployment, both in the city and in the construction industry. Union leaders, who must be responsible to the membership for their actions, cannot realistically be expected to seek out any applicants—Negro or white—when the union entrance doors already have more hopeful applicants in line than the membership wants to admit.

Thirdly, the actions of the civil rights groups in the city have shown few signs of encouragement for the resolution of the impasse. Despite strong leaders who have been able to marshal support behind their drives, the program set forth suffers from a complete lack of imagination and an apparent unawareness of exactly what apprenticeship programs are. Far more serious efforts to interest and to recruit applicants who desire to work in the trades are required than simply giving out handbills on the street corner and speaking to Sunday school classes. The work is tedious and frequently slow in demonstrating results. For these reasons, a civil rights group whose existence is often perpetuated by its ability to show quick results is not a desirable vehicle for successfully settling the long-run apprenticeship issue. Rather, what is needed is a continuing body which accumulates experience in recruiting and gains the confidence of both the applicants it recruits and the JACs with which it deals. Such a body has repeatedly proven itself to be the only agency through which demonstrable results can be accomplished.

Whether the HRC can assume this role and whether it will be given the support by the city government to exercise the responsibility for performing this thankless task will spell the difference between continued division between the parties and possible resolution of the problem. If the HRC continues to remain on the sidelines, the only hope for settlement will rest in the establishment within the city of a new body (similar to the Workers Defense League) to fill the void.

Given the experiences of human relations commissions elsewhere, however, the best long-term solution for the city would be the establishment of a WDL-type operation. The HRC represents the best existing channel for providing assistance to both sides. But, because of its multiple responsibilities, limited staff, poor image, and restricted powers, it could provide only short-run relief. The more challenging job—that of recruiting, tutoring, and establishing working relationships with JACs—requires an organization that can specialize on a continuing basis on these complex issues. Serious consideration should be given to such an undertaking.

CHAPTER IX

DETROIT

INTRODUCTION

As compared with our other study cities, Detroit has several unique features. Detroit's 1960 population of 1.6 million made it the nation's fifth largest city. Although nonwhites constituted 29.2 per cent of the city's population, Negroes comprised 53 per cent of public school enrollment in 1964. Detroit also has a large number of ethnic communities within its boundaries.

Although Detroit is a strong union town, because of the importance of the automobile industry, the industrial unions dominate the city's labor movement. In fact, it is estimated by Mr. William Sher, Director of the Apprenticeship Information Center in Detroit, that about 60 per cent of the apprentices in the city are industrial apprentices and 40 per cent are in the building crafts. Moreover, there are two separate public apprentice-training facilities in Detroit: the Washington Trade School for industrial apprentices and the Apprentice School for the building and printing crafts.

Fifteen of the thirty building trades in the city use the Apprentice School's facilities. The classes are all conducted during the daytime on a two-week cycle (i.e., the student works nine days on the job and attends class on the tenth day). Employers pay the wages of apprentices while they attend classes. The school operates on a twelve-month uninterrupted basis. The apprentice is required to begin classes immediately after his acceptance by a JAC.

Although both apprentice schools are part of the Detroit Public School System, they have operated without financial support from the city since 1963. Except for the federal funds received under the Smith-Hughes Act, the apprenticeship-related training costs in 1965 were defrayed by tuition charges of $151.40 a year (plus, in some instances, costs of certain instruction materials). Tuition charges are based on the cost of 144 hours of instruction a year (the minimum allowed under the Smith-Hughes Act). The students are allowed to pay their tuition in four installments.

Table 9-1

Employment in Selected Occupations by Race, 1960—Detroit Metropolitan Area

Occupation	Number Employed				Percentage Distribution			
	Total	White	Negro	Other nonwhite	Total	White	Negro	Other nonwhite
Selected occupations								
Carpenters	9,043	8,675	363	5	100.0	95.9	4.0	0.1
Plasterers and cement finishers	1,480	1,097	383	—	100.0	74.1	25.9	—
Structural metal workers	1,095	1,071	19	5	100.0	97.8	1.7	0.5
Electricians	8,121	7,916	193	12	100.0	97.5	2.4	0.1
Plumbers and pipefitters	6,566	6,307	255	4	100.0	96.1	3.9	<0.05
Construction laborers	7,547	4,722	2,811	14	100.0	62.6	37.2	0.2
Total employed	927,024	819,284	105,686	2,054	100.0	88.4	11.4	0.2
Total construction industry	50,716	44,788	5,867	61	100.0	88.3	11.6	0.1

Note: Percentages may not add to total because of rounding.   Based on data obtained from U.S. Bureau of the Census.

Prior to 1963, much of the cost of apprenticeship training was paid by the Board of Education. But when a millage proposal was voted down that year, the Board of Education discontinued its financial support of apprenticeship training and other programs deemed to be "nonessential." The tuition cost per pupil was therefore increased from $0.12 a class hour of instruction in 1963 to $1.05 a class hour in 1965.

To remain eligible to attend classes at the apprentice schools, apprentices must be employed. Unemployed enrollees may attend four classes, but thereafter they are given leaves of absence from classes until they are re-employed. However, there are a number of coordinators, paid by their respective industries, who assist apprentices in finding jobs.

Table 9-1 indicates the degree of Negro employment in the Detroit construction industry. As shown, Negroes comprised 11.6 per cent of the employees in 1960. Although these figures reveal a wider degree of Negro participation than found in many cities, they also show Negroes to be concentrated in the laborers, carpenters, plasterers, and cement finishers. As in Cleveland, both the commercial and residential phases of Detroit's building industry are largely unionized. Hence, there are few opportunities for Negroes to be exposed to occupations in the construction industry outside the orbit of the unions.

NEGRO PARTICIPATION IN UNIONS AND APPRENTICESHIP PROGRAMS

Since 1962, the Apprentice School has taken racial head counts of its students on a regular basis. Since all of the major trades use these facilities, the data is especially useful for this study. The reported aggregate totals are as follows:

Date	No. of Apprentices Enrolled	No. of Negroes
2/19/62	1,314	10
6/12/63	1,341	12
10/ 2/63	1,623	22
6/16/64	1,585	28
10/15/64	1,902	34
6/16/65	2,056	34
10/ 4/65	2,321	44
2/15/66	2,363	41

As is readily apparent, the training of Negroes in these apprentice-able trades is extremely small. The composition of the total figure by specific trades as of February, 1966, is given in Table 9-2. Besides the thirty-eight apprentices accounted for in the table, there are three Negro apprentices (out of a total of 134) in the printing industry attending the school.

Table 9-2

Negro Participation in Selected Building Trades Apprenticeship Programs, February, 1966

Trade	Total Apprentices	Total Negro Apprentices
Carpentry	872	19
Electrical	217	4
Glazing	32	0
Ironworking	132	0
Lathing	14	1
Painting	90	5
Plastering	15	2
Plumbing	305	2
Resilient floor decorating	86	3
Sheet metal working	315	1
Steamfitting	160	1
Total	2,238	38

Based on data obtained from the Apprentice School, Detroit Board of Education.

DEVELOPMENTS IN THE CONSTRUCTION INDUSTRY

Amidst the nation-wide publicity over the demonstrations in other cities, the Joint Construction Activities Committee of the Detroit Metropolitan area issued a public statement on July 9, 1963, endorsing the principle of equal employment opportunity. Besides acknowledging nondiscrimination as a desirable goal, the resolution pledged that the industry would take affirmative action to increase minority participation in the construction trades. In addition to adopting policies of equal employment opportunity, local unions were urged to recruit qualified nonunion craftsmen and all JACs were asked to make all apprenticeship qualifications and application rules available to the public. (Compared to other cities, Detroit was by far the easiest in which to obtain apprenticeship entry standards.)

It was not long afterward in 1963 that the Board of Education exercised its newly acquired powers by denying the use of its facilities to IBEW Local 58 because there were no Negroes in its apprenticeship classes. The thirty electrical apprentices who were removed from the Apprentice School received no classroom instruction for one year. When the Board of Education and the IBEW local reached an accord after a year, the electrical apprentices reentered the school and special classes were held on Saturdays to make up for the lost class time.

Some unions do not use the public school systems for reasons having no apparent connection with the race issue. In 1965, for example, Bricklayers Local 2 withdrew their apprenticeship program because, according to union officials, "we did not want our boys to go to school during the summer. Under our new program our classes are held at the McComb County Community College.... All classes are held during the winter because this is our slack period. We [also] pulled out of the public school system because the tuition rates are too high."[1] Moreover, Plumbers Local 98 is in the process of building its own training facilities, which are scheduled for completion in late 1966.

In the summer of 1966 there were four Negro apprentices in the electrical program. The first Negro admitted (to be discussed later) was—after working several regular construction jobs—assigned to the Board of Education. He was told that the job was a choice assignment available only to apprentices with good records. However, once he accepted the post, he found that Board of Education apprentices work only a 35-hour week and had virtually no opportunity for overtime employment. As a result, he feels his earnings have been sharply limited relative to his fellow apprentices. Moreover, after he was assigned to the Board job, the right of an apprentice to refuse to accept a job assignment was taken away, and a special union official was given the authority to make unilateral job assignments to apprentices. Subsequently, we are informed, the industry's other three Negro apprentices have also been assigned to the Board of Education. There is a feeling among civil rights spokesmen that the action of the union is a form of revenge for the Board's earlier action in banning the union from the training school.

[1] Field interviews, August 11, 1966.

DEVELOPMENTS IN THE
INDUSTRIAL SKILLED TRADES

As mentioned earlier, Detroit is somewhat unique among our study cities in having a high proportion of apprentices in the machinist trades. Although most of these are directly associated with programs in the automobile industry, there are other opportunities for skilled tradesmen in the small "jobbing shops" scattered throughout the city. Most of the apprenticeship programs are a part of the program of the Skilled Trades Department of the United Automobile Workers (UAW). While statistics on Negro participation in these programs are sketchy, UAW spokesmen provided the following estimates:

Program	Total Apprentices	Total Negroes
Ford	2,000	160
Chrysler	1,751	119
General Motors	3,400	N.A.
Jobbing Shops	600	6

Throughout our interviews in the city, it was commonly acknowledged that Ford has long been a leader in encouraging Negro participation in its programs. Chrysler and GM were consistently classified as laggards. The small jobbers are seen to constitute the most difficult area.

There was a severe shortage of skilled tradesmen in Detroit in 1966. This shortage has come from both an increase in demand because of general economic prosperity and restrictions on supply because the UAW's early retirement program, won in bargaining settlements in late 1965, started in 1966. A substantial number of employees with thirty years of employment have taken advantage of the opportunity to retire at age fifty-five. Indicative of the manpower shortage is the fact that at Ford, where the contracted ratio of journeymen to apprentices is eight to one, the ratio was one to one in the summer of 1966.

Entry into the automobile industry apprenticeship programs is by two routes; one is upgrading production-line employees into apprenticeship training, and the other is direct entry into the program by interested individuals. Strong preference is given to the former. In fact, it seems that entry for Negroes into the skilled trades has come far more easily by the upgrading route than by the direct application route. Although UAW skilled trades officials claim that younger applicants who typically apply directly for apprenticeship programs tend to do better on written qualifying examinations, the UAW's experience has shown that the older apprentices drawn from production lines tend to be more serious about learning, tend to catch on more quickly, and therefore, tend to do better once admitted to an apprenticeship class than the younger apprentices. Thus, the UAW's experience would suggest that qualification tests are not good predictors of competency.

Apprenticeship Information Centers

Although Detroit has had an AIC since July 17, 1964, its operations have been a continual source of controversy. From our interviews with the staff and members of the advisory committee, it is apparent that the Center has been mainly active with industrial apprenticeship programs and has had limited co-operation from the building trades unions. As of February, 1966, the only construction union placing orders with the AIC was the IBEW, which had just begun to use the Center's facilities.

Indeed, it is apparent that, other than the industrial programs, few organizations are either referring applicants to the AIC or requesting Negro applicants from it. It is estimated that about 35 per cent of the applicants found qualified for apprenticeship are Negroes and that most of these are "walk-ins" rather than referrals from civil rights groups. A report issued by a BES and BAT team, which evaluated the AIC in July, 1965, concluded "that the AIC personnel have, to a great degree, ignored the minority community and have been remiss in their responsibility to promote the announced tenets of the Center."[2] The report was highly critical of the Michigan Employment Service's operation of the AIC and of the activities of the Center's personnel.

THE TRADE UNION LEADERSHIP COUNCIL (TULC)

Virtually all efforts to supply Negro applicants to the building crafts seem to center around the activities of Mr. Horace Sheffield and his work with the Trade Union Leadership Council (TULC).[3] While not always successful in all of his efforts, it does seem that, where entry has occurred, Sheffield has usually been involved. The

[2] Formal Joint Evaluation of the Detroit Apprenticeship Information Center (July 21–23, 1965) (mimeographed), p. 2.

[3] For details concerning the history and general objectives of this organization, see Ray Marshall, *The Negro and Organized Labor*, pp. 68–70.

TULC has undertaken the initiative to advertise the AIC in the Negro community's newspapers and radio programs, has convened conferences with school counselors to acquaint them with apprenticeship, and has recruited Negro applicants for apprenticeship openings. Because of its background and composition, the TULC also has served an important function in dealing with the Negro community. Due to the fact that its membership consists largely of Negro union members (typically from industrial unions), the TULC has been able to educate civil rights spokesmen about the institution of apprenticeship. It has been apparent from our study that one obstacle to increasing Negro participation in these programs has been the limited knowledge of the nature of apprenticeship by civil rights leaders. Without a thorough understanding of the anatomy and physiology of the patient, it is difficult to prescribe realistic remedies. The TULC does have this understanding—both of apprenticeship training in particular and of the labor movement in general.

As an example of Sheffield's work, take the case of the first Negro to be admitted to the apprenticeship program of IBEW Local 58. Acting on his own initiative, Paul Crutcher, a young Negro, went to the union hall to pick up an application form for the program in November, 1963. He was told they were "fresh out of applications" and therefore was asked to write his name and address on a blank sheet of paper and leave it with the union official in charge. After several weeks had passed and no word was heard, Crutcher's father contacted Sheffield. Together with several other Negro community leaders, Sheffield went to the union headquarters. They were told there was no record of Crutcher's application. A meeting was called with public school officials which resulted in the local being denied the use of the Apprentice School. Several months later, Crutcher was sent an application. Later he was given an aptitude test and was interviewed by the JAC. The TULC also had a committee on hand which was permitted to review his examination. He passed both requirements and was admitted to the program. Had it not been for the intervention of Sheffield acting through the TULC, it is doubtful that the outcome would have been so successful.

IBEW TESTING PROGRAM

The IBEW's selection procedure is somewhat different from that used by most other unions. As mentioned above, prior to 1963, much of the testing was done by the city, but this program was also found to be "expendable" in 1963 when the School Board curtailed its activities for financial reasons. As a consequence, several unions (and thirty-five other private companies not in the construction industry) prevailed upon the man who had supervised the public testing program to set up a private testing company to continue his work. The man, Dr. Richard Dresher, also serves as Assistant Superintendent of Schools for the Detroit Board of Education in charge of guidance and counseling. In addition to the IBEW, Dresher does the testing for the cement finishers and the pattern makers. According to Dresher, his tests (based on eighteen years of testing experience) "do not discriminate against anyone." They are nonverbal tests designed to check perception and, to some degree, comprehension. The cut-off point for entry, however, is determined entirely by the people for whom he does the testing. They establish the minimum score deemed to be acceptable and they lower the score until they get enough people to meet their needs.

NEGRO ELECTRICIANS' ORGANIZATION

Many of the nonunion Negro electricians in Detroit belong to an organization known as the Associated Electricians of Detroit (AED). Founded in 1937, it today is comprised of about twenty-five Negro contractors, thirty Negro journeymen, and several other interested people working in the electrical field. In 1966 the Association began the process of establishing its own apprenticeship program "independent of the IBEW and if necessary from BAT." Exploratory talks were held with the IBEW and the BAT, but negotiations broke off. The IBEW had agreed that it would accept AED applicants provided they could pass the IBEW written and oral examinations; that the AED applicants would be indentured by AED contractors; that when the training program was completed the Negro apprentices would be referred by AED contractors and not by the union; and that AED would pay the union scale. The AED turned down the IBEW proposal because it was "separate but equal" and because its representatives felt that "the union age, education, and testing requirements were unreasonable."

COUNSELING AND RECRUITING
NEGRO APPRENTICES

In addition to the use of punitive measures against discriminating locals, the Board of Education has also discussed ways to assist in recruitment of Negro apprentices. One suggestion was made in 1965 to place special vocational counselors in each high school.[4] Their purpose would be to single out potential Negro candidates for apprenticeship who are not planning on going to college. Furthermore, it was suggested that an effort be made to enlist retired Negro journeymen to act as school aides to advise Negroes who are interested in jobs in these areas. In addition, in 1965 the Board of Education wrote individual letters to all JACs and contractors in order to determine how the school system could help them to place more Negro apprentices. The Board of Education also launched a "crash program" in 1965 to compile a list of a hundred potential Negro candidates for apprenticeship. The seven inner-city schools (whose student bodies are predominantly Negro) were to be contacted for a list of all of their graduates in June, 1965. Dr. Dresher was asked to compile the list. He replied to the Superintendent that the assignment would be impossible since:

1. Negro youths who graduate from high school are highly motivated to college.
2. There has been discrimination in the past, and as a result, Negroes are hesitant to apply.
3. There has been a poor job by unions of letting the Negroes know that their doors are now opened.

Dresher did agree, however, that a study needed to be made of the problems of Negro high school graduates in the city. Since unions are currently looking for high school graduates, the apprenticeship question would be tied closely to the findings of the study. He decided to study all high school graduates for the past year and those males found to be unemployed would be told to go to the AIC. It was his feeling, however, that few of the unemployed Negroes in the city would be high school graduates. The study was still in progress in the summer of 1966.

[4] Regardless of the merits of the specific proposal for vocational counselors, more counselors are definitely needed. Dr. Richard Dresher, Assistant Superintendent of Schools in charge of guidance and counseling for Detroit, reported that in 1965 there was only one counselor for every 329 students in the senior high schools and one for every 499 in the junior high schools. He warned, however, that with respect to the apprentice area, it was his experience that more counselors alone is not going to help a great deal. The real question is the approach to be used by the counselor. It was his opinion that parents have a far greater influence on vocational choice than do counselors, since the counselor may suggest that a pupil prepare himself to become a carpenter, while his parents may have an entirely different view.

PRE-APPRENTICESHIP PROGRAMS

There has been some experimentation with pre-apprenticeship programs in Detroit although they have been limited to industrial trades rather than the building trades. UAW officials, unlike some building trades leaders, do not consider pre-apprenticeship to be a dirty word. In fact, several UAW skilled trades interviewees referred to these programs as "an answer to a major social problem." They stated that, since many Negro applicants have never seen a machine, they and other underprivileged children cannot "stack up" on the qualification tests. Pre-apprenticeship, therefore, is seen to be a potential bridge over this gap, making it possible for Negroes to compete on a more nearly equal basis.

In early 1965 a pilot pre-apprenticeship program was jointly sponsored by the UAW and the Detroit Tooling Association. The project was financed with a grant from the Area Redevelopment Administration. The AIC did the selection work. Fifteen people were chosen to participate in the six-week training program. When it was completed, the Detroit Tooling Association accepted seven enrollees into its program, and the Chrysler Motor Company admitted seven, while one enrollee dropped out.

In September, 1965, the City of Detroit and the UAW received an MDTA grant for a pre-apprenticeship class for tool-and-die work involving about 120 youths who were selected by the AIC from about 1,000 applicants. Five per cent of the enrollees were Negroes. Instruction, mainly in mathematics and the use of machines, lasted eight hours a day, five days a week, for fifteen weeks. Sections of fifteen enrollees each were formed at staggered beginning dates. Based upon the results of the first six sections (or eighty graduates), placement has averaged about 85 per cent. Originally, it was felt that most of those who completed the program and who were then able to pass the union qualification examination would be placed in one of the "big three" automobile plants. In fact, however, about half of the placements have been with one of the automobile plants while the other half went to the unionized small job shops in the city. There was less delay in finding immediate employment with the small jobbers. Thus, the pre-apprenticeship program seems to be successful in its prime mission: to assist disadvantaged youth to compete on an equal basis on apprenticeship qualification examinations.

It was reported in 1966 that Chrysler has been considering the establishment of a pre-apprenticeship class for people who just barely failed to pass the qualification tests.

COMMUNITY DEVELOPMENTS

Lastly, there are several significant community developments that are working to increase Negro participation in these programs. One of these was the convening of a special citizens' committee composed of business, labor, and civil rights representatives from the "power structure" in the city. The committee is chaired by Reverend Richard T. Emorich (an Episcopal priest) and is concerned with the race issue of which the apprenticeship area is felt to be potentially one of the most explosive. Similarly, in May, 1965, the Archbishop's Committee on Human Relations for the Catholic Church in Detroit recommended that a nondiscrimination code for its construction projects be implemented. Archbishop John F. Dearden agreed to this recommendation and issued the directives. The program calls for employers and unions to undertake affirmative action to demonstrate their compliance with the principle of equal opportunity.

GENERAL CONCLUSIONS

While there have been few dramatic public confrontations with the building trades unions, it is apparent from our work in Detroit that the issue is far from resolved. To date, it appears that the Negro community, as represented by its civil rights groups, is content to allow time for the various remedial projects to take form. Moreover, the availability of a large number of industrial apprenticeships has become a safety valve for pent-up Negro frustrations in entering the skilled trades ranks. Due to the strong demand for industrial apprentices that has characterized the mid-sixties and to the progressive attitudes of the UAW leadership toward assisting disadvantaged youth to compete on a more nearly equal basis, Negroes have had more successful experiences gaining entry to the industrial programs.

The civil rights groups and the AIC in the city have likewise followed the path of least resistance and concentrated upon industrial programs rather than upon the building trades. Even the TULC has focused upon the industrial programs, but it does offer its assistance when a Negro of his own volition expresses interest in the construction industry. As for the Board of Education, it has been concerned with apprenticeship programs in general and with the building trades who use its facilities when pressed to act. To date, however, the Negro community has been satisfied to make piecemeal forays, but it has made no organized assault on the building trades. Whether this pattern will continue or whether Negro organizations will undertake the more difficult task of promoting, recruiting, tutoring, and pressing for access to the building unions remains to be seen. The issue appears to have been simmering in the summer of 1966 but has not yet reached the boiling point.

CHAPTER X

WASHINGTON, D.C.

INTRODUCTION

According to the 1960 census, Washington, D.C., was the only city of over 100,000 inhabitants which had a greater percentage of nonwhites (54.8) than whites in its population. In 1966, nonwhites were estimated to be approximately 60 per cent of the city's total population and approximately 88 per cent of its school enrollment.

The construction industry is one of the major industries in the city. Most government construction and much commercial construction is done by union workers, while most residential construction is nonunion. Table 10-1 shows that 27.9 per cent of employment in the construction industry in the Washington Metropolitan Area in 1960 was nonwhite. This participation rate was by far the highest of any city included in this project. The highest concentration here, as elsewhere, was in the laborer, trowel, and carpenter occupations. Yet, as Table 10-1 shows, there are a number of Negroes in the electrician and plumbing trades. Presumably, most of the Negroes are to be found in the nonunion sector.

THE EXTENT OF NEGRO PARTICIPATION IN APPRENTICESHIP PROGRAMS

The degree of Negro participation in apprenticeship programs for the years 1963 through 1965 is presented in Table 10-2, which shows that, with the exception of the Sheet Metal Workers Local 102, there has been a significant reversal of earlier patterns.

SPECIAL ACTIVITIES

The most climactic showdown to date in Washington occurred in 1960 with IBEW Local 26. AFL-CIO President George Meany, officers of the international union, officials of the AFL-CIO Civil

Table 10-1

Employment in Selected Occupations by Race, 1960—Washington, D.C., Metropolitan Area

Occupation	Number Employed				Percentage Distribution			
	Total	White	Negro	Other nonwhite	Total	White	Negro	Other nonwhite
Selected occupations								
Carpenters	6,830	6,218	604	8	100.0	91.0	8.8	0.2
Plasterers and cement finishers	1,550	682	864	4	100.0	44.0	55.7	0.3
Structural metal workers	347	335	12	—	100.0	96.6	3.4	—
Electricians	3,439	3,232	207	—	100.0	94.0	6.0	—
Plumbers and pipefitters	3,672	3,389	283	—	100.0	92.3	7.7	—
Construction laborers	9,229	2,382	6,842	5	100.0	25.8	74.1	0.1
Total employed	447,004	334,497	109,251	3,256	100.0	74.8	24.4	0.8
Total construction industry	46,248	33,303	12,897	48	100.0	72.0	27.9	0.1

Note: Percentages may not add to total because of rounding.   Based on data obtained from U.S. Bureau of the Census.

Rights Committee, and the President's Committee on Government Contracts (PCGC) had tried repeatedly during the late fifties to break the race barrier of the local. In December, 1958, the AFL-CIO officials admitted that all of their efforts had been to no avail. During this period, Meany had gone so far as to propose that he would recruit nonunion Negro electricians if the PCGC would direct a governmental contractor on a public housing project to employ them. Even this drastic step failed, because Meany and interested civil rights groups could not locate any such people. But when plans were projected into the future to secure nonunion Negro electricians for federal projects, the union issued a work permit to a Negro journeyman in 1960.

As of the end of 1965, the construction unions without Negroes in their apprenticeship programs were: Sheet Metal Workers Local 102; Asbestos Workers Local 24; Glaziers Local 963; Painters Council 51; Lathers Local 9; Stone and Marble Masons Local 2; and the Tile and Terrazzo Workers Local 3.[1]

REMEDIAL PROGRAMS

Washington's Apprenticeship Information Center (AIC) was set up as a demonstration project on June 17, 1963, and was one of the first federally financed AICs in the nation. The operation of the AIC in Washington is of special consequence because it is the only center to be operated entirely by federal employees. Since the nation's capital is not a state, the U.S. Employment Service in the Bureau of Employment Security of the Department of Labor assumes the obligations and duties that are performed by state employment bureaus elsewhere. As of June 17, 1966, 72 per cent of 5,522 applicants to this center were Negro. Of this number, 1,868 were found qualified for referral (1,214 or 65 per cent of these were Negro). A total of 1,679 qualified applicants were actually referred (out of which 1,150 or 68 per cent were Negroes). Of the 609 applicants eventually placed into union programs, 403 (or 66 per cent) were Negroes.[2]

Based on earlier figures available for 324 placements (of whom 207 were Negroes) for the period through January, 1966, 89 per cent of the AIC's placements were into building trades apprentice-

[1] Report of the Office of Liaison, U.S. Department of Labor (January 26, 1966) (unpublished mimeographed material), p. 29.
[2] Figures in this paragraph supplied by Mr. Robert Borden, Director of the District of Columbia Apprenticeship Information Center.

Table 10-2

Negro Apprentices in Apprenticeship Programs in Selected Trade Unions in Washington, D.C., 1963, 1964, 1965

Local Union	Apprentices, 1963		Apprentices, 1964		Apprentices, 1965	
	Total	Negro	Total	Negro	Total	Negro
Carpenters, D.C.	312	5	263	16	320	23
Columbia Typographers 101	228	50	—	—	182	33
IBEW 26	125	2	124	9	180	9
Pipefitters 602	120	2	150	4	294	8
Operating Engineers 77	95	18	160	20	66	19
Stationary Engineers 99	95	5	—	—	49	3
Plumbers 5	80	2	100	2	199	8
Sheet Metal Workers 102	77	3	80	0	124	0
Ironworkers 5	58	2	62	2	49	2
Bindery Workers 42	40	10	42	1	40	0
Asbestos Workers 24	31	0	51[a]	21[a]	52	8
Bricklayers 1	30	7	30	0	60	0
Painters 51	30	0	27	0	22	0
Stone Masons 2	28	0	20	1	18	2
Rodmen 201	23	1	25	0	18	0
Lathers 9	23	0				

Cement Masons 2	21	10	31	20	51	30
Photoengravers 17	21	0				
Bakers 117	17	3				
Plasterers 96	17	2	15	2	21	2
Glaziers 963	16	0	14	0	27	0
Web Pressmen 6	14	0				
Bookbinders 4	13	4				
Bricklayers 4	11	5	a	a	62	44
Pressman 72	10	4				
Iron Shopmen 486	10	2	10	0	11	1
Machinists 193	10	1				
Mailers 29	10	1				
Auto Mechanics 1486	9	2				
Tilesetters 3	9	0	12	0	8	0
Sign Painters 1129	5	1				
Stone Cutters 2	2	0				
Electrotypers 17	1	0				
Total	1,591	142	1,216	100	1,853	192

1963 data obtained from Commissioners Council on Human Relations, Washington, D.C. 1964 and 1965 data obtained from Office of Liaison of the Equal Employment Opportunities Commission. (The 1965 data was supplemented by a report from the Washington Apprenticeship Information Center.)

a Figure for Bricklayers Local 1 and Local 4 combined in 1964 only.

Table 10-3

Placements into Apprenticeship Classes in the Building Trades
by the Washington AIC, June, 1963, to January, 1966

Trade	Apprentices Placed	
	White	Negro
Bricklaying	22	62
Carpentry	26	101
Cement mason	0	1
Electrician	3	3
Ironworker	1	0
Operating engineer	4	3
Plumbing	20	7
Steamfitting	20	5
Total	96	182

Based on data obtained from the Apprenticeship Information Center, Washington, D.C.

ship programs. A breakdown of those specific building trades programs is given in Table 10-3. A comparison of Table 10-2 with Table 10-3 shows that the major channel by which Negroes entered these apprenticeship classes was through the AIC. For whites, the AIC provided only minimal assistance. It should be kept in mind, however, that the AIC is located in the center of the Negro population, which is convenient to the vast majority of Negroes, and that the jurisdictions covered by the unions are much broader than the geographical boundaries of the city. The area included within the jurisdiction of the JACs includes parts of Maryland and northern Virginia, which have large white populations to draw upon. Accordingly, it would be logical for the AIC to show a disproportionately large number of Negro placements.

With regard to the recruitment issue, there is no indication of any formal effort being made by any group to place Negroes. The void is partially explained by the fact that there has been some degree of success in placement. Sterling Tucker, Executive Director of the Washington Urban League, stated that the apprenticeship issue "is slightly relaxed but still grave."[3] Although the Urban League has a representative "with a direct line" to its headquarters in the Bureau of Employment Security office (the same building which houses the AIC), there have been little active recruitment

[3] Personal interview, September 8, 1965.

efforts by any of the civil rights groups in the city to find Negroes interested expressly in apprenticeship. The most notable efforts have been those led by Robert Harlan who served in the capacity of Area Coordinator for the now-defunct President's Committee on Equal Employment Opportunity. His efforts were centered mostly on Sheet Metal Workers Local 102, which at last reports did not have any Negro members. The Council on Human Relations has not been engaged in any type of recruitment program.

In Washington there has been some experience with pre-apprenticeship training classes in carpentry and in bricklaying, both of which have had special pre-apprenticeship classes to prepare Negroes to qualify for apprenticeship openings. The carpenters' program, however, was a failure as a job placement venture. Only twenty-two (twenty of whom were Negroes) of the original hundred enrollees (eighty-two of whom were Negroes) completed the program and were placed in apprenticeship classes. Its demise was ascribed to the fact that it admitted dropouts from the tenth grade, it started during the winter months when work was scarce, and it was hastily conceived, with the participants rounded up in less than one week's time. As an object lesson of what not to do, however, the program had positive value. The bricklayers' program, on the other hand, was far more successful due, it is felt, to the fact that even though the high school diploma requirement was waived, there was more time for the AIC to obtain and to screen applicants for the program. Thirty-four of the original forty participants ("most of whom were Negroes") completed the program and were admitted to the apprenticeship class of Bricklayers Local 4. A second pre-apprenticeship class subsequently has been started. These programs have been a combination of institutional and on-the-job training. The success of the bricklayers' program is due in part to the high degree of likelihood of placement after completion, and an incentive given for diligent effort by the bricklayers union which promised that if the participants performed well in their training work, one year of the three years of their apprenticeship would be waived.

GENERAL CONCLUSIONS

Washington represents a unique case. Its public schools and most dining areas were not desegregated until 1955. Accordingly, it is not surprising that many of the local unions would still be practicing discrimination by the late fifties. Yet, for a variety of reasons, integration came quickly to the city once the formal barriers were removed. Apprenticeship, while lagging behind progress in other areas of its own city life, has taken significant strides when compared with many other Northern cities in which the legal obstacles to integration had long ago disappeared.

The reasons for progress can be attributed to the extremely high proportion of Negroes that now comprise the city's population, to a booming construction industry, over-full employment in the local labor market, proximity to federal authorities and international union and federation officials who are headquartered there, and to the high proportion of federal construction in the city.

With some signs of weakening resistance by unions to change in past exclusionary policies, the civil rights groups have turned their attention in the mid-sixties to the issue of "home rule." As a result, the apprenticeship question has not been of high priority, and it is unlikely (with the possible exception of the case of the sheet metal workers) that it will become a controversial issue in the near future. Moreover, with the AIC apparently being successful in its ability to obtain information and disseminate it to the community, the recruitment issue appears in general to be solving itself. The case with the sheet metal workers again represents the exception.

CHAPTER XI

SAN FRANCISCO-OAKLAND

Although the San Francisco-Oakland Bay Area of California has a relatively large and diverse minority population, it did not have many Negroes before World War II. A 1963 study reported about 30 per cent of San Francisco's 800,000 population to be members of minority groups, equally divided among Negroes, orientals, and Mexican-Americans. Oakland's total population has remained fairly stable at about 400,000, but this stability conceals significant internal racial shifts. The decline in Oakland's white population of about 58,000 between 1950 and 1960 was partially offset by an increase in its nonwhite population of about 46,000. Nonwhites constitute about 25 per cent of Oakland's population, and almost all of these nonwhites are Negroes.

The Negro's economic conditions in the Bay Area are reported to be very bad. A committee appointed by Mayor John F. Shelley of San Francisco reported in 1963 that "as a group Negroes are in a crisis comparable to the great depression of thirty years ago."[1] The economic conditions of Negroes in Oakland are undoubtedly as bad as those in San Francisco, if not worse, because Oakland has had unemployment rates far above the national average, and many Oakland Negroes have sought employment in San Francisco.

Table 11-1 shows Negro participation in the Bay Area construction industry to have been approximately 9.2 per cent in 1960, which is a lower proportion than all but two of our other survey cities. It will be noted, moreover, that 74 per cent of the Negroes working in the San Francisco–Oakland construction industry are in the carpenter and laborer occupations.

BACKGROUND

San Francisco has had its share of civil rights demonstrations, but for the most part they have not yet centered upon the apprentice-

[1] "Report of the Interim Committee on Human Relations" (October 8, 1964), p. 3.

Table 11-1

Employment in Selected Occupations by Race, 1960—San Francisco-Oakland Bay Area

Occupation	Number Employed				Percentage Distribution			
	Total	White	Negro	Other nonwhite	Total	White	Negro	Other nonwhite
Selected occupations								
Carpenters	13,762	12,754	802	206	100.0	92.7	5.8	1.5
Plasterers and cement finishers	1,718	1,349	353	16	100.0	78.5	20.5	0.9
Structural metal workers	1,730	1,558	123	49	100.0	90.1	7.1	2.9
Electricians	6,422	6,000	240	182	100.0	93.4	3.7	2.9
Plumbers and pipefitters	5,066	4,886	145	35	100.0	96.4	2.9	0.7
Construction laborers	7,498	4,463	2,991	44	100.0	59.5	39.9	0.6
Total employed	699,777	624,613	44,992	30,172	100.0	89.3	6.4	4.3
Total construction industry	56,979	50,910	5,258	811	100.0	89.4	9.2	1.4

Note: Percentages may not add to total because of rounding.　　　Based on data obtained from U.S. Bureau of the Census.

ship question. In the spring of 1964, when there were a number of demonstrations in hotel lobbies, supermarkets, automobile show rooms, and drive-in lots to protest the lack of minority group employees. Mayor Shelley appointed a fifteen-member Interim Committee whose purpose was to "put out fires, prevent fires." At the conclusion of its brief, five-month life span, the Committee issued a mild warning that it felt the practices of some unions (none were specified) needed to be mended.[2]

Because a permanent Human Rights Commission (HRC), recommended by the Interim Committee, was not established until September, 1964, the HRC has not figured as a recruitment body in San Francisco as similar agencies have in most of our other study cities. In fact, it seems that no public or private organization in either Oakland or San Francisco has actively sought to locate applicants for apprenticeship programs.

The organization which seems to have most actively pressed this issue is the San Francisco Archdiocesan Catholic Interracial Council. In April, 1965, this group requested the state FEP Commission "to conduct an extensive investigation into the membership, apprenticeship, and other programs and practices of certain construction unions."[3] The Council identified the suspected culprits as Plumbers and Pipefitters Local 38, Ironworkers Local 790, Sheet Metal Workers Local 355, IBEW Local 6, Glaziers Local 718, Operating Engineers Local 3, and Building Material and Construction Teamsters Local 216. The Council reported that "our research shows beyond any doubt that many construction industry unions have stubbornly refused to take any meaningful action to eliminate racial discrimination."[4] In September, 1965, the Council enlarged its complaint to include the practices of contractors, JACs, the California Apprenticeship Council (CAC), and the California Division of Apprenticeship Standards (DAS).[5]

The Archdiocese had earlier announced that all future construction contracts to which it is a party must contain a fair employment clause. The clause requires that the contractors take affirmative action, that they make their records accessible to compliance review, and that all subcontractors must also meet both requirements.

[2] "Report of the Interim Committee on Human Relations," pp. 13–14, and Appendix I, pp. 3–4.
[3] News release, San Francisco Archdiocesan Catholic Interracial Council, July 19, 1965.
[4] *Ibid.*
[5] Press release, San Francisco Archdiocesan Catholic Interracial Council, September 19, 1965.

Complying with the request of the Catholic group, the FEPC started an investigation beginning on May 4, 1965. In mid-July, 1965, an FEPC spokesman was quoted as saying that dealing with labor unions is the "toughest problem FEPC faces."[6] He went on to elaborate by saying: "Labor unions in reality are responsible only to themselves. Their elected officials are put in by the membership and no one else. They reflect the status quo feeling of the membership."[7] The investigation, however, was dropped because it lacked specific complaints.

A major showdown on the issue appears to be looming when the Bay Area Rapid Transit project begins in 1967. Besides the construction of a tunnel under the bay, there will be extensive construction of depots and trackage throughout the entire Bay Area. In 1965, a coalition of civil rights and religious groups formed a committee known as Job Opportunities Bay Area Rapid Transit (JOBART) for the purpose of pressing for the training and hiring of local workers to supply the labor needed for the mammoth task. JOBART felt that the project "offers a unique opportunity" to prepare local workers to qualify for employment in the project. This group hoped that, with the availability of federal training funds and a large unskilled work force (made up largely of minority people), minority participation in the trades could be increased immeasurably. By December, 1966, however, JOBART appeared to be moribund.

Aside from the transit project, it was announced in April, 1966, that Oakland had been selected as the first city to be rebuilt as a part of the Great Society's city refurbishment project. The Economic Development Administration (EDA) made available $15 million for a port-expansion project and a new airplane hangar. Tied to the loans, however, was a stipulation made by EDA that employers on the project must give priority to Negroes and other minority people in filling these new jobs. Hiring plans for upwards of at least a year in advance would be required of the employers who would submit these plans to a special EDA-sponsored review panel. An EDA spokesman has been quoted as saying: "It's the first time that this sort of requirement has been made. It has never been tested in court."[8]

To assist Negroes to qualify for these jobs in the construction

---

6 *The Monitor,* July 7, 1965.

7 *Ibid.*

8 "Administration Selects Oakland as First City in Rebuilding Program," *Wall Street Journal,* April 25, 1966, p. 1.

industry and other industries in the area, it was announced in early 1966 that a "skill bank" would be set up. The program was to be a major expansion of the Oakland Adult Minority Project. A $5 million program of job training was to be sought through the provisions of the Manpower Development and Training Act.

The Oakland Building Trades Council, however, does not share the optimism of either JOBART or the Oakland Adult Minority Project supporters. Its spokesman, J. L. Childers, has been quoted as saying that the talk of shortages of construction workers was "mostly hot air" and "hullabaloo."[9] At one point, another representative for the Council testified before a special legislative committee that the plan to expand the Adult Minority Project was launched "just to get U.S. cash."[10] Ultimately an accord was achieved when the Alameda County Manpower Development and Training Act Advisory Committee adopted an amended version of the original proposal. The amendment occurred after the Central Labor Council and the Building Trades Council had both appealed to Governor Brown to intervene. The change occurred when it was announced that training would take place only for specific occupations and after a detailed survey had been conducted of occupational demands.[11] Only eight occupations were immediately identified as having shortages: six were in the field of repairing office machinery and the other two were draftsman occupations. Conspicuously absent was any mention of training in the construction trades.

In spite of its opposition to these programs, the Alameda County AFL-CIO became the first central labor council in the nation to sponsor a community action program. In conjunction with the "war on poverty," the labor body initiated an on-the-job work-experience project during the summer of 1965 for 200 youths, most of whom were from minorities.

THE CALIFORNIA PLAN FOR EQUAL OPPORTUNITY

At its 1957 meeting, the California Apprenticeship Council (CAC) adopted a proposal that apprenticeship training be made available to all qualified youths regardless of race, creed, or color. At this

9 "Plenty of Workers to Construct BART," *East Bay Labor Journal*, January 7, 1966, pp. 1, 7.

10 "Project Launched Just to Get U.S. Cash," *East Bay Labor Journal*, January 28, 1966, p. 1.

11 "Skills Center Approved—with Labor Safeguards," *East Bay Labor Journal*, February 4, 1966, pp. 1, 7.

same meeting it was decided to investigate the feasibility of holding a biennial statewide conference of apprenticeship committees. From these efforts came the decision to hold such a conference in 1960.

Prior to the actual convening of the first biennial California Conference on Apprenticeship (CCA) in 1960, the president of the state labor federation recommended the inclusion of a workshop on the subject of equal opportunity. Accordingly, with added support from civil rights groups and some management associations, the decision to include a workshop on the topic was agreed upon. At the CCA meeting, the workshop presented its first recommendation which was accepted by the conference and later by the California Apprenticeship Council.

The recommendation called for the establishment of a special study committee on the employment of minorities. It was done. Meeting in January, 1961, the study committee immediately realized that the first problem was one of actually determining the existing degree of participation. "There were no accurate records or statistics available on the status of minority groups in apprenticeship training."[12] Accordingly, it was decided to request that such a study be made immediately (to be discussed below). At a later meeting in 1961, the study group recommended that a state-wide committee and local committees be established to encourage equal opportunity for minority applicants to apprenticeship programs.

As a consequence, the Statewide Committee for Equal Opportunity in Apprenticeship and Training for Minority Groups (SCEOATMG) was created. The SCEOATMG has established Apprenticeship Information Centers, initiated a speakers' bureau to supply speakers to local JACs, engaged in a publicity program (including the publishing of the *Apprenticeship News Letter,* which is issued quarterly and distributed to all news media), supervised the establishment of local communities for equal opportunity, requested that special surveys of apprenticeship programs be conducted, and pressed for greater promotion of apprenticeship programs in general. The total of its activities in this area is referred to as the California Plan for Equal Opportunity.

Mention also should be made of the related fact that in 1961 the CAC amended its state program for apprentice selection. The new provision called for fair and impartial treatment through the use of uniform selection procedures applicable to all who seek admittance.

[12] Division of Apprenticeship Standards, "The California Plan for Equal Opportunity" (undated), p. 2.

THE 1964 CALIFORNIA CONFERENCE
ON APPRENTICESHIP

The California Conference on Apprenticeship (CCA) is a permanent organization that meets biennially. Established in 1957 by the California Apprenticeship Council, the CCA is composed of members of the CAC and of all apprenticeship committees in the state. The CCA is important in that its members are responsible for the local implementation of general directives formulated at the higher state and national levels. For this reason, the actions of this group are seen as bellwethers for the thinking of the rank and file. In this context, developments during the third meeting of CCA were very eventful with respect to the issue of equal opportunity in apprenticeship.

The third CCA meeting began with a strong statement by Governor Edmund G. Brown on this issue. Reminding the delegates of their 1960 conference pledge to seek ways to expand apprenticeship opportunity for minority youth (which led subsequently to the California Plan for Equal Opportunity), the Governor stated that "we must press for absolute fairness in the selection of apprentices. Young people, without regard to race, creed, or color, must have equal opportunity to receive training for skilled employment."[13] In one of the associated workshops—entitled Equal Opportunity in Apprenticeship and Training for Minority Groups—the specific question of eliminating discrimination and expanding the number of apprenticeships was taken up in detail. Charles F. Hanna, chief of the Division of Apprenticeship Standards, told the workshop: "For those groups who have built in discrimination we will continue to break down these evil practices. The time for them to voluntarily abandon these practices has just about run out."[14] In addition, he is quoted as saying: "We are well aware of the fact that more would apply if they could believe they would receive fair and impartial treatment."[15] In summing up the 1964 status of minorities in apprenticeship programs in the state, he said that progress made to date is "far from satisfactory."[16] It was the consensus of the workshop that one of the best ways to increase minority participation was to press for an expansion of apprenticeship—especially in the public sector (e.g., state highway department,

[13] *Proceedings: Third Biennial California Conference on Apprenticeship*, San Francisco, May 20, 21, and 22, 1964, p. 19.

[14] *San Francisco Chronicle*, May 22, 1964.

[15] *Oakland Tribune*, May 22, 1964.

[16] *San Francisco Chronicle*, May 22, 1964.

federal defense programs, etc.).[17] To this dual goal, Resolution No. 51 was adopted by the workshop and forwarded to the Conference for promulgation.

Resolution No. 51 called first for an expansion of apprenticeship and resolved that the "conference [would] urge all groups interested in apprenticeship to bend every effort to study, encourage, and effectuate every possible means to insure fair and equal opportunity to qualified minority youth to enter apprenticeship programs."[18]

The vote on Resolution No. 51 was one of the last to be taken up by the Conference. Only about 200 of the 400 voting delegates were present when the vote came, and the unexpected opposition exposed itself. The night before, a caucus of dissidents—led by Dominic Soffieto of the Southern California Journeymen-Apprentice Pipe Trades Trust Fund and William Reedy of the San Francisco IBEW—had met to muster opposition to the resolution. When the vote came, the resolution was tabled. It was clearly a reversal from the expressed tenor of the meeting. Hanna was quoted as saying that he was "deeply disappointed"[19] and that "we've got to persuade these people to come along with the progressive position."[20] In addition, Hanna stated: "It [the action of the conference] raises a serious question as to whether we can continue to extend state services to the conference in view of the Governor's code of fair employment practices. It forbids us to provide services to organizations or private bodies which discriminate."[21]

Following the adjournment of the CCA the eighteen-member California Apprenticeship Council met and unanimously supported the recommendation that the Conference on Apprenticeship had turned down the day before. Although the Council's action did something to counteract the Conference's rejection of Resolution No. 51, the CCA's action in rejecting the equal opportunity proposal darkened the building trades' already unfavorable image in the Negro community.

It is not, however, clear to what extent the opponents of Resolution No. 51 were motivated by racism and to what extent they were motivated by opposition to outside interference with apprenticeship programs. There can be little question that both motives were present.

17 *Proceedings: Third Biennial California Conference on Apprenticeship*, p. 27.
18 *Ibid.*, p. 59.
19 *Oakland Tribune*, May 23, 1964.
20 *San Francisco Chronicle*, May 23, 1964.
21 *San Francisco Examiner*, May 24, 1964.

THE APPRENTICESHIP
INFORMATION CENTERS

The Bay Area Urban League's experiences convinced it that one of the most pressing problems confronting minority youth interested in apprenticeship was the lack of information concerning such matters as eligibility, application procedures, details concerning specific programs, and general information about the benefits that accrue to those who undertake such training. The Urban League suggested that there was a need for some sort of information clearing-house. As conceived by Arthur Bradford, the originator of the information center idea, the clearing-house would be staffed not only by people knowledgeable about the details of apprenticeship but also by psychologists, vocational counselors, and education experts.

Although it did not accept all of Bradford's ideas, the 1960 California Conference on Apprenticeship recommended that an Apprenticeship Information Center (AIC) be established. A pilot program was set up in Fresno, followed shortly afterward by another in San Francisco in 1963. Operated jointly by the Division of Apprenticeship Standards of the State Department of Industrial Relations, the State Department of Education, and the State Department of Employment, the functions of the AIC were:

1. To maintain a library of information on apprenticeship,
2. To provide counseling services and to make available details on how and where to apply, and
3. To refer applicants to JACs who request such action.[22]

Although the first effort in 1963 to get funds from the California legislature to establish a series of Centers on a permanent basis failed to pass, the 1964 session approved AICs for California's major cities.

SURVEYS OF MINORITY PARTICIPATION

As noted earlier, the initial recommendation of the study group on equal opportunity was to gather data. The recommendation was approved by the Executive Board of the CCA and the CAC for the

[22] "Report of the California State Advisory Committee to the U.S. Commission on Civil Rights on California Program for Equal Opportunity in Apprenticeship" (prepared by William Becker), reprinted in Senate Committee on Labor and Public Welfare, *The Role of Apprenticeship in Manpower Development: United States and Western Europe,* p. 1,240.

first survey in 1960. The second survey was taken in 1961 at the request of the CAC and the SCEOATMG. The DAS actually conducted both studies. "Aware of the controversial nature of the question on minority backgrounds," the DAS secured a legal ruling which assured them that *post*-employment ethnic information was not illegal.[23]

The First Survey

The pioneering study conducted by the DAS was made in 1960 of apprentices who completed their training in 1955. During that year, 3,018 journeymen certificates were awarded by the CAC. Questionnaires were sent to one-half of these; 756 completed the form. Of those responding, seventy-seven, or about 9 per cent, listed themselves as belonging to minority groups. These seventy-seven were distributed as follows: Mexican-American, forty-five; Negroes, eleven; Jewish, nine; oriental, six; Indians, three.[24] The eleven Negroes represent 1.1 per cent of the total. There was no breakdown by union affiliation for the minority members.

The Second Survey

In 1961 the DAS was again requested by the CAC and the State-wide Committee for Equal Opportunity in Apprenticeship and Training for Minority Groups to conduct a survey of active apprentices. Of the 20,575 active apprentices, 7,166 returned completed questionnaires (about 34 per cent). The minority breakdown was as follows: Indians, 283; Chinese, 18; Japanese, 31; Jewish, 58; Mexican, 521; Negro, 150; other, 32.[25] The total minority participation was 17 per cent, but Negroes constituted only 2.1 per cent of the total. Again, there was no breakdown of union affiliation released to the public. Commenting on the validity of this survey, the California State Advisory Committee to the U.S. Committee on Civil Rights stated:

The survey of apprentices currently in the program in 1962 did not result in a valid sample. It was decided not to try to do it by mail with the 20,575 names but to pass out the surveys to those apprentices attending classes of related instruction. Some school systems notably San Francisco would not allow the questionnaires to be distributed in their classes. A

[23] Division of Apprenticeship Standards, "The California Plan for Equal Opportunity," p. 4.

[24] Division of Apprenticeship Standards, "Survey of Completed Apprentices" (1960), p. 19.

[25] Division of Apprenticeship Standards, "The California Plan for Equal Opportunity," p. 21.

few large apprenticeship committees refused to cooperate in any way. . . . As a result of these factors the second survey does not come close to being a valid statistical sample.[26]

Commenting on the status of the Negro, the report stated: "The progress made to the beginning of 1962 has not allowed anyone concerned with the program to lose sight of how much work remains to be done, especially for Negro youth."[27]

Continuing Ethnic Survey

In December, 1964, the State-wide Committee again solicited the CAC to report on the ethnic composition of the apprenticeship programs in the state. DAS again conducted the survey. Of the 24,673 registered apprentices, 18,430 (about 74 per cent of the total) were included in the visual head count obtained by actually visiting the apprenticeship classes and counting the minority youth (see Table 11-2). The report found that 14.56 per cent of the apprentices were minority members. Of those in the survey, 2.88 per cent of the total (or 531) were Negroes. Of the 531 Negroes, 239 were in the Los Angeles District, 83 were in the Oakland District, 80 in the Petaluma District, and 77 in the San Francisco District. Thus, 90 per cent of the Negroes were in these districts, which contained about 70 per cent of the total apprentices in the survey. The highest concentration of Negroes was in the carpentry trade, which reported 215 Negro apprentices (about 3 per cent of the total in the trade). Bricklaying reported 3.2 per cent Negro apprentices; plasterers and cement masons reported 16 per cent Negro apprentices, and roofing 6.5 per cent Negro apprentices. The report held that in certain geographical areas, "the degree of integration has been limited"— specifically in the electrical, ironworkers, operating engineers, pipe trades, and sheet metal workers trades. Again, there were no figures for specific programs in any city given.[28]

In its quarterly meeting in July, 1965, the CAC recommended that DAS undertake a program designed to provide up-to-date statistics on apprentices. The project would be referred to as a "con-

[26] "Report of the California State Advisory Committee to the U.S. Commission on Civil Rights on California Program for Equal Opportunity in Apprenticeship," reprinted in Senate Committee on Labor and Public Welfare, *The Role of Apprenticeship in Manpower Development: United States and Western Europe*, p. 1,244.

[27] *Ibid.*

[28] The data presented in this paragraph are based upon a four-page release from the State Department of Industrial Relations, October 29, 1965.

tinuing ethnic survey." Unless this data is broken down by the specific trades in specific geographical areas it is extremely difficult to appraise the status of minority participation from this new data.

Table 11-2

Negro Participation in Apprenticeship Programs
in California, December, 1964

		Negroes	
Industry or Trade Group	Total in survey	Total in survey	Per cent of total in survey
Asbestos workers	7	0	—
Auto repairing	1,070	52	4.02
Barbering	161	1	0.02
Boilermakers and blacksmiths	33	0	—
Bricklayers and tile setters	370	12	3.24
Carpentry and wood trades	4,240	124	2.92
Carpet and linoleum layers	569	4	0.70
Cooks and bakers	53[a]	10	18.87
Electrical trades	2,133	36	1.69
Electronics technicians	124	16	12.9
Ironworkers, field	422	0	—
Ironworkers, shop	94	6	0.33
Lathers	450	7	1.53
Machinists, tool and die	720	38	5.28
Meatcutting	491	24	4.89
Metal plating	20	2	10.0
Molding and coremaking	54	7	12.93
Office machine and appliance repair	30	2	6.67
Operating engineers	259	2	0.77
Painters and glaziers	1,069	20	1.87
Pattern making	15	1	6.67
Pipe trades	2,832	13	0.45
Plasterers and cement masons	635	101	15.01
Printing	491	15	3.03
Roofing	216	14	6.48
Sheet metal workers	1,381	16	1.16
Surveying (chief of party)	291	1	0.34
Upholsterers	18[a]	1	5.55
Telephone installers	55	0	—
Miscellaneous	30	6	20.0
Totals	18,430	531	2.88

Source: December, 1964, survey by the California Division of Apprenticeship Standards.

[a] Variance in data due to "Unregistered Apprentices in Class" as of survey date.

San Francisco–Oakland Area

The results of visual head count made of the apprenticeship classes in Oakland conducted under a study made by the University of California in 1964 are presented in Table 11-3. The pattern is quite similar to that revealed in the other survey cities: few, if any, Negroes in the electrical, plumbing, steamfitting, and sheet metal trades (there were no figures available for the ironworkers); and a concentration of Negroes in the carpentry, painting, and trowel trades.

Table 11-3
Enrollment in Apprenticeship Classes in Oakland, April, 1964

Trade	Total Apprentices	Total Negroes
Carpenters	119	25
Cement masons	46	5
Electrical workers	117	1
Lathers	35	0
Painters	28	3
Plumbers	63	1
Roofers	27	4
Sheet metal workers	98	3
Steamfitters	88	0
Plasterers	38	7

Data obtained by head count in Oakland schools.

The DAS has been consistently reluctant to provide specific data to this study and, apparently, to other interested parties in the state. Indeed, the DAS even refused to provide statistical information to the California FEP Commission. The DAS, by its desire for secrecy, is implicitly saying that it feels that there is serious cause for concern. In addition, it is clear that DAS—which receives its state appropriation on the basis of the number of registered apprentices in the state—does not want to do anything which might cause any JAC to cancel or to de-register its program.

Field Work Findings

It was, however, possible to arrive at the approximate number of Negro apprentices in various programs by a process of elimination. The 1964 DAS survey reported that Negroes constituted 3.67 per cent of the apprentices in San Francisco. Our field interviews uncovered the following numbers of Negro apprentices in San Francisco as of January 1, 1966: carpenters, eighteen; cement masons, fourteen; plumbers, two; and machinists, four. We have thus accounted for thirty-eight of the Negro apprentices. Subsequently, it has been reported that in 1966 two additional Negro apprentices were admitted to the plumbers' program and that seventeen Negroes were among 265 applicants tested for the electricians' apprenticeship program. With respect to the latter, seven of the Negro applicants met the electrical workers requirements and were advised that they could take the examination; however, only two appeared for the test, both of whom passed and were admitted. The IBEW Local 6 agreed to give the names of the other fifteen Negro applicants to any civil rights organization willing to help prepare them to meet the requirements. But no civil rights organization accepted the union's proposal.

GENERAL CONCLUSIONS

The San Francisco-Bay Area is heralded throughout the United States for its accessibility and openness to outsiders. But if it takes an exception to prove a rule, the apprenticeship question is certainly that exception. In no city has information been more difficult to gather. The impasse, however, is by no means limited to our study. It is denied, it seems, to all. The sole possessor of the data needed to evaluate the prevailing picture—the state Division of Apprenticeship Standards (DAS)—guards the information with zealous secretiveness. While the DAS does conduct its regular surveys, the information that is released to the public is so broad that it can only be evaluated with great care. The refusal of a public agency to release information that pertains to a vital social question is hard to comprehend. If public review was as potentially explosive as the DAS apparently believes it is, why has similar data been so accessible elsewhere? Racial tension in other cities has certainly been greater than here, yet the data can be obtained. Possibly, the cloak of secrecy can be explained by the fact that the DAS has not been sufficiently pressured by civil rights groups and other public officials to release the information.

For an area its size, there is an amazing lack of organized concern over Negro participation in the apprenticeable trades. Piecemeal efforts have cropped up at times. These programs, however, have been more concerned with placing Negroes in immediate employment. There has been no serious attempt to date to promote, to seek out, to tutor, and to follow up Negroes who might be interested in employment in the trades. The advent of JOBART and the skills bank projects may spur more concern for such placement activity. Yet, to obtain results of consequence, attention must be focused now on the development of recruitment channels. Experience elsewhere shows that unions cannot be expected to actively recruit applicants of any race, that the Negro community is almost completely unaware of the traditions, processes, and procedures surrounding apprenticeship, and that without direction nothing more than token entrance at best can be expected. In other words, the civil rights groups need to give attention to the establishment of machinery tailor-made to the apprenticeship issue. Until such time as such a specific body is formed, little will change and no one should be surprised or complain over the low participation figures.

173

CHAPTER XII

HOUSTON AND ATLANTA

HOUSTON

Introduction

Houston not only is the largest city in the South but also has a rapidly expanding economy. According to the 1960 population census, Houston was the seventh largest city in the United States. About 23 per cent of Houston's 900,000 inhabitants are classified as nonwhites. The National Aeronautics and Space Administration complex has given rise to many related industries which have served to spur on the already rapid pace of development. Opportunities in apprenticeship have increased with the growth of the industrial sector, but Negro participation in these programs can at best be described as infinitesimal.

Part of the explanation for the paucity of Negroes in these programs can be found in the school system, which had been following a grade-a-year desegregation program up to the fall, 1965, when Grades 7 and 9 were integrated. Actually, however, there has been little real integration of student bodies because of community racial patterns.

For many years, virtually all apprenticeship training classes were held at San Jacinto High School, which is still the city's main vocational high school. San Jacinto's admission policy has until only the most recent times been "white only." One interviewee, a nonunion Negro apprentice, related the story of the difficulties he encountered in gaining admission to San Jacinto's classes in electrical work. In November, 1964, when he applied for admission to these classes, he was told by the principal that if he entered the white students would walk out en masse. It was only through the persistent efforts of his employer, a nonunion Negro electrician and a community leader, that in January, 1965, he was finally admitted. Needless to say, the white students made no attempt to leave their classes.

175

According to Dr. B. A. Turner, Dean of the School of Industries at Texas Southern University (located in Houston), all four of the high schools attended primarily by Negro students "have always been poorly staffed and financed in comparison with the other schools in the city."[1] Furthermore, Dr. Turner states that vocational training opportunities for Negroes at the high school level "have been poor and limited to only a few traditional occupations such as cooking and food preparation." A 1961 study by the Southern Regional Council lends support to Turner's appraisal:

Discriminatory conditions which materially affect occupational opportunity begin early for Houston Negroes. They are barred from the city's only full-time vocational high school [San Jacinto High School], and vocational courses offered in their own schools are limited to skills which the school system defines as most appropriate for them as adults. Industry, for its part, feels little obligation either to employ Negroes at jobs for which they are training or to provide inservice training.[2]

Civil rights spokesmen feel that the recent introduction of technical courses at the predominantly Negro schools was in response to efforts of Negro youth to transfer to predominantly white schools for this training.

In defense of school officials, it should be added that the public school system has not received strong community support, perhaps because there are many excellent private schools in the city which have led Houston's "power structure" to be somewhat ambivalent about the quality of the public schools. For example, a recent government report on Houston concluded that its "vocational education is wholly inadequate."

As compared with most of our other survey cities, Houston is not in any sense a union town. It is estimated by the state AFL-CIO that no more than 15 per cent of the city's labor force is organized. Probably, the construction industry comes closest to being one of the best organized, although there is a large nonunion sector in this industry. Virtually all residential construction is done by nonunion labor. Table 12-1 shows that almost 18 per cent of those employed in the construction industry in 1960 were Negro. This figure is the third highest (exceeded only by Atlanta and Washington) of our ten survey cities. Since we have uncovered little evidence of Negroes in most of the crafts, it can only be deduced that the nonunion sec-

[1] Interview of January 25, 1966. (The four schools he is referring to are Washington, Wheatley, Worthington, and Yates.)
[2] Art Galenher, Jr., "Houston: The Negro and Employment Opportunities in the South," report written for Southern Regional Council (November, 1961), p. 6.

Table 12-1

Employment in Selected Occupations by Race, 1960—Houston Metropolitan Area

Occupation	Number Employed				Percentage Distribution			
	Total	White	Negro	Other nonwhite	Total	White	Negro	Other nonwhite
Selected occupations								
Carpenters	5,905	5,484	425	—	100.0	92.8	7.2	—
Plasterers and cement finishers	728	377	391	—	100.0	46.3	53.7	—
Structural metal workers	586	520	16	—	100.0	97.0	3.0	—
Electricians	2,558	2,494	64	—	100.0	97.5	2.5	—
Plumbers and pipefitters	2,764	2,542	217	5	100.0	92.0	7.9	0.1
Construction laborers	5,241	2,150	3,091	—	100.0	41.0	59.0	—
Total employed	318,703	263,792	54,053	863	100.0	82.8	17.0	0.2
Total construction industry	33,243	27,266	5,948	29	100.0	82.0	17.9	0.1

Note: Percentages may not add to total because of rounding.   Based on data obtained from U.S. Bureau of the Census.

177

tor has become the source of employment for the vast majority of Negroes in most of the crafts shown in Table 12-1 except the cement masons. It should be noted, however, that the 1960 census figures show that 58 per cent of the Negroes in the Houston construction industry were working as cement masons and laborers.

Table 12-2 presents the data gathered through our field interviews on the degree of Negro participation in selected building trades in Houston.

Table 12-2

Minority Participation in Building Trades Apprenticeship
Programs in Houston, April, 1966

Union	No. of Journeymen		No. of Apprentices	
	Total	Negro	Total	Negro
IBEW 716	1,000[a]	0	160	0
Pipefitters 211 } Plumbers 68	60[b]	1	184[b]	0
Sheet Metal Workers 54	630	0	91	0
Ironworkers 84	700	0	86	0
Carpenters 213	2,900	1	199	0
Painters 130	1,000	0	42	0
Plasterers 79	170	1	24	0
Lathers 224	130	0	16	0
Bricklayers 7	364	0	47	0
Cement Masons 681	700	60	26	2

Based on data obtained in field interviews in Houston, 1966.

[a] There are an additional 1,000 journeymen in the union who are in manufacturing industries. Of this number, six are Negro journeymen.

[b] The apprenticeship training program is a joint program between the employers and the unions in both trades.

As in most cities, there is a wide gulf between the views expressed by civil rights groups and those expressed by labor spokesmen on the apprenticeship question. When one attempts to find concrete evidence to support either view, the only conclusion that can be drawn is that there is virtually no minority participation. The study conducted by the Southern Regional Council in 1961 found that the plumbers, painters, sheet metal workers, lathers, carpenters, and bricklayers "ban Negro membership under all circumstances."[3] The findings presented earlier in Table 12-2 show that by 1966 little had

[3] *Ibid.*, p. 14.

changed. The surprising conclusion to be drawn from this table, however, is not the absence of Negro apprentices in the electrical, pipefitters, plumbers, sheet metal workers, and ironworkers unions. Rather, it is the absence of Negroes from some other programs which in most other cities are not even considered problems, that is, the carpenters, plasterers, bricklayers, lathers, and painters. The only two Negro apprentices uncovered by our survey of the city were in the cement masons' program. They were brothers and their older brother is a journeyman in the union. The conspicuous absence of Negroes in almost all unions and apprenticeship programs casts strong suspicion about the optimistic rhetoric expressed in the interviews with union officials in the city. Indicative of the dichotomy between words and action was the experience of J. C. McDaniel, President of Laborers' Union Local 18, who raised the question of the lack of Negroes in the industry before the city's building trades council. Shortly afterward, the council wrote to his international that he had stepped beyond his bounds as a representative of his trade and urged that they reprimand him for his inappropriate remarks. His international did not comply with the request.

The one Negro journeyman in the plumbers' union did not enter the union by the apprenticeship route. He graduated in 1947 from Prairie View A. & M. College, where he had taken a two-year course in plumbing. He later worked as a nonunion plumber for sixteen years at that institution. In September, 1965, he applied for admission to Local 68. He was tested and subsequently admitted in November, 1965. For some time he did not have steady employment due to the fact that employers are able to call for men by name and he, like other new men, was relatively unknown. In 1966, however, he was able to get more employment.

The one Negro journeyman carpenter transferred to Houston from a carpenters' local in Hobbs, New Mexico, at the urging of a Houston employer. He had difficulty gaining admission to the Houston local, and it was not until his employer and the business representative of Laborers Union Local 18 intervened that his application was approved in November, 1965. On the job, he has received a considerable amount of "static," but he feels it is diminishing.

In 1962, Carpenters Local 213 attempted to prevent a Negro contractor from working on a large hotel being built in Houston but relented when the contractor threatened to get an injunction against the local. The contractor and his Negro employees were forced to join Carpenters Local 724, whose business agent was described as sympathetic to Negroes. However, the Negro members of Local 724 were not referred by the local to jobs.

A few years ago, IBEW Local 716 picketed a job on which a nonunion Negro contractor was working, claiming that nonunion labor was being employed on the job site. When the Negro employer offered to associate with the local, the union refused to admit his employees. In the words of the business representative for the local, "We were caught with our pants down."

In 1964 IBEW Local 716 accepted into its apprentice program the first Negro in the union's history when Theodore Ingram, who had a college degree in industrial education and who was working as an electrician for a nonunion firm, passed the written and oral entrance examination. When offered a position in the apprenticeship class, however, he declined. He had secured a teaching job in the interim and told our interviewer that he plans to go on to graduate school.

During the course of our Houston investigation, there were many indications that Negroes did participate in industrial apprenticeship programs. While exact figures are not available, there were indications that a few Negroes could be found employed in a variety of programs but not many in any particular program. Compared to the building trades, access to industrial apprenticeship opportunities in Houston—as elsewhere—seems more possible. Access to and entrance into them are two different matters. The industrial apprenticeship programs in Houston and the experience of Negro applicants demonstrate again the qualifications bottleneck. Even where barriers to access are minimal, Negro applicants have not fared very well.

In Houston, for example, NASA took 750 applications for its apprenticeship program in 1964; 407 applicants showed up for the written examination given by the U.S. Civil Service Board of Examiners. It is estimated that between one-third and one-half of the applicants were Negroes. Of the 407 tested, 140 passed with a grade of 70 per cent or better. Of about fifty Negroes who applied to the program, only two passed the test. One of the two did not show up for the interview and was dropped; the other declined to accept the position after he had passed the interview because he had gotten another position in the interim. In 1965, there were 175 applications to the NASA apprenticeship program, with the same percentage estimated to be Negro (between one-third and one-half of the applicants). Of the twenty-one who passed the test, two were Negroes.

One of the two was turned down for health reasons and the other was admitted and is currently serving a machinist apprenticeship.

With respect to Negro participation in Houston's industrial apprenticeship programs, mention also should be made of the now famous NLRB decision in the Hughes Tool Company case. Ivory Davis, the complainant in the Hughes case, told our interviewer that in 1962 he had been a laborer at Hughes for over twenty years, during which time he became well aware of the advantages of apprenticeship training, when he decided to apply for the company's apprenticeship program. At the time, Davis was a member of a Negro local of an independent union that had been certified jointly by the NLRB with a white local as bargaining agent at Hughes. The Negro local, however, had not agreed to allow all apprentices to be restricted to the white local. When Davis was denied permission to apply to the apprenticeship program, he filed charges against the union with the President's Committee on Equal Employment and with the NLRB. In his petition to the latter body, he claimed that the union had failed to represent him fairly by discriminating against him on the basis of race. Accordingly, he argued that this failure represented an unfair labor practice. In a three-to-two decision, the NLRB concurred with Davis' position and rescinded the union's certification. The independent union has subsequently been replaced by a local of the United Steel Workers. Davis, in the meantime, passed the apprenticeship examination. After some initial hostility by some of his supervisors, he reports that he has been fully accepted and is having no problems performing his work and getting along with his associates.

General Conclusions

All in all, there is little to be optimistic about concerning the current status and the potential prospects for Negro participation in apprenticeship programs in Houston. There is no apparent effort to inform the Negro community of the professed "change in attitudes" of union officials, and there is little effort being made by any group, civil rights or otherwise, to recruit applicants for any of these programs. If the initiative is to come for change, the vacuum that now exists must be filled by Negro leadership. There are some indications, however, that craft unions in Houston will, perhaps reluctantly, accept applications for membership and apprenticeship positions if these are forthcoming and that members will be permitted to transfer in from other locals.

181

ATLANTA

Introduction

Atlanta is not a typical Southern city in terms of its racial attitudes. But, although it has acquired a reputation for having more enlightened racial policies than most other Southern cities, the city exhibits some characteristics which are typically Southern. For one thing, Atlanta, like many other Southern cities, has a large Negro population; nonwhites—all of whom are Negroes in the South —constituted about 38 per cent of the city's more than one-half million people in 1960. Moreover, the construction industry in Atlanta has followed the Southern pattern of providing extensive employment opportunities for Negroes in the trowel trades, as laborers, and in nonunion sectors of other crafts. As can be seen from Table 12-3, Negroes comprised almost one-fourth of Atlanta's construction employment, a proportion exceeded only by Washington, D.C., among our ten survey cities.

While there is a significant dispersion among the trades, when compared with those in many Northern cities, it is apparent that Negroes in Atlanta, as elsewhere, are concentrated in the laborer and trowel trades. Although Negroes in the trowel trades tend to be unionized, Negroes in the electrical, metal working, and plumbing trades are employed mainly in the nonunion sector. There are, moreover, many nonunion Negro carpenters, bricklayers, and plasterers doing residential work in Atlanta. Except for the plumbers and electricians, the Atlanta building trades unions are relatively weak.

Negro Participation in Unions' Apprenticeship Programs

There are very few available sources of information on Negro participation in Atlanta's apprenticeship classes. The data that is available is presented in Tables 12-4 and 12-5. All of the programs reported on by the 1964 field teams sent out by the President's Committee on Equal Employment Opportunity in 1964 are contained in these tables. These statistics do not represent complete coverage; they depict the sample selected by these teams. However, our interviews indicate that the statistics are essentially accurate and that, by the summer of 1966, no Negroes were in any of these programs except the carpenters, who had taken some Negro apprentices at that time.

Table 12-3

Employment in Selected Occupations by Race, 1960—Atlanta Metropolitan Area

Occupation	Number Employed				Percentage Distribution			
	Total	White	Negro	Other nonwhite	Total	White	Negro	Other nonwhite
Selected occupations								
Carpenters	4,372	4,035	337	—	100.0	92.3	7.7	—
Plasterers and cement finishers	549	84	465	—	100.0	15.3	84.7	—
Structural metal workers	240	224	16	—	100.0	93.3	6.7	—
Electricians	1,801	1,776	25	—	100.0	98.6	1.4	—
Plumbers and pipefitters	1,419	1,317	102	—	100.0	92.8	7.2	—
Construction laborers	4,362	1,412	2,950	—	100.0	32.4	67.6	—
Total employed	250,180	202,797	47,198	185	100.0	81.0	18.9	0.1
Total construction industry	25,118	19,143	5,963	12	100.0	76.2	23.7	0.1

Note: Percentages may not add to total because of rounding.   Based on data obtained from U.S. Bureau of the Census.

Table 12-4

Negro Apprenticeship Applications and Selections
in Five Atlanta Building Trades, 1964

Union	Total Applied	Total Negroes Applied	Total Selected	Total Negroes Selected
Plumbers	60	4	33	0
Electricians	73	0	38	0
Sheet Metal Workers	50	2	28	U
Ironworkers	58	0	29	0
Carpenters	30	0	24	0

Based on data obtained from President's Committee on Equal Employment opportunity.

Table 12-5

Negro Participation in Apprenticeship Classes in Selected
Building Trades in Atlanta, 1965

| Union | Apprentices Enrolled in Class | | | |
	Total 1965	Negro 1965	Total 1964	Negro 1964
Plumbers and pipefitters	37	0	33	0
Sheet metal workers	30	0	26	0
IBEW	25	0	27	0
Ironworkers	15	0	20	0
Total	107	0	106	0

Based on data obtained from President's Committee on Equal Employment Opportunity.

In 1962, the Southern Regional Council (SRC), a long-established, Atlanta-based civil rights organization, reported that "as far as is known, except for the lathers, there are no apprenticeship programs —integrated or segregated—for Negroes in Atlanta."[4] The report of the SRC's survey quoted a spokesman for the carpenters local, which had never had a Negro apprentice, as saying, "You know how things are in this area."[5] Moreover, the study found that Negroes were barred altogether from the sheet metal workers' and the

[4] "Atlanta Report by the Southern Regional Council on the Negro and Employment Opportunities in the South" (April, 1962), p. 3.
[5] Ibid.

plumbers' unions and that the electricians' union permitted Negroes to hold membership in the industrial sector but not in the construction craft sectors.[6]

Although union officials in Atlanta report considerable receptivity to change in the construction industry as a result of the civil rights ferment of the 1960's, not many concrete changes have taken place, because few movements have been initiated to get more Negro apprentices and journeymen into these trades. The Atlanta bricklayers locals were segregated until 1961, but there were no Negro bricklayer apprentices until 1965, when seven were admitted to that program. The bricklayers had eight Negro apprentices in September, 1966. The lathers had fourteen apprentices in 1966, half of whom were Negroes. The plasterers and cement masons programs were predominantly Negro, and had eight Negro apprentices in September, 1966. The operating engineers had some Negro journeymen members and had accepted Negro applicants for their new apprenticeship program in the summer of 1966. Although their local unions are segregated, the Atlanta painters' apprenticeship program is integrated and has two Negroes. The carpenters also have segregated local unions, but has an integrated apprenticeship program containing three Negroes. The number of Negroes in other Atlanta apprenticeship programs in October, 1966, were: roofers, eight; electricians, none; printers, none; ironworkers, none; sheet metal workers, none; and plumbing and pipefitting, none.

The white carpenters local has announced that it would accept all Negroes who apply. The carpenters' international union has a representative working full time in Atlanta and other Southern states to merge segregated locals. Although mergers have been accomplished in New Orleans and other Southern cities, the Atlanta locals remain segregated.

The only pre-apprenticeship program in Atlanta has been an effort by the Road Machinery Company, which started a project with three Negroes and three whites. The Negroes were recruited from the Carver Vocational School. Unfortunately for the program's sponsors, however, the three Negroes dropped out to take jobs with the post office because they felt that the post office gave them greater job security. The ironworkers have accepted a Negro applicant but he failed the test for admission to that program.

The joint apprenticeship committees in the Atlanta area apparently have had very little trouble complying with the BAT's

6 *Ibid.*, p. 7.

185

nondiscrimination regulations as stipulated in 29 CFR 30. The BAT regional director takes the position, which he says is supported by the Bureau, that a written statement claiming to be in compliance is all that is required of apprenticeship sponsors. It is not surprising, therefore, that all of Atlanta's JACs are considered to be in compliance.

Efforts to establish an apprenticeship information center in Atlanta have met opposition from a number of sources. Some civil rights groups have opposed the idea because an AIC was unnecessary and because AICs have not accomplished very much in other cities. But the most important of this opposition has been overcome by those who feel that a center would be an effective way to get Negroes into apprenticeship programs. The most significant remaining opposition apparently is from the Georgia Apprenticeship Council, which has rejected the idea of a center, and the Georgia Employment Service, which is studying to see if a center is necessary. Although there is not much awareness of the apprenticeship problem among civil rights groups in Atlanta, the Urban League and a few individuals from labor and the Southern Regional Council were attempting to generate support for such a center in the summer of 1966.

Another activity in Atlanta which could increase Negro participation in construction apprenticeship programs is an agreement by the laborers local to add Negro college and high school students for summer work. The Laborers approved this project and have agreed to help form a pre-apprenticeship program, even though it means that they will lose some of their best members to other unions if the students succeed in getting into apprenticeship programs.

Our interviewees in Atlanta feel that the construction trades are receptive to the idea of admitting Negroes, but they will do so only if they get really outstanding applicants. Since this is a risky undertaking for business agents, they want to be sure the Negroes will be admitted before formally accepting them. There is a danger, of course, that Negroes who are overqualified will not remain in apprenticeship programs.

The Lockheed Corporation

There have been some efforts to get Negroes into the apprenticeship and training program at the Lockheed Aircraft Corporation at Marietta, near Atlanta. In 1961, a number of charges were filed with the President's Committee on Equal Employment Opportunity against Lockheed and the International Association of Machinists, which represent the Company's employees for collective bargaining purposes, alleging a pattern of segregation and discrimination against Negroes. The Air Force investigated these charges and found that although the plant's 494 Negroes (among its 10,319 employees) were mainly in the low-wage categories, "the pattern in the Marietta facility . . . was far from being one of rigid racial segregation. Much progress has been made. . . . Nonetheless, serious limitations still exist, both in diversity of assignment and extent of upgrading at the production level."[7]

The Air Force report found that Lockheed's training program, which was controlled exclusively by the Company, had been integrated since early 1955. However, racial restrictions continued in the programs conducted jointly with the Cobb County Board of Education's vocational service. No Negro had ever participated in Lockheed's apprenticeship program, which was not operating at the time of the Air Force investigation.

As a result of the complaints with the PCEEO, the Company agreed, among other things, to desegregate its training program, which was offered in the Company's classrooms after hours in conjunction with the Cobb County Board of Education under the Smith-Hughes Act. Shortly after this investigation, Lockheed announced that two Negroes were among eight apprentices selected for four-year apprenticeships.[8] The Company later accepted three Negroes among thirty apprentices, but one of these Negroes dropped out. In a 1965 class of twenty-six electrical apprentices, there were five Negroes, but one of these had a degree from Tennessee State College and dropped out of the apprenticeship program to join the Company's engineering staff. The first Negro graduated from Lockheed's electrical apprenticeship program in June, 1966. In the summer of 1966 the Company had five Negro apprentices. Lockheed was reported to have undertaken a vigorous search for qualified Negro employees. By the middle of July, 1961, the Company had increased its total employment to 11,000 and its Negro employment to 530.[9] In May, 1963, the Company had about 1,300 Negro employees among a total of 14,500.[10] In January, 1963, the Southern Regional Council reported that Lockheed was one of the few companies in Atlanta as signers of "Plans for Progress" with the PCEEO

[7] President's Committee on Equal Employment Opportunity, "Summary Report," May 24, 1961.
[8] *Atlanta Constitution,* June 23, 1961.
[9] *Atlanta Journal,* July 13, 1961.
[10] *Chicago Defender,* May 4–10, 1963.

which had "demonstrated what appeared to be a vigorous desire to create job opportunities."[11]

In spite of the Company's efforts, however, it admits that relatively few Negroes have been found for its apprenticeship and training programs. One Company spokesman reported that few Negroes applied for the company's training programs and that many of those who did apply failed to show up for classes. Some of the classes were conducted on company time; others were conducted on the employees' own time. But, in all cases, the self-improvement programs were financed entirely by the Company.

The Company also reports it has had virtually no response in its efforts to recruit Negroes for its apprenticeship program. Those who have applied have had great difficulty passing the screening tests. The Company has sent recruiters to Negro colleges; Negro students and instructors from technical colleges throughout the South have been brought to the Company's facilities and given tours; Negro high school counselors likewise have been given day-long tours and explanations of the industrial uses of classroom subjects; and the Company has worked with the Urban League to help motivate Negro applicants and to inform them of available opportunities, and to improve counseling and to sponsor student visits and other activities designed to help Negro youths overcome disadvantages they suffer because of past discrimination. So far the efforts have had few results, but it is encouraging to know that they will continue.[12]

Our interviewees in Atlanta reported considerable difficulties getting Negro youngsters interested in apprenticeship programs. Counselors in the Negro schools rarely counseled Negro youngsters to go into the skilled trades. Most of them emphasize college for the qualified Negro high school graduates. The Atlanta school system also regards the predominantly Negro vocational school as a "dumping ground" for those who lack academic abilities.

General Conclusions

Little can be said about Negro participation in apprenticeship programs in Atlanta, because little has been done. The area has a long legacy of denial of equal opportunity, but at the same time

11 Southern Regional Council, "Plan for Progress, Atlanta Survey" (January, 1963) (mimeographed), p. 8.

12 For a discussion of Lockheed's experience by a company representative, see E. G. Mattison, "Integrating the Work Force in Southern Industry," in Northrop and Rowan (eds.), *The Negro and Employment Opportunity*, pp. 147–65.

Atlanta has become a symbol of progress for the entire southeastern part of the United States. The apprenticeship area, however, appears to be one of the city's least progressive areas. Although there are some plans for an Apprenticeship Information Center, this effort apparently faces opposition from the apprenticeship establishment and the state employment service. The laborers' program to provide summer employment for 800 youths seems to meet a real need, but was stymied by a strike in the summer of 1966. It is possible that the rapid growth of the local economy, which has offered many rural Negroes opportunities that they have not hitherto known, has meant that little attention is being centered upon the limited opportunities available in apprenticeship.

The Lockheed experience suggests, however, that the problem of getting Negroes into apprenticeship programs will not be easy, because of the shortage of qualified Negro applicants. It should also be observed that Lockheed has not restricted its efforts to the Atlanta area but has recruited throughout the South.

Because of the number and quality of Negro educational opportunities in Atlanta, however, we are convinced that some qualified Negroes can be found, if some group in Atlanta is willing to devote the necessary time to recruitment, counseling, tutoring, and providing the necessary information and detailed assistance required to get Negroes into these programs. Our interviews in Atlanta suggest a receptivity to Negro applicants by apprenticeship programs from which they previously have been barred. But there needs to be some recruitment activity to test the genuineness of their attitudes. There are some efforts by labor and civil rights groups to establish an apprenticeship information center and take other measures to increase the number of Negro apprentices, but these efforts were still in the planning stages in November, 1966.

CHAPTER XIII

POLICIES TO INCREASE
THE NUMBER OF NEGRO APPRENTICES

As noted in Chapter I, civil rights groups devoted increasing attention to the apprenticeship problem during the 1950's and 1960's. Since it was assumed that the absence of Negroes from these programs was due mainly to discrimination, much of the early public policy sought to combat discrimination, especially by unions. However, as time went by and apprenticeship sponsors adjusted their policies to comply with these regulations, and as surprisingly few Negroes either filed charges of discrimination with regulatory agencies or applied for apprenticeship openings when they became available, it became increasingly clear that antidiscrimination policies would have to be supplemented with other policies to recruit, counsel, and sometimes supply remedial tutoring programs, if progress was to be made in this area. The first part of this section deals with various antidiscrimination measures and the last part deals with programs designed to increase the supply of applicants.

SANCTIONS

State Laws

Although the laws against discrimination in employment adopted by twenty-six states and many municipalities prohibit discrimination in apprenticeship training programs, there have been very few complaints under these laws. For example, the New York Commission, the oldest and most active of the state FEPCs, had only three cases involving apprentices between 1946 and 1965. One reason for this paucity of complaints is a reluctance to file complaints; the other is that apparently very few Negro youngsters even know about state antidiscrimination agencies.

Moreover, traditional FEPC complaint procedures are not likely to get many Negroes into apprenticeship programs. Even if Negroes filed complaints, these cases are likely to be time-consuming and uncertain as to their outcome. The apprentice selection procedure has been so diffused and irregular, and selection is based on so many different and sometimes nebulous standards, that it has been very difficult to prove discrimination. State and city human relations officials agree that discrimination by unions is very difficult to combat by conciliation and threats of public hearings, which are more effective with employers. Craft unions can be relatively impervious to public pressures, because they derive their power from control of skilled labor supplies and not from sales directly to the public; businessmen are more vulnerable to these pressures, because they are afraid that public hearings will damage their reputations and cost them sales. Although their punitive enforcement powers have not been particularly successful in getting Negroes into apprenticeship programs, some city FEP agencies have been important threats to discriminating JACs and have performed valuable functions in mediating disputes, investigating the extent of Negro participation in these programs, recruiting Negro applicants and working with other governmental and private agencies to help solve this problem.

The Courts

The U.S. Supreme Court has ruled that the Constitution imposes upon the unions which acquire the privilege of exclusive bargaining rights under the National Labor Relations Act or the Railway Labor Act the duty to represent all members of the bargaining unit fairly.[1] Some federal courts also have held that employers are jointly liable with unions for the duty of fair representation, and aggrieved minorities have brought suit against unions for damages resulting from violation of their legal rights. Although court action requires a great deal of time, is uncertain as to its outcome, and has rarely resulted in damages to the plaintiffs, lawsuits are valuable to aggrieved minorities as threats to discriminating employers and unions, and injunctions have been used to make it possible for Negroes to retain their jobs. Moreover, because injunctions can lead to fines for contempt of court, they are more effective against local unions which are impervious to the more conciliatory approaches normally employed by antidiscrimination commissions.

The NLRB

Probably because of Congress's repeated refusal to give it specific authority to deal with racial discrimination, the National Labor

[1] See *Steele* v. *L & N*, 323 U.S. 192 (1944); *NLRB* v. *Wallace*, 323 U.S. 248 (1944); *Syres* v. *Oil Workers*, 350 U.S. 892 (1955).

Relations Board traditionally has not done much to eliminate employment discrimination.

In a number of recent cases, however, especially the 1964 Hughes Tool decision, the Board has made an important departure, which could have important consequences for discrimination in employment. Specifically reversing a previous NLRB position, the Board ruled, in a split decision, in Hughes Tool, that *a violation of the duty of fair representation is also an unfair labor practice* (147 NLRB, No. 166 [1964]). Previously, the NLRB had interpreted its authority in such cases as limited to the relatively weak and rarely used penalty of revoking a union's certification. The NLRB's Hughes Tool ruling came in spite of the 1962 Miranda case,[2] which did not involve the race issue, in which a U.S. Circuit Court of Appeals refused to enforce the Board's ruling that a violation of the duty of fair representation was an unfair labor practice. But, if sustained by the courts, the Hughes Tool theory would, in effect, give the aggrieved person an administrative remedy for the duty of fair representation, making it no longer necessary for him to seek relief in the courts. Relying on the Hughes Tool doctrine, the Board ruled in 1964 that a rubber workers' local in Gadsden, Alabama, had committed an unfair labor practice by refusing to process grievances against job discrimination and segregated plant facilities (150 NLRB, No. 18 [1964]).

The NLRB has been involved in other race cases. In the New York Plumbers case, discussed in Chapter IV, the Board ruled that it was a violation of the Act for union members to refuse to work with nonunion Negroes and Puerto Ricans. This ruling is important, because unions often strike to enforce their rules against nonunion workers who are barred from membership.

The President's Committee on Equal Employment Opportunity (PCEEO)

President John F. Kennedy created the PCEEO in March, 1961, to administer a merit employment system for federal employees and to secure compliance with nondiscrimination clauses in government contracts. The PCEEO's functions were expanded in 1963 to cover nondiscrimination and merit employment where federal funds were being used in private construction projects.

Although the PCEEO had no power to deal directly with labor organizations, because they were not parties to governmental contracts, the Committee adopted a number of measures designed to

2 See "The Miranda Case," *Pennsylvania Law Review,* 112 (1964), 711.

combat racism by unions. The committee had the power to "hold hearings, public or private, with respect to the practices and policies of any such labor organization" and to "recommend remedial action." The Committee also required federal contractors to ask unions bargaining for their employees to sign statements that their "practices and policies do not discriminate on the grounds of race, color, creed or national origin" and that the labor organizations "would cooperate within their legal and contractual authority in the implementation and policy" of the executive order. If such statements were not given, the employer was required to report the union's refusal to the contracting agency and the PCEEO.

The PCEEO also sent field teams to help implement nondiscrimination policies in construction projects in thirty Southern and seventeen non-Southern cities in the summer of 1964 (the statistical results of this survey are shown in Chapter III). The teams met with contractors, unions, and joint apprenticeship committees performing work on federally involved construction projects.

The teams also discussed the PCEEO's Rules and Regulations on apprenticeship programs, which became effective in July, 1964. It was explained that compliance with the BAT's regulations (29 CFR 30, discussed below) would be required for compliance with the executive orders. "Thus, the enforcement powers of Executive Orders 10925 and 11114 are placed behind the apprenticeship standards set out by BAT, and these standards apply to *all* the apprenticeship programs of a contractor while he is covered by the Orders, not just those registered with BAT." It was explained that under the new apprenticeship regulations, "where the sponsoring parties of the apprenticeship program use a 'nonobjective' system for selecting apprentices (i.e.: father–son requirement), the absence of any minority group persons will be strong evidence of discrimination; however, the presence of some minority group persons in this situation would be evidence that their requirement is being met. This concept, like that of 'affirmative action' generally, is one for a case-by-case approach."

In 1965, President Johnson abolished the PCEEO and transferred its government-employee nondiscrimination functions to the Civil Service Commission and its contract-compliance functions to the U.S. Department of Labor. The Plans for Progress program was continued as a separate program on voluntary, private basis. By that time the Civil Rights Act was passed and the various government antidiscrimination functions became more co-ordinated than previously.

Title VII of the Civil Rights Act of 1964

Title VII of the Civil Rights Act of 1964 became effective for employers or unions with a hundred or more employees or members one year after passage. The Act provided for gradual extension to firms and unions with less than twenty-five employees or members by July, 1968. However, unions which operate referral systems or hiring halls were subject to the Act one year after passage regardless of the number of members. Unions with fewer than twenty-five members not operating hiring halls are not subject to the Act at any time.

The Act made it an unfair employment practice for the union to exclude, segregate, or classify, or attempt to cause an employer to discriminate against, any individual because of his race, color, religion, sex, or national origin. Employers also are prohibited from discriminating in any manner for racial reasons and employment agencies cannot discriminate in referring workers to jobs. Joint Apprenticeship Committees, employers, and labor unions are prohibited from discriminating in any apprenticeship or other training program.

Complaints filed under Title VII are first referred to state antidiscrimination commissions, where they exist, and thereafter action may be taken by the Equal Employment Opportunity Commission (EEOC). The EEOC has the power to investigate charges and attempts to conciliate cases when the state or local agencies either do not exist or where they have not been able to resolve the issues involved.

If conciliation by the EEOC fails, the aggrieved individual may sue in a federal district court. At his discretion, the district judge may appoint an attorney for the complainant. Reasonable attorney's fees may be allowed the prevailing party unless the United States is the prevailing party.

If the court finds that the discrimination has been intentional, it may enjoin the violation and order the hiring or reinstatement of the employee with back pay.

Any EEOC Commissioner who has reasonable cause to believe an unlawful discriminatory employment practice is occurring or has occurred may file a charge in writing with the Commission. If the discriminatory act occurs in a state with an antidiscrimination law, the EEOC, before taking any action with respect to the charge, must notify the appropriate state or local authority and offer to refer the charge to it.

Title VII also authorizes the Attorney General to bring a civil action in the federal courts when he has "reasonable cause to believe that any person or group of persons is engaged in a pattern or practice of resistance to the full enjoyment of any of the rights" secured by Title VII. The first suit under this provision was filed in February, 1966, against the St. Louis Building and Construction Trades Council and several of its affiliates. This complaint alleged that the unions had violated Title VII of the Civil Rights Act and were interfering with a nondiscrimination agreement between the United States and a contractor. Action was brought against the unions because their members walked off the Gateway Arch job to protest the hiring of a Negro plumbing contractor and his employees, who were represented by the Congress of Industrial Unions (CIU), an integrated union not affiliated with the AFL-CIO. The unions offered to take all CIU members who were qualified, and argued that their strike was for jurisdictional reasons and not because of race. However, the Justice Department alleged that the walkout, which shut down the project, was staged "to prevent and discourage the employment on construction projects in the St. Louis area of plumbers who are members of nondiscriminating unions." The Justice Department brief alleged that: Pipefitters Local 562 had over 1,000 members, none of whom is a Negro; Sheet Metal Workers Local 35 had 1,250 members, of whom only two apprentices were Negro; International Brotherhood of Electrical Workers Local 1 had 1,963 members, only one of whom was a Negro; and Plumbers Local No. 35 had 1,200 members and 102 apprentices, none of whom were Negroes. The Justice Department asked for injunctions to prevent these unions from frustrating the contractor's nondiscrimination clause in his federal contract and to prevent the unions from discriminating against any member or potential member. The charges alleging discrimination in the specific dispute were dismissed by the federal district court, but the charges alleging a pattern of discrimination in violation of Title VII were still pending in August, 1966. It should be noted that no specific charges of discrimination by Negroes were filed in this case and that action was taken by the Justice Department on its own initiative.

The NLRB was involved in this case because the walk-out violated the secondary boycott provisions of the Taft–Hartley Act. The Board therefore obtained an injunction which sent the strikers back to work.

Title VI of the Civil Rights Act of 1964

Title VI of the Civil Rights Act prohibits the use of federal funds to support a discriminatory activity. Section 601 of this title declares: "No person in the United States shall, on the grounds of race, color or national origin, be excluded from participation in, be denied the benefits of, or be subjected to discrimination under any program or activity receiving Federal financial assistance." This title, therefore, makes it unlawful for federal funds to be used to support related training for apprenticeship programs in public schools, if the union practices discrimination.

However, this power, though not completely insignificant, is limited by the fact that many apprenticeship sponsors provide their own related instruction, and others would do so rather than submit to what they considered to be onerous regulations.

Federal Apprenticeship Regulations

Some form of antidiscrimination provision in federal government contracts has existed since President Roosevelt's Fair Employment Practice Committee (FEPC) was set up during World War II. These committees did not, however, pay much attention to the apprenticeship question until 1961, when Secretary of Labor Arthur J. Goldberg announced that all federal contractors would thereafter be required to include a specific nondiscrimination clause in their apprenticeship standards.

In response to President Kennedy's instructions the previous June, when racial demonstrations were staged at a number of construction sites in large Northern cities, Secretary of Labor W. Willard Wirtz, over the heated objections of some union leaders, approved new standards which provided that apprentices must be selected on a nondiscriminatory basis. These regulations (29 CFR 30) became effective January 17, 1964, and provide that all apprenticeship programs registered on or before that date had to meet the following requirements:

1. The selection of apprentices on the basis of qualifications alone, in accordance with objective standards which permit review after full and fair opportunity for application, unless the selections otherwise made would themselves demonstrate that there is equality of opportunity.

2. The taking of whatever steps are necessary, in acting upon application lists developed prior to this time, to remove the effects of previous practices under which discriminatory patterns of employment may have resulted.

3. Nondiscrimination in all phases of apprenticeship and employment during apprenticeship after selections are made.

Selection on the basis of "qualifications alone" means, according to 29 CFR 30, that apprentices must be chosen solely on the basis of qualifications, which may be determined by such means as "fair aptitude tests, school diplomas, age requirements, occupationally essential physical requirements, fair interviews, school grades, and previous work experience." "Objective standards" means that qualifications must be based on "specific requirements so that questions of discrimination can be fairly adjudicated. . . . Requirements must be established and disseminated publicly prior to selection."

In order to permit review of objective standards, 29 CFR 30 requires the keeping of "adequate records of the selection process" which must be made available to the BAT on request. The records must be retained for a period of at least two years.

The meaning of "after full and fair opportunity for application" depends upon when the application lists were established. Those lists established before 29 CFR 30 became effective (January 17, 1964) met this requirement if they "had publicly disseminated information about the availability of apprenticeship opportunities and had allowed a substantial period of time for applicants to apply." For programs established *after* January 17, 1964, compliance requirements are satisfied if:

the program sponsor, prior to the time of selection and at least once annually, except in years when no selections are made, has allowed a substantial period of time for new applicants to apply and former applicants to reapply for apprenticeship, has publicly disseminated full information about the availability of apprenticeship opportunities, and has ranked the new applicants thus received along with previous applicants on the basis of their cumulative qualifications.

Those apprenticeship programs established *before January 17, 1964, that do not wish to select on the basis of qualifications alone* can meet the requirements of 29 CFR 30 by *either* selecting from *existing employees* or *"demonstrating equality of opportunity"* in their selection procedures. This requirement is not defined in detail but obviously permits program sponsors to discriminate in favor of relatives and friends so long as they also discriminate in favor of enough Negroes to satisfy the Administrator of the BAT.

The Secretary's regulations permit the selection from existing employees or some other "restricted pool," provided "admission to the pool as well as selection of apprentices [are] on a nondiscriminatory basis after January 17, 1964. Selections from the pools may be on the basis of seniority of employment."[3]

[3] For an example of this procedure, see our discussion of the New York Printing Industries program in Chapter IV.

The Secretary's regulations also provide that there shall be no discrimination in the operation of apprenticeship programs. This means that there can be no discrimination in such things as "job assignment, promotion, layoff or termination, rates of pay or other forms of compensation and conditions of work." All registered programs are required by 29 CFR 30 to contain formal nondiscrimination provisions.

Programs registered *after* January 17, 1964, "must select apprentices on the basis of *qualifications alone* in accordance with *objective standards which permit review after full and fair opportunity for application* and must adopt a nondiscrimination clause" (emphasis added). In other words, all new programs do not have the option of demonstrating nondiscrimination or selecting from existing employees, but must use objective standards alone as the sole standards for selection.

In addition, the federal apprenticeship regulations require the BAT to undertake a "systematic field review of existing federally registered programs, inform program sponsors of the equal opportunity standards, encourage their adoption and take appropriate action regarding programs which do not adopt and operate in accordance with the standards." After efforts at conciliation and provisions for a hearing, the Administrator of the BAT is authorized by 29 CFR 30 to

render a final decision in writing based on the file or the record as the case may be. If the decision is that the program is in nonconformity and that satisfactory action to achieve conformity has not been undertaken, the program shall be deregistered. . . . In each case in which deregistration is ordered the Administrator shall make public notice of the order and will notify the President's Committee on Equal Employment Opportunity and the Solicitor of Labor.

Apprenticeship programs in the State Apprenticeship Council (SAC) states are required by 29 CFR 30 to adopt standards consistent with the Secretary's regulations. If BAT's Administrator "determines that a State program is not consistent with such standards, he shall notify the Secretary of Labor that a question exists as to whether the Federal Government should continue to recognize for Federal purposes programs registered by the State agency."

Although our information concerning the effectiveness of 29 CFR 30 is rather sketchy, our evidence suggests that, although there was some resistance to the standards, all state programs were approved after eighteen months and most joint apprenticeship committees have adopted standards in compliance with these regulations. The New York and Pennsylvania apprenticeship standards are in many ways more stringent than the federal, but there have been few cases of noncompliance with either the federal or state regulations.

It would be very surprising, however, if many programs failed to comply with the federal standards, because it is possible to be in compliance and continue to bar Negroes from membership through the use of selection procedures. The Labor Department insists that the selection procedures be objective, but it has left the determination of qualifications and the content of the tests and their interpretation to the JACs. In addition, the apprenticeship sponsors apparently have been able to comply with these standards by formal notice of their intention to do so. No penalties have been imposed on JACs for failing to comply with these requirements or to make the reports which they require.

It is also possible for apprenticeship sponsors to avoid including Negroes in the apprenticeship programs by following the alternative of selecting from existing employees when it is known that Negro employees are either unwilling or unqualified to apply for apprenticeship training.

There is a prevailing belief that a major deterrent to implementing the nondiscrimination standards is the fact that the BAT and the state apprenticeship agencies are not sympathetic to the enforcement of such policies. It is argued that the BAT is staffed mainly by ex-construction trades unionists who consider themselves to be "fronts" for the unions rather than agents to carry out nondiscrimination policies. Others in the apprenticeship agencies consider enforcement of antidiscrimination policies to be inconsistent with their main function of promoting apprenticeship programs.

As a consequence of their failure to produce more than formal changes, some observers argue that the adoption of 29 CFR 30, by encouraging tests and objective standards, actually has provided apprenticeship sponsors a means for perpetuating discrimination. This observation is based upon the conclusion that, without special preparation, Negroes do not do well on written tests and therefore are most likely to get into apprenticeship programs where standards are flexible and no tests are required.

Although these standards apparently have had the result indicated by their critics, they cannot really be regarded as the causes of inadequate Negro representation in apprenticeship programs. We are convinced that tests are less important than the attitude of the people administering the tests. If apprenticeship sponsors want to take in qualified Negroes, they can use the tests to do so. Under present conditions, on the other hand, apprenticeship sponsors also can and have used tests to continue to bar Negroes. The real problem with apprenticeship regulations is that the nature of apprenticeship programs is such that it is very difficult to impose punitive regulations which would *require* apprenticeship sponsors to take action against their will. We have noted that the BAT's main power over these programs—deregistration—really is not likely to mean very much. Moreover, there seem to be few other penalties which would really be effective against recalcitrant apprenticeship programs without destroying their flexible nature by having governments determine qualifications, give the tests, pay for the training and provide the training facilities. Although governments could do more than they do to train apprentices in their own facilities, it is doubtful that governments can provide an adequate apprenticeship program without private support. It would be easy enough for governments to provide the academic part of apprenticeship training, but this is much less important to most apprenticeship programs than on-the-job training.

In conclusion, although there is considerable dissatisfaction with the results of the apprenticeship regulations, they have not been completely ineffective. The fights over these regulations have had important educational results for all of the parties involved. They have created an attitude by the apprenticeship establishment that changes are inevitable and that the apprenticeship sponsors had better prepare their followers to accept some Negroes. These regulations, along with the 1964 Civil Rights Act and the various state apprenticeship regulations, have created attitudes in the industry which are conducive to change, even though the actual changes have been minimal.

On the other hand, civil rights leaders and government officials outside the apprenticeship establishment have learned something about apprenticeship programs. They know that the apprenticeship establishment will fight to preserve its traditions and that it has considerable ability to resist change. Civil rights leaders and their governmental allies also have learned that getting more Negroes into apprenticeship programs is not simply a matter of lowering racial barriers. On numerous occasions, very few qualified Negro applicants have come forward in response to efforts to recruit Negro applicants for apprenticeship programs.

Preferential Treatment Issue

One of the most controversial issues surrounding antidiscrimination regulations has been the question of preferential treatment, which some civil rights groups have advocated to compensate Negroes for the cumulative influences of discrimination. Demands for quotas and preferential treatment are based upon the realization that even with nondiscriminatory employment policies, Negroes would not be able to change their employment patterns very rapidly.

Although preferential treatment is usually condemned by employers, union leaders,[4] and most government agencies, it has not been uncommon. Indeed, in the past, when Negroes have brought pressures for more jobs or official positions in unions, formal or informal racial quota arrangements sometimes have seemed the logical compromises to settle these disputes. The federal government, in spite of vigorous assurance to the contrary, has at least left the impression that it expects government contractors to give preferential treatment to minorities.

The Civil Rights Act of 1964 is not clear with respect to the legality of preferential treatment. The Act merely declares that preferential treatment is not *required* by Title VII, though it presumably would be legal. However, in order to be consistent with other provisions of the Act, preferential treatment which discriminates against whites presumably would be unlawful.

Preferential treatment for Negroes is opposed, of course, because it might discriminate against whites. But *special* programs for Negroes need not discriminate against Negroes or whites. For example, apprenticeship sponsors who have not recruited among Negroes in the past and who have no Negro employees, trainees, or members might make special efforts to recruit Negroes or to help them acquire training. This would be special treatment to include Negroes in the recruitment pattern, but it would not be preferential treatment because it would extend to Negroes benefits which whites already enjoy.

Special programs by unions and employers to prepare Negroes and other disadvantaged groups for apprenticeship or other training programs also would not seem to be "preferential treatment." However, industry spokesmen claim that the following government contract compliance example of "affirmative action" contemplates quota systems: "The Company will assist at least *three* youths with

---

[4] In 1963, for example, when the Secretary of Labor's apprenticeship regulations were first announced, they were interpreted by labor leaders as requiring preferential treatment. Union and employer representatives in the plumbing industry drafted a statement declaring: "We will accept no dictation. We reject any imposition of quotas based on racial or population percentages by any Government agencies or private business group. . . . We consider quotas undemocratic, unreasonable, unwarranted, and unworkable. . . . We do not believe in rejecting an applicant because of his race, color, or creed. . . . And we likewise cannot be expected to admit an applicant because of his race, color, or creed" (*New York Times*, August 20, 1963).

minority group identification to enter each apprenticeship program in which it is involved."

There would seem to be a continuum of policies ranging from hostile discrimination against Negroes in favor of whites to hostile discrimination against whites in favor of Negroes. Between these extremes there exist various combinations of policies that might be adopted, some of which will discriminate against whites a little now in order to give the Negro a more nearly equal chance. Of course, preferential treatment that causes either whites or Negroes to be displaced is objectionable, but the measures to improve the economic opportunities of Negroes need not take this form and need not ignore the qualifications of Negroes or whites. But, since qualifications are difficult to determine with precision, there will always be a considerable margin within which decision-makers can exercise judgment for or against particular groups.

Whatever one's judgment concerning the desirability of preferential treatment, the pressures on civil rights organizations, the federal government, employers, human rights commissions, and unions are such that Negroes *will* receive preferential treatment in many cases. All of these groups face certain pressures to show results in terms of including Negroes in jobs and training programs from which they were previously excluded. Legalistic barriers, tests, and qualifications thrown up to make it more difficult for Negroes to enter these programs will not relieve these pressures. Employers or unions, therefore, will be compelled to relieve the pressures by all available means. All parties can present moral reasons why they should either take action or avoid it. But, as in most cases of conflict resolution, the problems will be solved only through compromises and not by moral arguments.[5]

Other Policies

As noted earlier, the meager tangible results of antidiscrimination measures and the use of sanctions by government agencies made it abundantly clear that policies based entirely on the assumption that discrimination was the only problem were inadequate. It not only became increasingly clear that the apprenticeship establishment was relatively impervious to various sanctions, but that antidiscrimination policies operated only on the *demand* for Negro apprentices without doing anything to increase the supply. This realization was

[5] For an excellent article on this topic see George Strauss and Sidney Ingerman, "Public Policy and Discrimination in Apprenticeship," *The Hastings Law Journal,* XVI (February, 1964), 285–331.

brought home to some civil rights groups by their inability to produce many qualified applicants when unions and employers challenged them to do so. Since demand and supply must operate together to produce results, various organizations started taking measures to recruit and tutor Negro applicants for apprenticeship programs. Some of these, such as the Workers Defense League program in New York, we have discussed in connection with our city studies. Others, including various governmental and private programs, are discussed in this section.

Advisory Committee on Equal Opportunity in Apprenticeship and Training

The Advisory Committee on Equal Opportunity in Apprenticeship and Training (ACEOAT) was created by Secretary of Labor W. Willard Wirtz in February, 1963. The ACEOAT's functions were defined as follows:

The Committee shall advise the Department of Labor with respect to the development, review, and promotion of more effective programs and policies for establishing and maintaining equal opportunities in apprenticeable and other occupations. It shall recommend actions for implementing the policies of the Department of Labor in the specific area of skilled manpower development on a nondiscriminatory basis.

The Committee has fifteen members, appointed by the Secretary of Labor: four from labor, four from management, five from the minority community, and two from the general public. Secretarial, technical, and other services to the Committee are provided by the BAT, and Under Secretary of Labor John F. Henning has served as its chairman. Harold Barrett, Jr., from the BAT's staff, is the Committee's Executive Secretary.

The ACEOAT's meetings generally have been involved with acquainting Committee members with developments in the apprenticeship field, as they relate to equal employment opportunities, and with the formulation of policies to help deal with this problem. The Committee's most comprehensive recommendations came out of its eleventh meeting in San Francisco, October 4–5, 1965. At this meeting, a special subcommittee developed the following eight-point program:

1. Direct neighborhood recruitment and promotion activity by the BAT-BES-AIC personnel;
2. Conferences each school semester with all school counselors to advise on the realities of local apprenticeship opportunities, conditions and requirements;

3. Similar periodic conferences with leaders of the organized minority community;
4. Development of a promotional and explanatory film;
5. A systematic reporting procedure to assess progress in the field in carrying out the program;
6. The creation of independent testing agencies for objectifying and validating grading and testing of apprentice candidates;
7. Setting aside specific time in each Regional and State Apprenticeship Conference for the advancement of equal opportunity;
8. Informal assemblies of key leaders involved in any way with apprenticeship and civil rights, for the purpose of communications and problem-solving.

The subcommittee also requested specific information on the extent to which BAT-registered programs had complied with 29 CFR 30; it is significant that two years after 29 CFR 30 went into effect the ACEOAT did not have this information. On October 1, 1966, however, the BAT reported that field compliance reviews had been satisfactorily completed with 7,201 programs. There were at that time 40,437 registered programs, only 6,727 of which had five or more apprentices.

The ACEOAT's January, 1966, session was preceded by a public meeting at Howard University in Washington, D.C., attended by representatives of all civil rights groups except the Urban League and the Southern Christian Leadership Conference (who were invited but did not attend) and was designed to give these groups an opportunity to speak on the Negro's perception of, experience with, and expectations from apprenticeship sponsors.

The civil rights groups attending the Howard meeting were extremely critical of the lack of progress in increasing the number of Negro apprentices. At its executive session the following day, the ACEOAT concluded: "The essence of the public meeting was a clear indication that Negroes do not really understand the nature, operations and purposes of apprenticeship; that their experiences have been extremely frustrating and disappointing; and that they wanted more opportunities *now*."[6]

In response to its concern over the civil rights leaders' "cry for action," and the implicit charge that the ACEOAT had produced no results in its two years of operation, a proposal was made for a

[6] Advisory Committee on Equal Opportunity in Apprenticeship and Training, "Annual Report, 1966" (dittoed), p. 6.

program to obtain four "specific, attainable goals for calendar year 1966."[7] These goals were:

1. Aim to have minorities in every registered apprenticeship program by the end of calendar year 1966.
2. For those programs now employing minority-group apprentices, sustain the same proportion of minorities, or better, in this year's new apprentice classes.
3. Select pilot test-areas [which the Committee defined as all those cities with active AICs] and try out the ideas in the [special] subcommittee report's proposed "affirmative action program."
4. If, after we have set out goals, and have promoted cooperation with local programs, and have *not* achieved these goals in specific instances, *then* we should bring sanctions to bear on the offending programs.

ACEOAT's January, 1966, meeting also adopted the special subcommittee's report. The Committee's executive secretary, Harold Barrett, subsequently proposed to the BAT that it adopt the action program, but, for a variety of reasons, especially a claim that it had inadequate funds and staff, Bureau officials did not accept the ACEOAT's program.

With respect to the usefulness of the Committee, ACEOAT's 1966 *Annual Report* concluded:

The committee proposals, although they may be addressed to the practicalities of need, are sometimes not sufficiently sensitive to the budgetary limitations of the Bureau and the Department. The establishment of priorities within the Bureau and the Department as to which way funds will be directed and staff deployed are often the result of policy considerations unknown to, and inaccessible to, the Committee. As the result, Committee recommendations tend to be ahead of the practical implementation abilities of the Department and compete with other program areas which tend to have higher priority values than the equal opportunity issue. Nevertheless, the Committee serves the useful purpose of pointing in the direction of need, should the occasion arise with staff and budget and priority values which would permit the equal opportunity issue to be given its turn in the value structure of the Bureau and the Department.

Although the BAT, like all agencies, undoubtedly had budgetary limitations which made it difficult for it to implement such proposals as that made by the ACEOAT, civil rights advocates, within the Bureau and without, suspect that the BAT's refusal to act was based upon a reluctance to oppose those within the Bureau who are not sympathetic to equal opportunity measures and upon the fact

[7] Advisory Committee on Equal Opportunity in Apprenticeship and Training, "Report of the Twelfth Meeting, Executive Session" (January 28, 1966) (mimeographed), p. 4.

that Bureau officials are unwilling to assign civil rights policies efficiently high priorities. Some BAT officials, on the other hand, express the belief that the equal opportunities proposals are unrealistic because they contemplate preferential treatment in disregard of qualifications. Proponents of the latter point of view believe that the advocates of equal opportunity give too much weight to civil rights programs.

The Industrial Training Advisors (ITAs)

The racial position of the BAT was under attack from a number of sources, including the U.S. Civil Rights Commission, during the early 1960's.[8] These attacks came not only because the Bureau seemed to be doing so little to get Negroes into apprenticeship programs but also because it had very few Negroes on its staff. Since the Bureau's traditional staff qualifications resulted in the selection of people with mainly craft union backgrounds, Negroes previously were almost automatically excluded from employment on the BAT's field staff.

The Bureau met some of this criticism in 1963 by adding four race relations consultants, whose function it was to open up apprenticeship opportunities to Negroes. Other consultants, called Industrial Training Advisors (ITAs), were later added in all of the BAT's regions. A Negro also was appointed regional director of the region which contains Chicago.

The regional industrial training advisors are under the direction of the BAT's regional directors, but receive technical assistance from the National Training Advisor in Washington. There is a Special Assistant for Equal Opportunity to the BAT Administrator who has general responsibility for the Bureau's equal opportunity program. The selection of Negroes for most of the ITA positions resulted in a dramatic reversal of the BAT's traditional personnel policies.

If their objective was to get Negroes into apprenticeship programs, the ITAs clearly have not been a success. Indeed, the Deputy Administrator of the BAT, who has general responsibility for this program, told us in December, 1965, that he did not know of a single case where an Industrial Training Advisor had been responsible for getting a Negro admitted to an apprenticeship program. While they apparently are dedicated people, most of the ITAs interviewed by this study seemed too often to lack sufficient inde-

8 See U.S. Civil Rights Commission, "Reports on Apprenticeship, 1964."

pendence to carry out their activities. A major problem seems to be the lack of support for this program by many of the BAT regional staffs. Regional directors too often seem to resent the ITAs or to think they are unnecessary, and have not given them sufficient independence or resources with which to operate.

We have found, however, that the ITA in Atlanta has been able to do a fairly effective job in working with the Negro community and the trade unions. It is apparent, therefore, that the main problem with the ITAs is not the concept but the implementation of that concept.

There can be little question that the ITAs, or somebody with the backing of the BAT's top administration, need to take measures to advise the Bureau's field staff on minority group relations and bridge the wide gap which presently separates the BAT, the Negro community, and apprenticeship sponsors.

Someone on the BAT's staff undoubtedly could perform this function more effectively if: (1) the BAT had no enforcement powers under 29 CFR 30, because it is difficult to promote voluntarism while threatening punitive action; (2) some other organization, such as the EEOC or the OFCC, stood by to take punitive action if the BAT's promotional efforts failed; and (3) the nondiscrimination policy was instilled in the field staff by the BAT's top administrators and regional directors.

Apprenticeship Information Centers

There seems to be almost universal agreement that the lack of knowledge of apprenticeship is one of the most important reasons for the paucity of Negroes in these programs and for much of the controversy that surrounds this question. This lack of information is perpetuated by high school and employment counselors who, perhaps realistically in the past, have not advised Negro youngsters to interest themselves in apprenticeship training. Lacking members of the family who had served apprenticeships, it is not surprising that Negro youngsters should know so little about these programs.

Many skilled trades unions have intentionally perpetuated the ignorance of apprenticeship in order to continue excluding all except friends and relatives. Since many state and federal apprenticeship agencies apparently consider themselves to be agents of these exclusive unions, they have done very little to close this informational gap.

One of the first groups to concern itself with an apprenticeship information clearing-house was the Bay Area Urban League, which

argued that there should be a central location where a Negro youngster interested in apprenticeship could get information on qualifications, procedures, time and place of making application, or the
career possibilities in different trades. As a consequence, the establishment of apprenticeship information centers became one of the
first objectives of the California State-wide Committee for Equal
Opportunity in Apprenticeship and Training when it was established in 1960.[9]

Although city apprenticeship information centers had already
been established in California and New York City (discussed in
Chapter IV), the first federal center was opened June 17, 1963, in
Washington, D.C., as a co-operative effort between the District of
Columbia Apprenticeship Council, the District of Columbia Commissioners and school authorities, the U.S. Employment Service, and
the U.S. Department of Labor. While the Washington AIC was
intended for all persons regardless of color, Under Secretary of
Labor John F. Henning observed that "the Center should be of
particular value to Negroes and other minorities from whom the
knowledge of admission procedures and requirements often had
been withheld."[10]

Following the creation of the Washington Center, Under Secretary Henning, in his capacity as Manpower Administrator, issued
Manpower Administration Order No. 12, which established policy
for the operation of AICs in a number of cities. This order outlined
the joint responsibilities of the Bureau of Employment Security
and the BAT in operating these centers, and was based on the
premise that "There is a demonstrated need for providing a central
and easily accessible source of information, guidance and counseling
concerning apprenticeship opportunities, requirements and enrollment in labor market areas where apprenticeship trades are located." Manpower Order No. 12 also established the following
guidelines for the AICs:

a. Information centers will be established in appropriate labor market
areas, particularly in areas where there are substantial minority groups in
the work force.

b. The Centers shall secure, maintain, and publicize an up-to-date
compilation of apprenticeship information and make it available to high
school students, public school guidance departments, the minority, community, labor unions, employer associations, employers, and the general
public.

[9] The experience of this Committee is discussed in detail in Chapter XI.

[10] John F. Henning, "Expanding Apprenticeship for All Americans," *American
Federationist*, July, 1963.

c. The Centers shall place emphasis on developing cooperation with employers, unions, and minority groups, in order that these parties take action commensurate with the significant value of apprenticeship in relation to the National manpower situation.

d. The Centers shall determine the qualifications of applicants by interviewing, counseling, and testing, and refer only those qualified to available apprenticeship openings.

e. Centers shall be operated as separate entities within the organizational structure of Employment Service local offices and each one shall be prominently identified as "Apprenticeship Information Center," so as not to be confused with any other Employment Service function within which or near which it is located.

The operation of the Centers was placed under the joint control of the BAT and the BES. The BAT's responsibilities include taking "the initiative in stimulating local interest and securing community support from labor, management, civic, education and minority groups, and in publicizing the goals and attainments of the Centers." The BAT also was instructed to "secure and provide current and essential apprenticeship information, including local apprentice requirements, to the Centers."

The BES was given the responsibility of securing the co-operation of state employment security agencies with the establishment and administration of the AICs, and of informing them of the Center's objectives and operations. Special attention was given to labor market areas "with substantial minority groups represented in the work force." "Where necessary," the BES was instructed to "make financial arrangements to enable the State to participate without diminishing existing services" in the employment service offices selected to operate AICs.

Since the AICs require the co-operation of a variety of government agencies, Manpower Administration Order No. 12 provided for the establishment of an intergovernmental Agency Coordinating Group (ACG) for each center representing the BAT, the state employment service, the state apprenticeship agency (where appropriate), the public schools, and the minority advisors of the BAT and the BES. The local BAT field representative was made responsible for the formation and continuing operation of the ACG for providing the group with "essential information obtained from management, labor and the minority community, which will aid in guiding local operating practices."

Order No. 12 also provides for an AIC Advisory Committee (AICAC) to "assure the fullest community participation in the successful operation of each Center." It was recommended that the

AICAC be appointed by local civic authorities wherever possible and that it be made up of representatives of management, labor, minority, and civil organizations. Members of the ACG are instructed to attend AICAC meetings and to act as consultants from their respective organizations.

The AICAC is supposed to maintain close contact between the community and the AIC. Its specific functions, as outlined in Manpower Order No. 12, were to give advice on "(1) the reactions of various community groups to the activity of the Center; (2) the opportunities and outlook for apprenticeship in the area; and (3) possible modifications or improvements in the conduct of the Center."

In order to promote the idea of the AICs, teams from the BAT and the BES went into various communities to explain the purposes of the Centers and overcome opposition to them. Since much of the opposition initially was from the labor movement, special efforts were made to overcome the specific fears that the AICs were going to usurp the unions' prerogative of determining the qualifications for their programs. Much union opposition was due to the stipulation in Manpower Order No. 12 that "The Centers shall examine the qualifications of applicants by interviewing, counseling, and testing, and *refer only those qualified* to available apprenticeship openings" (emphasis added). As a consequence, BES Administrator Robert C. Goodwin issued a letter of clarification on March 11, 1964, which called upon all state employment security agencies to "Please notify the affected labor organizations and major apprenticeship sponsors . . . that there is no intent on the part of apprenticeship information centers to bypass or disrupt the traditional prerogative and authority of joint apprenticeship committees or other apprenticeship sponsors to make the final selection and placement of apprentice applicants."

Goodwin's clarification did not, however, allay the suspicions of industry spokesmen, many of whom expressed the fear that the AICs were simply the beginning of federal control of the apprentice-selection process.

As a consequence of continued industry opposition, BES and BAT teams attempted to sell the idea that the AIC was the best alternative facing the unions and that they should promote the establishment of centers in their areas in order to exercise some control over them. It was explained that the AICs would really be performing a useful function for the unions by screening applicants for them; the AICs' union advocates felt that it was better for the Centers to tell the Negro youngsters that they were not qualified than it was for the union leaders to incur the suspicion of discrimination by having to perform this disagreeable task. The unions also were told that the AICs were getting qualified Negroes into apprenticeship programs, whereas other training activities were producing Negroes to compete with those programs. It was also pointed out that the AIC was a part of the voluntary tradition of the American apprenticeship system, whereas alternatives to the AIC contemplated more direct government regulation.

In spite of continued opposition from the construction industry, the Labor Department funded AICs in the following cities by the end of August, 1966:

1. Baltimore[a]	13. Minneapolis[a]
2. Birmingham[a]	14. Nashville[a]
3. Boston[a]	15. Newark[a]
4. Bridgeport[a]	16. Norfolk
5. Camden[a]	17. Paterson[a]
6. Chicago[a]	18. Philadelphia
7. Cincinnati[a]	19. Pittsburgh
8. Cleveland[a]	20. Portland
9. Detroit[a]	21. St. Louis[a]
10. Houston	22. St. Paul[a]
11. Indianapolis[a]	23. Seattle
12. Kansas City[a]	24. Washington, D.C.[a]

[a] Operating in August, 1966. The balance of these were financed in the fiscal year 1966.

It will be observed that AICs had been funded for all of our study cities except New York and San Francisco-Oakland, where city or state centers are in operation, and Atlanta.

As may be seen in our discussions of those cities, Philadelphia, Houston, and Atlanta have had difficulties getting AICs established, but efforts were under way late in 1966 to establish centers in Philadelphia and Atlanta.

Evaluation of the AICs

It is, of course, very difficult to establish criteria by which to evaluate the AICs. Their most important objective obviously is to get youngsters in general and minorities in particular into apprenticeship programs. We cannot, however, use this as our sole cri-

212

terion, because the AIC's main function is to supply information and to act as a clearing-house; it has no power to compel apprenticeship sponsors to accept its referrals. Obviously, therefore, the AIC's success depends in large measure on the co-operation of the apprenticeship establishment as well as on the imagination and effectiveness of the Center's staff in recruiting, screening, referring, and getting applicants into these programs.

The most successful AIC that we have studied was the one in Washington, D.C. The Washington Center's relative success seems to have been due to a number of factors including the following: its director was director of both the AIC and the YOC, had himself served an apprenticeship, and had good contacts with the labor movement; much of the work done by the unions in the Washington area is on government contracts; there is a large Negro community in Washington, which has become involved in the Center's operations; and the Center does not have to contend with all the problems involved in a joint federal-state arrangement.

Between June 17, 1963, and September 17, 1965, the Washington AIC had 3,103 applicants, of whom 2,411, or 77 per cent, were Negroes. Of those who applied, 1,037 were qualified by the AIC for apprenticeship programs; of these 728 (70 per cent) were Negroes. Of those who were qualified by the AIC, 921 were referred to unions; 724 of these referees (79 per cent) were Negroes. Of the total referees, there were 291 placements; 205 Negroes (70.4 per cent) were placed. Although we have no information on the occupational breakdown of these placements, the Washington experience apparently was more productive than that of any other city with the possible exception of Chicago.

Between the establishment of the Center in Chicago in April, 1964, and June, 1965, the AIC had 4,278 applicants appear, had referred 4,278 and had placed 581 in apprenticeship programs. Although statistics on nonwhite placements in Chicago are not available for the entire period of its operation, the AIC in that city placed sixty-one nonwhites between September, 1964, and July, 1965, which was about 15 per cent of placements during that period. The Chicago AIC placed forty-seven Negroes in apprenticeship programs in a special concerted program between December 1, and August 1, 1966; the AIC had referred 219 Negroes to the construction trades, but some of these had dropped out and others were waiting to be placed on August 1, 1966.

The experience of other AICs in placing Negroes has been presented in the chapters dealing with the specific cities. The placement

213

experience of the nine active AICs in June, 1965, is shown in Table 13-1.

By the time of our survey, the AICs in most of our other study cities had been relatively less successful in placing apprentices,

Table 13-1

Placement Experience of Apprenticeship Information Centers, 1964 to 1965

Center	Cumu-lative 1964	Cumu-lative 1965	Total
Baltimore (from April, 1964)			
Appeared	279	321	600
Referred	303	396	699
Placed	97	80	177
Boston (from February, 1964)			
Appeared	1,289	351	1,640
Referred	213	152	365
Placed	7	5	12
Bridgeport (from January, 1965)			
Appeared		176	176
Referred		165	165
Placed		67	67
Chicago (from April, 1964)			
Appeared	2,118	2,160	4,278
Referred	455	875	1,330
Placed	232	349	581
Cincinnati (from April, 1964)			
Appeared	795	320	1,115
Referred	141	85	226
Placed	16	29	45
Cleveland (from December, 1964)			
Appeared	54	286	340
Referred	9	90	99
Placed	0	19	19
Detroit (from July, 1964)			
Appeared	569	573	1,106
Referred	95	341	436
Placed	8	74	82
Newark (from January, 1965)			
Appeared	63	127	200
Referred	59	205	264
Placed	24	50	74
Washington, D.C. (from February, 1964)			
Appeared	1,181	786	1,967
Referred	374	199	573
Placed	106	49	153

Based on data obtained from the Bureau of Employment Security.

white or nonwhite, and some of them appeared to be making little effort to publicize apprenticeship programs. In Oakland, the director of the AIC (which was not supported by the federal government) had been given the direction of the Center without guidelines on how to operate it. During its first six months, the Oakland AIC had 357 applicants, 167 of whom were Negroes; it referred seventy-five applicants to apprenticeship programs, thirty of whom were Negroes. However, over half of the Negroes were referred as a result of special recruitment launched to satisfy a request for boilermakers. Of those referred, only ten, four of whom were Negroes, were accepted by the JACs. Three of the Negroes were accepted by the boilermakers and a fourth by the automobile painters.

An investigation of the San Francisco AIC in July, 1965, by the California Employment Service showed that, in the two and a half years the AIC had been in operation, "a total of six youths have entered apprenticeships to the best of our knowledge." In the year ending July, 1965, 200 to 240 youths were introduced to JACs. But, except for the six known cases, it was not possible to verify another placement. The racial composition of the six placements is not known, but of 190 other referrals, forty (or 21 per cent) were Negroes. Of 323 referrals by all AICs in California made before "early 1965," twenty-one (or 6.5 per cent) were Negroes; four of these twenty-one Negroes were known to have been hired. The report on the investigation of the San Francisco AIC concluded that: "It appears that the Center is serving youths from the minority groups at least proportionately [to their distribution in the population], and that exposure to the JACs of youths from the minority community is occurring *provided* the youth is given the introduction and ever succeeds in seeing the JACs, a point about which we know nothing."

A sample of about 80 per cent of those introduced to JACs in one year by the San Francisco AIC was as follows:

JAC or Occupation to Which Introduced

	Total	*Negro*
Carpenters	34	5
Plumbers	10	3
Millman, cabinetmakers	6	1
Structural steel	1	0
Ironworkers	1	0
Painters and decorators	5	1
Bricklayers	1	0

JAC or Occupation to Which Introduced

	Total	Negro
Ornamental ironworkers	1	1
Lathers	1	0
Plasterers	1	1
Tilesetters	2	0
Electricians	23	3
Sheet metal	13	1
Machinist	32	8
Tool and die	1	0
Typographical	5	1
Compositors	7	4
Air conditioning and refrigeration	1	1
Welding	1	1
Auto mechanics	28	9
Body and fender	5	0
Meat cutters, butchers	7	1
Surveyor	1	0
S.F. naval shipyard	3	2
Metal polishers	2	0
Metal platers	1	0
Stationary engineers	2	1
Operating engineers	5	0
Aircraft maintenance	1	0
Not stated on card	2	0

This listing shows thirteen cases in which a youth was referred to more than one JAC or source for possible apprenticeship.

The main reasons for the meager results of the California AICs were similar to those of many of the federally supported Centers, namely, the refusal of apprenticeship sponsors to give the Center adequate notice of openings, so that actual referrals could be made, and the AICs' inability to verify the results of their referrals. A California employment service representative concluded that he had a feeling that the San Francisco AIC "may actually be serving to help preserve the status quo, rather than helping to integrate apprenticeships. Because the Center exists . . . it can be said that 'we're doing our part.' But six apprentices after two and one-half years?" A similar sentiment was expressed by a San Francisco building trades union official interviewed for this study, who told us: "The AIC is a failure. It is in the wrong location—the employment office, which already has a bad image in the Negro community."

As we have noted in greater detail in our studies of those cities, the federally supported Cleveland and Cincinnati AICs had been no more successful than those in San Francisco and Oakland. The director of the Cincinnati Urban League reported that the AIC there "has been a very regretful experience. It has not fulfilled any great need here in Cincinnati. There is a desperate need for good leadership."

According to the executive director of the Citizens' Committee on Youth of the Cincinnati Municipal Youth Commission: "The AIC is very unco-operative and inefficient. The AIC needs to be removed from the Employment Service system. It should be placed under another agency. . . . For one thing the AIC does not do follow-up studies. This is one fault we would correct immediately." The director of job development of the Pittsburgh Urban League told us "an AIC is not the answer to the apprenticeship problem, because it only goes through the motions."

An official of the Ohio State Employment Service told us: "We have not been able to place many Negro boys. We have tested several, and we have referred several to the different unions, but the unions have not accepted them. Many of the guys we sent out never show up for the exam. They simply lose interest. We do not make any effort to evaluate the result of our placement efforts."

James Abernathy, Director of Labor and Industry for the Cincinnati NAACP, told us: "With respect to the AIC, it seems that it has gone out of its way to go into neighborhoods where there is little likelihood of getting any applicants. It has tended to shy away from the Negro of the lower income bracket area."

In Cleveland, the AIC has been relatively ineffective and does not have the respect of the Negro community or civil rights agencies. An inspecting team in November, 1965, found that the Cleveland AIC had placed three Negro apprentices since December, 1964: two auto mechanics and one tool-and-die maker. A member of the Cleveland AIC Advisory Committee told us that the idea for the Center had originated with community organizations but that a local official of the BAT had controlled the selection of the Center's director—only one candidate was proposed for the job, and he was present in the meeting when he was nominated.

Conclusions on the AIC

Some of the AICs have not lived up to the expectations for them. A major obstacle has been opposition from the building trades

217

unions and at least some BAT officials. Unimaginative personnel also seem to have been put in charge of some of the Centers. These facts are not unrelated, of course, because it is often possible to frustrate a program one opposes by seeing that it is incompetently or inadequately staffed. But the main reason for the Centers' ineffectiveness is that they can do very little to get applicants into apprenticeship programs unless they have adequate information about openings, which information can be supplied only by the JACs. The JACs' co-operation also is needed to make it possible for the AICs to check the results of their referrals, and to make actual referrals to apprenticeship openings. Even with the co-operation of the joint apprenticeship committees, there will not be many qualified Negroes, but it should be a function of the AICs to locate them and to keep the Negro community informed on apprenticeship opportunities.

We conclude, therefore, that the AICs have succeeded in getting a few Negroes into apprenticeship programs but that the results have been disappointing, not because of any defect in the conception of the AIC but primarily because of a lack of co-operation from the apprenticeship establishments and state employment services and the lack of imagination by some of the Centers' directors. The experience of the relatively successful AICs suggest that the Centers can be made effective under the proper circumstances. Efforts should therefore be made to bring the ineffective Centers up to the standards of those in Washington, Newark, Baltimore, and Chicago.

Pre-Apprenticeship Programs

Depending upon with whom one speaks, the word "pre-apprenticeship" evokes a varied reaction ranging from ringing endorsement to thundering epithet. One union interviewee claimed, approvingly, that it is "an answer to a major social problem"; another official of the AFL-CIO warned us to avoid any reference to the term in our interviews.

The main objective of pre-apprenticeship programs is to equip disadvantaged youths with the knowledge and experience of a trade necessary to compete for apprenticeship openings on a more equitable basis. In most instances, the enrollees in these programs are unemployed and lack high school diplomas required for most apprenticeships, and in others they have graduated from substandard schools and cannot compete in written examinations with those from more fortunate backgrounds. Where the programs have been successful, however, the applicants have been carefully screened to select those with the aptitude and desire to learn. Since the Negro school dropout rate and the Negro unemployment rate both far exceed those of whites, the majority of the pre-apprenticeship enrollees have been Negro. From an economic viewpoint, pre-apprenticeship programs serve to increase the productive capacity and enhance the employability of the participants.

The goals and obstacles of pre-apprenticeship can be seen by reviewing the experiences of the National Institute of Labor Education (NILE) with such projects. NILE, in conjunction with its Youth Employment Program (YEP), contracted with the Office of Manpower, Automation, and Training "to establish pre-apprenticeship, institutional and on the job training programs for unemployed youths formerly unable to qualify."[11] The NILE program was known as Training for Apprenticeship (TFA). To overcome some early criticisms of pre-apprentice programs, that they are apt to fragmentize a trade, the TFA programs were tied directly to an on-going apprenticeship program. Accordingly, the graduates—as was the case in Washington's carpentry and bricklaying programs— were assured of job opportunities as apprentices when they completed the program.

The NILE program was supported initially by Neil Haggerty of the AFL-CIO Building and Construction Trades Department and, in fact, received a $10,000 contribution from the AFL-CIO. But shortly after the Construction Industry Joint Conference gave its approval to TFA as a model project for providing training opportunities for a large number of school dropouts, several building trades unions became very critical of the program. One union charged that the project was "injurious to the apprenticeship system."[12] Like the spread of a contagious disease, it became increasingly difficult for the NILE programs to gain acceptance. Local BAT officials also joined in the opposition. NILE attributes organized labor's veto of its efforts to: (1) a lack of endorsement by any official body of the labor movement; (2) a growing distrust by organized labor of all MDTA programs; (3) a sensitivity by organized labor about any outside intrusion into the apprenticeship area; (4) a fear that the admission of school dropouts would lower the prestige of their trades; and (5) prejudice by some union (and

[11] National Institute of Labor Education, "Final Report to the Secretary of Labor, United States Department of Labor, on OMAT Project P-3-63" (July, 1963), p. 3.
[12] *Ibid.*, p. 66.

employer) officials that "school dropouts were no-good, ignorant, and delinquent youngsters who had only themselves to blame for their lot, and who lacked the will and ability to learn a trade."[13] NILE concluded that the "small employer views apprenticeship training as a method of training journeymen craftsmen whereas the big employer uses apprenticeships for training foremen and supervisors."[14] Since the large employers apparently could not visualize a disadvantaged youth becoming a foreman, only the small employers were interested in the program. In addition, there was opposition from some BAT officials, who felt the program was an intrusion into their exclusive domain, and local vocational education officials, who were tied to established procedures and resented any attempted alterations. In any event, after about eighteen months, the project—receiving little support from the apprenticeship establishment—was abandoned in June, 1965.

It is somewhat ironic that, within a month after the abandonment of the NILE project due to union opposition, the Secretary-Treasurer of the AFL-CIO, William F. Schnitzler, spoke in the most laudatory terms of such programs, and said that "it is not enough to lean back and wait for the fully prepared, totally qualified Negroes to appear,"[15] but that employers, unions, and government needed to work together on pre-apprenticeship training programs that are designed to overcome the handicaps of inadequate educational opportunities. Schnitzler sharply criticized those—especially BAT officials—who "quietly supported" a sit-back-and-do-nothing policy of not encouraging Negroes to seek opportunities to enter apprenticeship programs. Equal opportunity in apprenticeship training must be "a living fact" and "not paper compliance," according to Schnitzler, and pre-apprenticeship training, in his estimation, was a way to make this a reality. Perhaps Schnitzler's comments reflect a moderation of union opposition based on better understanding of the nature of pre-apprenticeship programs.

Based upon NILE's experiences and upon those of the Detroit machinist program, it would seem that pre-apprenticeship has been prejudged as guilty of a host of evils with little opportunity given to prove or disprove its innocence. While certain trades may have subtle reasons for refusing to co-operate or to support such programs, there is little logic to the blanket condemnation of pre-apprenticeship per se.

[13] *Ibid.*, pp. 65–68.
[14] *Ibid.*, p. 69.
[15] "Schnitzler Presses Pre-Training Aid," AFL-CIO *News*, July 31, 1965, p. 2.

Even the most unsuccessful of these programs—the TFA carpenters' program in Washington—was able to place twenty-two formerly unemployed youths, of whom twenty were Negroes. It is our conclusion that pre-apprenticeship programs designed to compensate disadvantaged youngsters for their deficiencies are effective means of both providing opportunities to these youngsters and supplying qualified applicants to apprenticeship programs.

Manpower Development and Training Act

As Table 13-2 shows, there were very few building trades trainees in MDTA institutional programs in our study cities. Although there

Table 13-2

Approved MDTA (Institutional) Projects in Building Trades
in Selected Cities, July, 1966

Trade	City	Weeks	Trainees Provided for	Enrolled	White	Non-white
Plumbers	New York	15	48[a]	N.A.		
	New York	—	28	33	29	4
				33	29	4
Sheet Metal	New York	23	60[a]	N.A.		
	Philadelphia	48	24	37	15	22
	Philadelphia (area)	26	30[a]	N.A.		
	Washington, D.C. (area)	13	60[a]	N.A.		
					15	22
Bricklayers	Detroit	18	50	16	16	0
	Detroit	15	50	40	40	0
	Detroit	15	50[a]	N.A.		
	Detroit	21	96	125	117	8
	Washington, D.C. (area)	12	60	57	1	56
	Washington, D.C. (area)	12	60[a]	N.A.		
	Washington, D.C. (area)	12	120[a]	N.A.		
					174	64
Carpenters	San Francisco-Oakland	—	105[a]	N.A.		
	San Francisco-Oakland	2	70		57	13
	San Francisco-Oakland	6	180[a]	N.A.		
					57	13
Ironworkers,	Pittsburgh	38		36	29	7
Shop	Pittsburgh	38		28	18	10
					47	17
Metal Trades Apprentices	San Francisco-Oakland	13		46	15	31
Painters	San Francisco-Oakland	13	40[a]		24	16
	San Francisco-Oakland	13	28		13	15
						31
Total					374	182

Based on data obtained from Bureau of Employment Security.
[a] Number provided in contract, known totals, actual enrollment unknown.
N.A., not available.

were only 374 whites and 182 nonwhites (about 33 per cent) enrolled in these programs, it will be noted that a number of others
had been established which either were not operational or about
which there was no information in the Washington office of the
Bureau of Employment Security. Of the nonwhite enrollees, fifty-six
were in a virtually all-nonwhite bricklayers' program in Washington; an additional sixty-two were in a metal trades apprenticeship
and painters program in San Francisco-Oakland. Although there
are not many nonwhites being trained under these programs, the
proportion of nonwhites being trained in the construction trades
obviously was higher than the proportion of Negroes in the skilled
trades, and was higher than the rate of placement of MDTA
trainees in all skilled trades during 1965.

The Chicago Plan

A number of programs have been proposed in various cities to
get minority youths into apprenticeship programs. Sometimes the
programs are conducted by private organizations with financial
assistance from a variety of sources, including grants from the federal government. One of the most effective of these operations to
date has been that of the Workers Defense League in New York,
examined in detail in the chapter on that city. Other operations
organized along somewhat different lines were the Vocational Foundation in Cincinnati and the Cleveland Manpower Advancement
Program. The basic idea behind these plans is that concerted recruiting, tutoring, counseling, and study is necessary to get Negroes
and other youngsters into apprenticeship programs.

Since Chicago was not one of our study cities, we might mention
the "massive program" adopted in that city in December, 1965, to
provide apprenticeship opportunities in the building and construction industry for minority youth.

The Chicago program is a joint venture by the building and
construction trades unions and employers, the Chicago Board of
Education, the Illinois State Employment Service, the Manpower
Administration of the U.S. Department of Labor, the Chicago
Urban League and the NAACP, and similar groups.

The Chicago program encompassed several main activities:
(1) active recruitment of minority candidates by unions and employers visiting schools, addressing community meetings, and con-
ferring with interested groups; (2) surveys by the public schools to
locate potential applicants "who have graduated from vocational

schools"; (3) processing and referral to joint apprenticeship committees by the State Employment Office through the Chicago Apprenticeship Information Center; (4) co-ordination and provision by the Manpower Administration of technical personnel and services to interested groups. Additional assistance is provided through courses sponsored by the Chicago Board of Education for those found to lack the necessary qualifications to enter regular apprenticeship programs. Potential applicants are given information on such questions as aptitude testing, how to make application and be interviewed, and what the trade is all about.

The Chicago Plan also provides that a "broad and intensive drive to expand job openings for the employment of apprentices will be implemented."

Although the Chicago Plan is still in its infancy, and no conclusive evaluation can be made, several observations are possible. In the first place, the Chicago program supports the conclusion that a major obstacle is locating qualified applicants. Between December 1, 1965, and August 1, 1966, forty-seven Negroes are known to have entered various apprenticeship programs as a result of these activities, but others were in various stages of entry. All of the construction trades in Chicago had admitted Negro apprentices by August 1, except the small and declining terazzo workers. Between December 1, 1965, and August 1, 1966, the Chicago Apprenticeship Information Center had made the following referrals to construction programs in that city:

1. In the electrical workers, forty-seven Negroes had been referred, and the program had twenty-three Negroes among its more than 700 apprentices. Eleven Negroes had been placed, and the others were in various stages of being processed. A total of twenty-two Negroes had received appointments, one of the others had gone into the armed forces, and the others had either failed the test or failed to follow through with the opportunity to enter the electrical apprentice program.
2. The structural iron workers had received eighteen referrals from the AIC. This program had seventy-three apprentices and indentured its first Negro in its history on July 28, 1966.
3. The plumbers had received seventeen AIC referrals and had fifteen Negroes among their 200 to 250 apprentices. It is not known how many of these fifteen got in as a result of the Chicago Plan.
4. The sheet metal workers had accepted twelve referrals from

223

the AIC and had admitted three of these; this program had 220 apprentices.

5. The pipefitters had accepted thirteen Negro referrals and had indentured two of these; this program had about 300 apprentices in it.

6. The bricklayers had nineteen referrals from the AIC and had indentured two of these; these were the only Negroes among the seventy-two apprentices in the bricklayers program.

7. The glaziers had only one apprentice and he was a Negro accepted as a result of the Chicago program.

8. The cement masons had received eight AIC referrals and had ten Negro apprentices in a total of seventy-two. It is not known how many of these ten came in after December 1.

9. The architectural ironworkers had received six Negro AIC referrals and had indentured one of these; there were thirty-nine apprentices in this program.

10. The ornamental ironworkers had received one Negro referral from the AIC but had nine Negroes among eighteen apprentices.

11. The sprinkler fitters had indentured the one Negro referred to them, and he was the only Negro among forty apprentices.

12. The roofers had fourteen AIC referrals and had eight Negroes among 160 apprentices. The roofers had accepted eleven of the fourteen referrals, but all of them had not entered the apprenticeship program by August 1, 1966.

13. The painters and decorators had eighteen referrals and twenty-one Negroes of 178 apprentices. Although it is not known how many of these twenty-one came in after December 1, this program has had Negro apprentices in it for years.

14. The metal lathers had eighteen referrals and indentured one of these; he is the only Negro among twenty-five apprentices.

15. The plasterers, who are in a declining trade in Chicago, accepted three Negro apprentices after December 1, but they dropped out.

One's evaluation of the Chicago program will undoubtedly depend upon his perspective. Many Negroes naturally will minimize the results, because the absolute numbers involved are not impressive. Some of the more militant civil rights groups were critical of the program during its early stages, even though they were intentionally involved in the program in hopes, which failed to materialize, that they would aid in the difficult recruiting work and would help maintain communications on this problem with the Negro community.

The most difficult part of the program has been the location of qualified applicants. It has sometimes been difficult to retain those candidates once they have been recruited and screened. The reasons for failing to take advantage of apprenticeship opportunities cover the same range we have found in our survey cities (see Appendix).

Most observers would agree that, whatever its limitations, the Chicago Plan has been a qualified success in many ways. The achievement of a breakthrough in some of these programs is no small undertaking. These changes have had positive influence on BAT field representatives, who were deeply involved in the program and who had the confidence of the apprenticeship sponsors. Moreover, the program's sponsors feel that there have been important attitudinal changes in the apprenticeship establishment in Chicago and that long-range educational foundations have been laid which could produce a small but steady stream of Negro apprentices.

In spite of these optimistic beginnings, however, the long-term student of race relations in the building trades has seen the failure of too many hopeful beginnings to be more than optimistically skeptical about the chances for steady progress in these areas.

VOLUNTARY PROGRAMS OF COMPLIANCE

In an effort to establish machinery to solve their problems on a "voluntary" basis, the AFL-CIO has had an active civil rights department from its inception and a number of international unions and state and local central bodies have established such committees. Similarly, a number of companies and unions have adopted voluntary plans to deal with discrimination. Over 300 large companies signed so-called "plans for progress" contracts with the PCEEO in 1962, under which they agreed to take affirmative action to eliminate discrimination, and most international unions signed a joint union fair practices program the same year. Although the president of the IBEW refused to endorse this statement, on the grounds that the program was not truly joint because it was not jointly formulated and did not "provide for correlated and constructive undertakings by each party,"[16] he did join with other affiliates of the AFL-CIO Building and Construction Trades Department in June,

[16] Letter from Gordon Freeman to all inside and outside IBEW locals in the U.S.A., July 17, 1964.

1963, in formulating a plan for nondiscriminatory employment in the construction industry. Under this plan, which was later adopted by the management representatives of the Construction Industry Joint Conference (CIJC), the parties agreed to:

1. Accept all qualified members regardless of race, creed, color or national origin.
2. Permit no discrimination or racial identification in referral systems.
3. With regard to the application, or employment of, apprentices, local unions shall accept, and refer, such applicants in accordance with their qualifications and there shall be no discrimination as to race, creed, color or national origin, and the local unions shall adhere strictly to their apprenticeship standards.

The CIJC also adopted a model program to prevent discrimination in the selection and training of apprentices. The CIJC's program was adopted in 1963 in the hopes of forestalling tougher anti-discrimination clauses in their apprenticeship contracts and was to do the following:

1. Make applications available to all who are interested.
2. Notify school systems of when applications are being accepted.
3. Keep detailed records.
4. Adopt objective standards and follow prescribed procedures in the interviewing, scoring and selection of apprentices.
5. Abandon waiting lists unless objective standards were used and do not carry lists over from year to year.
6. Provide an appeals procedure with a committee made up of union, employer, and public members whose decision would be final and binding on the joint apprenticeship committees.

The CIJC also established a joint committee in July, 1963, to implement this program, to consult with various government officials, and to meet informally with the Secretary of Labor. In outlining its policies, the CIJC declared: "This committee believes that cooperation with the responsible national officers of labor and management will achieve substantial results if utilized in advance of resort to sanctions contained in the apprenticeship regulations and standards for contractor compliance. The industry recognizes the government's interest and its duty to correct economic injustice and pledges its good faith to work toward that goal."

After the passage of the Civil Rights Act of 1964, the CIJC worked closely with the Equal Employment Opportunity Commission, established to administer that Act, in handling nondiscrimination procedures in the construction industry.

Although these private procedures can hardly be called "voluntary," because they were adopted to forestall tougher regulations, they have certain advantages in overcoming racial discrimination because they are more flexible than legal procedures, which must observe due process of law, and they can take action that goes beyond legal requirements.

The Urban League–AFL-CIO Agreement

In February, 1966, an AFL-CIO agreement with the National Urban League provided, among other things, for a pre-apprenticeship training program for Negro youths. The AFL-CIO pledged $10,000 a year for three years to support the Urban League's program. The League announced that it would "guide Negro youth towards preparation for job opportunities in organized skill trades, assist in the placement of qualified individuals in suitable job categories."

CHAPTER XIV

RECOMMENDATIONS

ASSUMPTIONS

The following recommendations are based on a number of assumptions which we did not examine in detail. The first of these is that the paucity of Negro apprentices is due to a complex constellation of factors which are deeply embedded in the total American society. Successful programs to increase the number of apprentices therefore will require the co-operation—and sometimes the conflict—of a variety of governmental and private agencies.

Although there are many improvements that could be made in the nation's present apprenticeship programs, we assume the basic apprenticeship concept to be a good one. The combination of practical and theoretical training is, we are convinced, a good way to acquire skills.

While it is undoubtedly true that many apprenticeship programs are too inflexible, have unrealistic entry standards, and require unnecessarily lengthy training periods, the better programs probably turn out skilled craftsmen who have higher incomes and more stable employment, because they are better able to adjust to different work situations and to technological change. Although this question needs to be studied in greater detail, apprenticeship training probably is a relatively low-cost method of acquiring skills and probably yields high returns to individual craftsmen, unions, employers, and the nation. To the extent that the craftsman who is trained through apprenticeship is more productive, he helps reduce labor costs and increases the nation's economic welfare.

We also feel that the control of apprenticeship training, including the implementation of nondiscrimination policies, should remain primarily with the industry through the joint apprenticeship committees or through individual employers where no union exists. Industry representatives are in better positions than outsiders to devise training programs suited to their particular needs. Industry representatives also are likely to be highly motivated to devise and conduct realistic and effective training programs.

This is not to argue, of course, that government does not have an important role to play in apprenticeship programs. Government should undertake general measures to facilitate the development of human resources and should give specific aid to apprenticeship sponsors in performing certain functions that they cannot adequately undertake themselves. Although this question needs to be examined with greater care, if research demonstrates apprenticeship training to be an efficient and desirable system, the federal government should create an over-all environment and adopt policies that will lead to the expansion and improvement of apprenticeship programs.

Whatever one's judgment about the desirability of expanding apprenticeships, there is no question whatever that the elimination of discrimination is a valuable and necessary social objective. Apprenticeship sponsors benefit from including Negroes in their programs to the extent that more qualified Negroes are admitted than unqualified whites. Unions will benefit from nondiscrimination policies, not only by removing a moral stigma from which many of them presently suffer, but also because such policies could improve productivity and give them greater control over their jurisdictions. A policy of racial integration also would make it possible for many unions to strengthen their bargaining positions by taking in Negro competitors and potential competitors who have been forced to work under nonunion conditions.

A nondiscrimination policy is beneficial to the employer, because it relieves him of pressures from government contracting agencies and threats of civil rights demonstrations. Moreover, employers benefit to the extent that they are able to acquire a more dependable supply of productive workers.

It goes without saying that the national economy would benefit by a more productive work force as well as a relaxation of racial tensions which result from the Negro's unequal job opportunities.

Since our mandate was to consider means of increasing Negro participation in apprenticeship programs, we were not concerned directly with the problems of other disadvantaged groups. However, although Negroes obviously have special problems, much of our analysis also is applicable to other disadvantaged groups. We are persuaded, moreover, that public policies should be directed toward all groups similarly situated and not exclusively at a particular race.

Although we are persuaded, moreover, that racial discrimination continues to be an important problem, we are convinced that its relative importance has declined in recent years and that measures to recruit, train, and counsel qualified applicants currently are much more important. Our assumption is based on the belief that we already have adopted an imposing array of antidiscrimination policies which have done much to increase the demand for Negro workers by changing the thinking of apprenticeship sponsors about the necessity of admitting qualified Negro youngsters but have done relatively little on the supply side to get Negroes into apprenticeship programs. The weaknesses of punitive measures, when used against the apprenticeship establishment, have been discussed at length elsewhere, and it should be abundantly clear that such programs have not been very effective in dealing with programs which depend heavily on private, voluntary actions.

We do not mean to imply, however, that the Negro youngster has an *equal opportunity* to get into an apprenticeship program, because he suffers many handicaps other than current discrimination by apprenticeship sponsors. In other words, we do not believe that the Negro youngster has an equal chance of learning about apprenticeship training, of being motivated to try to enter these programs, of meeting the qualifications, of passing the tests, or, perhaps, of successfully completing these programs. Nor do we wish to imply that the "objective standards" imposed by many sponsors are not racially motivated. We are convinced that many of them are. But we are also persuaded that these barriers can most effectively be overcome if we concentrate on the supply of qualified Negro applicants. If a supply of qualified applicants is generated and continues to be barred from apprenticeship programs, public policy might have to devote more attention to the qualifications and testing procedures used to select trainees.

Our belief that punitive legal measures are not likely to be very effective in getting many Negroes into apprenticeship programs does not mean that we think sanctions are unnecessary; we believe that they are and that federal and state antidiscrimination measures should be strengthened to bring swift action against offenders— preferably fines, injunctions, denial of the use of public school facilities for related training, and perhaps other measures if they prove necessary. But we do not believe these measures by themselves will increase Negro participation in apprenticeship programs. Negative sanctions alone are likely to be ineffective, because they exaggerate the importance of discrimination, and create a defensiveness by the parties that will allow only token changes. Apprenticeship sponsors are likely to be particularly resentful when the symbolic nature of apprenticeship causes things to be said about these programs which are unrealistic and demonstrate ignorance of the apprenticeship system. Union officers also are likely to be resentful and defensive when it is implied that they are mainly responsible for the absence of Negroes when there have been few qualified Negro applicants and very few valid complaints against them before government antidiscrimination agencies.

The Significance of Apprenticeship Programs

The significance of Negro participation in apprenticeship programs depends to some extent on the number and quality of the positions that become available. There can be little question that those Negroes who complete apprenticeship programs would get more stable, high-paying jobs, and could probably advance to supervisory and contractor positions. As we noted in Chapter II, however, apprenticeship training is *not* at present a very important means of entry into the skilled trades, though it is important for some occupations. Our appraisal of the importance of apprenticeship programs for Negroes thus depends upon the perspective we take. Although we do not know how many apprentices of all kinds complete their training each year, registered and unregistered programs probably do not account for more than 50,000. If we assume that by all kinds of remedial programs Negroes could get 10 per cent of these, they would get 5,000 craftsmen jobs *a year* through this means, which is more than twice as many Negro apprentices *a year* as the total number of Negro apprentices reported by the census in 1960. The Bureau of Labor Statistics expects the increase in nonwhite craftsmen and foremen between 1965 and 1975 to be about 34,000 a year.[1] We have no information about the total number of Negro apprentices or the number of nonwhites among those who graduate each year. However, if we assume that Negroes constitute 4 per cent of the total and 5 per cent of the graduates, they would constitute about 10,000 apprentices and about 2,500 graduates. It is evident, therefore, that apprenticeship training will have to be greatly expanded for nonwhites if many of them are to reach craftsman status through this means.

Thus, although apprenticeship training will not mean very much

[1] Joe L. Russell, "Changing Patterns of Employment of Nonwhite Workers," *Monthly Labor Review*, May, 1966, p. 508.

in absolute terms in giving employment to Negroes,[2] the importance of these programs cannot be measured entirely in quantitative terms. Negroes can achieve *relatively* large increases in the number of apprenticeship positions they now hold. Moreover, apprenticeship programs are the only way that many Negroes can get into some of the better craft jobs, and apprenticeship training has gained great symbolic importance with civil rights groups. Obviously, however, measures to increase the *total* number of apprentices will give Negroes better opportunities to increase their proportions.

GENERAL POLICY RECOMMENDATIONS

We are convinced that, besides measures to increase the total number of apprentices, two of the most important *general and long-run policies* needed to increase Negro participation in apprenticeship programs are measures that would improve the quality of education available to disadvantaged youngsters and policies to maintain full employment and economic growth. As we shall see, these *general* policies facilitate the improvement of opportunities for Negroes, but they are *not sufficient* to produce the necessary changes. There can be little question that, in spite of the continuance of a very real and serious problem of discrimination, many of the Negro's most important disadvantages at present stem from his inadequate education. There can be no real equality in employment until this defect is corrected. Education must perform a much broader role for Negroes and other disadvantaged youths than it does for many whites; it must overcome some of the cultural handicaps which make it difficult for Negroes to benefit from basic educational programs.

Full employment and economic growth also are important general determinants of the extent to which Negro youngsters will get into apprenticeship programs, because a tight labor market exerts a powerful influence to overcome the barriers to the admission of Negroes to these programs. Labor shortages give employers motives to hire and train Negroes, while full employment reduces some of

[2] There were, in October, 1965, about 213,000 nonwhite male high school graduates between the ages of sixteen and twenty-one. Of these, 183,000 were in the civilian labor force and 18,000 were unemployed. (There were also 275,000 nonwhite male dropouts from high school in this age group, 41,000 of whom were unemployed.) There were about one million nonwhite males in the apprenticeable age group of 18–24 in 1965. (Harvey L. Homel, "Employment of High School Graduates and Dropouts in 1965," *Monthly Labor Review*, June, 1966, p. 646.)

the white workers' opposition to increasing the supply of apprentices in general and Negro apprentices in particular. Full employment would be particularly important in the building trades, whose aggregate unemployment rates have consistently been even higher than those of Negro males.[3]

Manpower Policies

Full employment alone will not solve this problem fast enough, however, and special manpower programs must be continued to improve the operation of the labor market. With respect to Negro youths, we feel that manpower policies should concentrate on specialized programs to overcome their general educational disadvantages and prepare them for apprenticeship and other training programs. Pre-apprenticeship and other remedial programs obviously are necessary to salvage dropouts and others who have basic abilities but are inadequately prepared for apprenticeship and other training programs. We are also impressed by the possibilities of recruiting apprentices from such programs as the Job Corps.

Youngsters with relatives in the skilled trades often have an advantage in taking apprenticeship tests because they have gained experience in the trades through summer and other part-time employment. We therefore feel that programs designed to give youths an opportunity to gain first-hand experience around a variety of jobs would be particularly valuable to minority-group youngsters. In this way, prospective trainees would be in a better position to select a field that is best suited to their interests. Where possible, companies and unions might be induced to hire youngsters during the summer months, even if they did no more than menial tasks on the job. In the construction industry, for example, it would seem to be useful to explore the possibilities of promoting programs like that of the Laborers in Atlanta, to give high school and college youngsters summer employment in the construction industry.

Programs also might be adopted to increase the prestige of the skilled crafts. There is a certain feeling of craftsmanship which many skilled occupations have that can be communicated only by

[3] For example, the relative employment rates for the construction industry as compared with nonwhites for the 1961–65 period were as follows:

Year	Nonwhite Males	Construction
1961	12.9%	14.1%
1962	11.0%	12.0%
1963	10.6%	11.9%
1964	7.1%	9.9%
1965	7.6%	9.0%

demonstration. In addition, the status of the skilled trades might be improved by making them open-ended through training programs that would make it possible for the young apprentice to continue his upward advancement after he finishes his training. Indeed, the available evidence is that many apprentices in the construction industry in fact become supervisors and contractors. But they should also have opportunities and be encouraged to become engineers and architects if they have the interest and ability. The prestige of the crafts might be enhanced by films, demonstrations, and other programs in junior high schools and high schools to emphasize the advantages of the skilled trades.

SPECIFIC RECOMMENDATIONS

Public Policy

Role of City Governments. Although federal and state governments have important roles to play in increasing the number of Negro apprentices, municipal governments should play the primary role, at least in the construction industry, because most race problems are problems of cities, and, although there is some similarity in problems, each city has its own reality, with many unique features which require detailed familiarity and constant attention. Problems in the construction industry seem particularly amenable to local solution because the market tends to be local in scope.

In order to carry out their functions properly, however, city governments must have assistance from federal, civil rights, industry, union, and state officials, and must have appropriate support for their antidiscrimination programs. Like other entities in conflict situations, city governments often need the help of outside agencies in order to break local paralyses or stalemates. In other words, city governments often can take action in a desired direction if they can shift the blame to others or point to the threat of punitive action by another agency.

In addition to their usual roles of handling complaints, some city civil rights agencies have served useful mediatory functions and have attempted to keep open the lines of information among civil rights organizations, unions, and employers. These commissions also have worked with high schools to recruit Negro applicants, have seen to it that qualified applicants were kept informed about important dates and other necessary matters, have checked to see what happened when Negroes applied to take tests, and have checked their progress after they began on the job.

City governments thus can do a number of specific things to improve Negro participation in apprenticeship programs. These include:

1. If not already established, create a city human relations agency with adequate support from city officials.
2. Carefully study the extent of Negro participation in apprenticeship programs and attempt to ascertain the reasons for the absence of Negroes where they do not participate.
3. Withhold city funds from building projects which exclude qualified Negroes. City governments also should deny the use of public schools to discriminating apprenticeship programs.
4. Maintain close relations with the Negro community and provide realistic information on the advantages and limitations of apprenticeship training as a means of getting jobs for Negroes.
5. Provide mediation facilities between unions, employers, joint apprenticeship committees, and the Negro community.
6. Provide realistic counseling in the city schools.
7. Encourage MDTA, OEO, EDA, and other programs designed to prepare interested Negro youths to meet the qualifications to enter apprenticeship programs.
8. Be prepared to get help from the AFL-CIO Civil Rights Department, international officers of unions operating in the city, industry associations, organizations like the Construction Industry Joint Council, state and federal antidiscrimination agencies, and perhaps the National Labor Relations Board.
9. Be prepared to follow up the results of actions taken to get Negroes admitted to these programs.

Federal Policies. In addition to the general measures to facilitate full employment, improve education, and enlarge and expand apprenticeship programs, the federal government could take a number of specific measures to improve Negro participation in these programs:

Antidiscrimination Policies. Federal authorities should encourage the development of voluntary nondiscrimination programs by unions and employers. Of course, the availability of a variety of sanctions gives the parties some incentive to develop "voluntary" programs. Indeed, the reality of the threat of sanctions strengthens those union and management representatives who *want* to solve their own problems by making it possible for them to use the threat of prosecution by governments to bring recalcitrants into compliance. Nevertheless, as compared with punitive government action, the parties have many advantages in attempting to solve their racial problems, because they understand their own situation better than government agents, can acquire information more easily, can employ more informal and flexible procedures to gain compliance, and can do many things which could not be required by law. Voluntary programs are particularly important in the apprenticeship field, because few sanctions are likely to be really effective in gaining entry for Negroes if industry and union officials resist. Since these programs are purely voluntary, and since many employers apparently are not strongly motivated to finance training from which they might benefit only indirectly, strong sanctions might cause apprenticeship programs to be discontinued altogether. Even if sanctions were effective, they would be no substitute for affirmative action by apprenticeship sponsors and organizations like the Construction Industry Joint Council and the printing industries councils in various cities. It could be, of course, that strong sanctions will have to be imposed against offenders to demonstrate that the government agencies mean business. But we are persuaded that sanctions should be imposed only as a last resort and after the sponsors have had a chance to bring the recalcitrant parties into line.

Apprenticeship sponsors should be encouraged to adopt certain procedures to avoid the suspicion of discrimination. There would perhaps be some advantage to letting the AICs or some other agency inform the rejected applicant of the reasons for his failure. Moreover, apprenticeship sponsors also might follow the electrical industry's example and provide an appeals procedure for rejected applicants who think they have been discriminated against.

A major impediment to getting the apprenticeship establishment actively to encourage Negro applicants is the defensiveness built up by state, federal, and local governments' emphasis on punitive measures to get Negroes into these programs. There can be little question that these punitive measures have done much at least to lower the formal racial barriers to Negroes. At the same time, however, they have created certain fears and suspicions by unions, employers, and government apprenticeship agencies which make it difficult to implement co-operative efforts to open job opportunities to Negroes. Antidiscrimination agencies have generated hostility in the construction industry particularly by giving the impression that the government is going to use "blackmail" (by threatening to revoke or withhold federal contracts) in order to require preferential treatment of Negroes, which could not legally be done under the law. Apprenticeship sponsors also are concerned that the federal government is attempting to "fragment" their trades (by training programs designed to produce narrow specialists instead of general craftsmen), force them to take "unqualified" apprentices, and impose federal controls over apprenticeship training. The industry's suspicions are intensified by the lack of clarity which surrounds the concept of "affirmative action." It would therefore seem to be highly useful for apprenticeship sponsors to be given assurances that they will retain control of the determination of qualifications unless those qualifications are used for discriminatory reasons, and that, although *special* programs are going to be taken to help Negroes and other disadvantaged groups compete on an equal basis in apprenticeship programs, these special programs will apply to all persons similarly situated and will not favor any particular racial group. In other words, it should be emphasized that measures will be taken to help disadvantaged groups prepare for apprenticeship programs, but that all who are admitted must meet the industry's qualifications.

The BAT. It is doubtful that the Bureau of Apprenticeship and Training's power over apprenticeship programs can be strengthened in such a way as to make it an effective enforcement agency for antidiscrimination measures. It is especially doubtful that deregistering apprenticeship programs, which is the BAT's main punitive power, would mean very much to unions or employers. The BAT also is limited by the fact that it has no control at all over unregistered apprenticeship programs. Moreover, the use of punitive powers probably would be incompatible with the BAT's traditional promotional activities, and too much confusion is created by having discrimination in apprenticeship subject to regulation by several state and federal agencies.

We therefore recommend that all enforcement activities under 29 CFR 30 be removed from the BAT. Antidiscrimination agencies should concentrate on securing reliable information on apprenticeship programs and the extent of Negro participation in those programs. But, since the implementation of equal apprenticeship opportunities must be based on an understanding of the apprenticeship system, we recommend close co-operation between antidiscrimination agencies and the BAT.

As presently constituted, the Industrial Training Advisors within the BAT do not have sufficient independence to function properly.

Probably, either they should be made independent of the BAT regional directors, by giving them independent budgets and having them report directly and only to the National Industrial Training Advisors, or they should be assigned to some other agency, perhaps the Apprenticeship Information Centers. We are convinced, however, that the BAT should seek to gain voluntary compliance with nondiscrimination policies and should take measures to educate its own staff on the need to give minorities equal opportunities in apprenticeship training.

Apprenticeship Information and Counseling. Great difficulties in adopting proper apprenticeship policies are created by the lack of reliable information on these programs. Many of our interviewees blamed high school counselors and the exaggerations of civil rights leaders for ignorance on this question, but these parties obviously cannot get information which the apprenticeship establishment does not make available. Realistic information should be readily available on such matters as the number of apprenticeship openings likely to be available each year in a given city, as well as qualifications and procedural details for applying to these programs. In order to accomplish this objective we recommend strengthening of the Apprenticeship Information Centers by:

1. Seeing to it that their advisory committees really represent the community groups they are intended to represent and appointing people who will take an active interest in the Centers;
2. Taking measures to gain the active support of local employment service and BAT officials; (if this fails it might be desirable to remove the Centers from the direct control of local employment services and BAT representatives and to place them directly under the control of the BES and the BAT national offices);
3. Making it a violation of Title VII of the Civil Rights Act for apprenticeship sponsors to fail to supply the AICs with the necessary information for the Centers to operate properly (especially adequate advance notice of apprenticeship tests or other selections and information on the reasons for applicants' being rejected for apprenticeship programs);
4. Making sure that the Centers' personnel actively disseminate information to schools and other community organizations and check the results of their recommendations to the JACs.
5. Also giving some consideration to better national co-ordination of the work of the AICs. At present there seems to be

very little national co-ordination, and the quality of the AICs is much too uneven.

Tests and Qualifications. Until we get more information about the validity of tests, and assuming that it can be demonstrated that the tests are not designed to discriminate, testing and standards should remain the prerogatives of the sponsors. However, it would seem to be useful to lay down certain guidelines to determine the legality of testing procedures. Tests should, for example, be administered and interpreted by trained personnel who understand the uses and limitations of various kinds of tests. The parties should make an effort to validate the tests in the setting in which they are used to see if they really are predictive. Tests also should rarely be the sole criteria for selecting candidates. Moreover, although the parties should be *encouraged* to use outside testing services, we would not *require* them to do so and would leave the cut-off scores and determination of qualifications up to the parties.

Counselors. While counselors cannot be blamed for all of the ignorance surrounding the apprenticeship question, very few of them seem to give realistic advice to Negro youngsters concerning apprenticeship training. In part this is because counselors have become convinced that Negroes cannot get into these programs. However, our evidence also indicates considerable bias by high school and other employment counselors against apprenticeship programs. This bias is based upon the mistaken belief that the skilled trades are for dropouts, delinquents, and others who do not have the qualifications for college, and lead only to dead-end manual jobs. Few counselors seem to realize the supervisory and managerial opportunities open to the skilled journeyman or of the rewards of the skilled trades themselves. The bias against trades is not limited to high school counselors but extends also to some employment services. In 1966, for example, the Workers Defense League in New York discovered, in checking on the reasons why some of its recruits who were sent to the employment service for testing failed to follow through with their apprenticeship plans, that employment service counselors had advised the Negro youngsters, recruited by the WDL with considerable effort, against the skilled trades.

We conclude that Negro youngsters rarely will come forward when merely invited to do so. Negroes have learned through long experience that public announcements that "everybody is invited" does not necessarily mean that Negroes are welcome. It will therefore be necessary for Negroes actually to get into programs and for

Negro youngsters really to feel that they are welcome. As in over-coming any institutionalized form of human behavior, considerable time, effort, and thought is required to convince Negro youngsters that it is possible for them to get into these programs. Negro young-sters also must be convinced that apprenticeship is a worthwhile activity because they, like many white youngsters, often do not aspire to the skilled trades.

Conclusions. We note in conclusion that, in addition to various general public policy measures to maintain adequate conditions—such as full employment, measures to increase the total number of apprentices, active manpower policies (including antidiscrimination measures), and improved education for disadvantaged youngsters—there are a variety of specific things that can be done by govern-ments, educators, employers, unions, and civil rights groups to in-crease Negro participation in apprenticeship programs. We have also noted that there is a logical governmental division of labor in accomplishing these objectives. In the construction industry, be-cause of the local nature of the market and the structure of the unions, we feel that primary governmental responsibility rests with the cities. In manufacturing industries with broader markets and different structures, state and federal agencies should play a larger role. Even in the construction industry, moreover, the city govern-ments might be paralyzed by local political situations or for other reasons which make it necessary for state or federal governments to intervene to get programs off dead center.

The Department of Labor and other federal agencies obviously should support those activities which seem to give the best results. Grants to private programs have many advantages of adaptability and flexibility over activities conducted exclusively by government agencies.

Other Agencies. Let us conclude by noting some other specific functions which might be undertaken by other agencies.

Educators. In addition to improved academic course offerings, educators can enhance the Negro youngster's chances of getting into apprenticeship programs by providing better counseling, co-operat-ing in the search for potential applicants, providing special remedial classes to help overcome educational deficiencies, and using their influence to ensure that discriminatory apprenticeship classes are not permitted to use public school facilities. Our evidence also sug-gests the need for adequate instruction in vocational schools to prevent these schools or programs from becoming (or continuing to be) dumping grounds for poor students.

Employers. Employers usually are primarily responsible for hiring and training employees and for operating their firms efficiently. The main exception to this is in casual industries like construction where unions perform many employment and training functions. Although it is difficult to lay down hard and fast rules for successful equal-employment programs, a 1966 study, *Company Experience with Negro Employment,* by the National Industrial Conference Board, concluded that "All of the programs studied by the Board that appear to be effective have one thing in common: a chief executive determined that the program produce results, and willing to commit himself to its success for an indefinite period of time." Although it would be difficult for top management to eliminate the more subtle forms of discrimination that cause lower-level supervisors and rank-and-file workers to give preferences to whites, top management officials can do much to make their nondiscrimination policies clear to all levels of supervisors and can see to it that testing and other selection procedures are not unnecessarily restrictive to minorities. Some companies, like Western Electric in its activities with the WDL in New York, have furnished staff personnel for programs to help Negroes prepare for examinations and meet other entrance requirements. Many employers will find it useful either to utilize the services of experts in racial employment relations or to add such persons to their staffs. Employers often will find it helpful to establish working relationships with civil rights organizations and representative Negro leaders to publicize their nondiscrimination policies. Although it requires considerable finesse in order to avoid stigmatizing favored Negro leaders as "Uncle Toms," employers can do much to strengthen the more responsible civil rights organizations. Management should realize that the most effective relationships often can be established with the more militant organizations that really represent the thinking of their followers.

Those employers who understand the nature of, and take positive measures to deal with, minority employment problems will incur some added expense in the shortrun but probably will find that the benefits exceed the costs in the long run. Where management has taken fair and firm measures, racial trouble rarely has been significant, because few employees are prepared to sacrifice good jobs for racial reasons. Unionized employers are strengthened in their nondiscrimination policies when they solicit the aid of international unions. Those employers who decide to resist the pressures for equal employment opportunities or make only token compliances will probably have the most trouble in the long run, and

242

might be forced to accept less qualified people or to lose some control of their employment and training processes.

Unions. Within the labor movement the main problem of discrimination is at the local level. The AFL-CIO has adopted a strong antidiscrimination policy and, although any program can be improved, the federation seems to be actively doing what it can to implement that policy. The trouble with the AFL-CIO is that it has severely limited power over the discriminating locals. And the trouble with the local unions, especially in the building trades, is that their leaders too often are afraid they will be voted out if they adopt nondiscrimination policies. Clearly, therefore, the international unions should bear the greatest responsibility for eradicating discrimination, because within the labor movement only they have sufficient power to accomplish this objective. The excuse of local autonomy should be no more permissible in cases of racial discrimination than it is where locals violate other trade union policies or federal, state, and local laws, especially now that unions can point to the threat of increasing government regulation and severe damage to the entire labor movement unless they deal with this problem. It would also seem that the discrimination issue is currently sufficiently critical that the internationals should move to eradicate the problem before crises develop. No other agency has the ability to learn as much as the international officers about discrimination in local unions. It would seem to be better strategy for the internationals to proceed vigorously—through trusteeships—against the worst offenders than to let discriminating unions damage the whole labor movement.

In addition, some positive measures are as applicable to unions as they are to employers; local unions should, for example, be encouraged to take the following steps:

1. Make it clear to the Negro community that all qualified applicants will be accepted.
2. See to it that tests and interview procedures are fair and realistic in terms of the requirements for the trades. Tests might be administered by outside organizations, as is already done in many cases, or outside observers might be present.
3. Local unions should have printed material which clearly explains the qualifications for membership and apprenticeship training programs. Apprenticeship openings should be announced to various community relations organizations, civil

rights organizations, and Negro community leaders. Appeals procedures might be maintained for those who are rejected for membership or apprenticeship training.

4. Unions might also maintain channels of communication and effective working relations with Negro leaders in order to clear up misunderstandings.

5. Locals should also keep careful records which would be available for inspection to authorized persons.

6. A really affirmative nondiscrimination program would not passively process Negro applicants who might show up, but would actively search out qualified Negroes for membership as journeymen or apprentices. The unions could, in this way, organize their jurisdictions more effectively and more nearly see to it that they get the kinds of applicants they want rather than taking only those referred by civil rights groups. Unions might also encourage their journeyman members to serve as instructors in various remedial training programs.

7. Unions should encourage their Negro journeyman and apprentice members to give realistic information or apprenticeship training to civil rights groups. Negro union members can do much to clear up misunderstandings about apprenticeship training and can give Negro youngsters reliable information on the advantages and disadvantages of the skilled trades.

The Civil Rights Movement. Civil rights organizations also have major responsibilities in this area. They can effectively work with the Negro community to produce qualified applicants for apprenticeship openings and improve information and counseling. If Negroes are encouraged to take advantage of the opportunities open to them, they can produce the labor supplies which, experience demonstrates, do more than anything else to reduce overt acts of discrimination. The experiences of the WDL in New York, the TULC in Detroit, and the concerted activities of various groups in Chicago demonstrate that, although recruiting qualified applicants for apprenticeship openings requires considerable effort, a flow of applicants can be found in the Negro community if some organization devotes itself full time to this problem. Moreover, the WDL's experience also shows that many unions actually are relieved to find a responsible civil rights organization which can supply qualified members of minorities.

The specific things that civil rights organizations can do include the following:

1. Work closely with employers, unions, and FEP agencies to gather information, bring pressure, and supply applicants.
2. Pay careful attention to facts and analysis in order to present strong cases in adversary situations. Civil rights groups should acquire realistic information on apprenticeship programs in order to inform Negro youngsters of the advantages and limitations of this form of training.
3. Take advantage of poverty and manpower programs to provide pre apprenticeship and other training opportunities for Negro youngsters.
4. Wherever possible, civil rights organizations might establish close working relationships (based on co-operation and not hostility or collusion) with various sympathetic representatives of human relations agencies, companies, employers' associations, and unions. Private civil rights agencies can do many things to promote the upgrading of Negro youngsters (that would not be legally permissible or required), and many apprenticeship sponsors could profit from effective alliances with responsible civil rights groups. Many union and employer representatives probably would be willing to form alliances with civil rights groups which understood their problems and needs and gave evidence of wanting to work out problems rather than to issue public attacks against them.

THE INTERVIEWS

I: THE BACKGROUND

As outlined in the Introduction, 127 interviews were conducted during the course of the project with Negroes who were associated in varying ways with apprentice programs. To recapitulate briefly, there were sixty-one interviews with Negro apprentices, eleven with Negroes whose applications were pending, twenty-five with Negroes who were rejected when they applied, twenty with those who failed to complete the application procedures after initially expressing an interest in apprenticeship, and ten with Negroes who dropped out of an apprenticeship class after having been formally accepted.

Although these matters should be explored in greater detail by more extensive investigation, these interviewees afforded us some insight concerning their preparation for and awareness of apprenticeship programs. Much of the information by its nature is subjective and nonadditive. Yet, we have been able to prepare several tables that indicate some of the results of these interviews and the conclusions we have drawn from them.

Initial Information Concerning Apprenticeship

One of the most important questions which we sought to study pertained to how the Negro community learned about employment opportunities in the apprenticeable trades. With their low participation rates in such programs, it has long been recognized that there are few chances for Negroes to learn about and to prepare for vocations in these areas. Indeed, it was the recognition of this lack of awareness that was largely responsible for the establishment of Apprenticeship Information Centers in many cities discussed in Chapter III.

Table A-1 indicates the initial sources of general information provided about apprenticeship to each of the interviewees. It was from this initial information that the interviewees later sought entry into a specific apprenticeship program.

Our main conclusion from Table A-1 is that there is no pattern of information channels. Negroes learn of apprenticeship from a host of different sources. The most often mentioned source (twenty-six instances or 20 per cent of the total) was high school counselors, teachers, or principals. Yet, as is shown in columns 4, 5, and 6 of Table A-1, nineteen of the twenty-six (or 73 per cent) of those who received initial information from this source were subsequently rejected when they applied, failed to complete the application procedures, or dropped out after being accepted.

247

Table A-1

Source of Initial Information on Apprenticeship in General

Source	In Apprentice Program	Application Pending	Rejected by Union	Failed to Complete Application Requirements	Dropped Out After Being Accepted
Advertisement in newspaper	2			1	1
Bulletin board announcement	4		1		
City Human Relations Commission (or equivalent)	3	2	1	4	
Civil rights group	1		3		1
Community center official	1	1			
Does not remember	1			1	
Employer's suggestion	1		1		
Federal Civil Service official	1				
Friend (in same union)	4				
Friend (in another union)	1				1
Friend (not in union)	4	2		2	1
High school counselor, teacher, or principal	6	1	12	6	1
MDTA class				1	
Letter from minister					1

Neighborhood Youth Corps official			2		
Nonunion work in trade	4				
Parent or relative (in same union)	5		1		
Parent or relative (in another union)	1		1		
Parent or relative (not in any union)	8				1
Radio announcement	1				
Read newspaper account on demonstrations on subject		1			
Personnel office		1	1		
Special public programs	3	1	1		
Special private programs[a]		1	1		
State employment service					
General	3	1		2	2
AIC	1			2	
Stranger's recommendation		1	1		
Talk by AIC official in school				1	
Union's request	1				
Working in another sector of same trade	2	1			1
Information not obtained in interview	3	1	1		1
Total	61	11	25	20	10

[a] Refers to such programs as those of the Workers Defense League in New York and the Trade Union Leadership Conference in Detroit.

Table A-2

Source of Specific Information on the Apprenticeship Program Applied to by Negro Interviewees

Source	In Program	Application Pending	Rejected by Union	Failed to Complete Application Requirements	Dropped Out After Being Accepted
Applied directly to employer	3				
Applied directly to union	3	4	2	2	1
Bulletin board announcement	2				1
Civil rights group	3		1		
City Human Relations Commission (or equivalent)	4	2	16	12	
Did not formally apply				3	
Employer suggestion	2				
Federal Civil Service official	2				
Friend's suggestion	2				
High school counselor, teacher, or principal					
Letter from minister	1				
Newspaper account of demonstrations					1

Neighborhood Youth Corps			1		
Parent or relative (same union)	2				
Parent or relative (not in union)	3				
Radio announcement					1
State employment service:					
General	4			1	2
AIC	4	1	2		
Special public program	10				1
Special private program[a]	3		2		1
Working in another sector of trade	1				1
Trade association office	2				
Union official	1				
Union organizing campaign	3				
Union member	2				
Information not obtained in interview	2				1
Total	61	11	25	20	10

[a] Refers to such programs as those of the Workers Defense League in New York and the Trade Union Leadership Conference in Detroit.

It would seem, therefore, that the advice given by the school officials must not have been of very high caliber or informative.

The most successful source of information, in terms of actual placements, was that provided by parents and relatives. Also, the fact that five out of six applicants had a relative in the same union in which they were eventually placed indicates that the "father–son" principle seems to apply indiscriminately to both Negroes and whites. The problem is that Negroes do not have enough relatives in these trades to rely solely upon this avenue.

It is noteworthy that only two of the 127 interviewees learned of apprenticeship through an AIC office. Seven more, however, were informed of it through contact with an employment service office.

Specific Information on the Apprenticeship Program to Which Entry Was Sought

Having become interested in apprenticeship in general, the prospective applicant selects a specific apprenticeship program to which to apply. Table A-2 indicates the sources of specific information for our 127 interviewees. Again, the sources of this type of information are widely dispersed, yet the data suggest several observations. First, the most singularly successful source of specific placements of Negroes has come from the special private programs such as the Workers Defense League in New York and the Trade Union Leadership Conference in Detroit. Ten of the sixty-one successful placements who were interviewed came by this route. Of the thirteen applicants who got their specific information from special private programs, only two were rejected by the unions and one dropped out. Secondly, the most often mentioned source of specific information was provided by municipal human relations commissions (or their equivalents). But only four of the thirty-four (about 12 per cent) referred to specific apprenticeship programs were actually placed. Thus, it would seem that these commissions have been an active source of supply of applicants but a poor source of successful placements. It would seem that these commissions—because of an absence of private programs in their respective cities—have been forced to assume recruitment and referral responsibilities among their numerous other tasks, and often they have paid more attention to sending as many individuals as they could locate who expressed any interest in apprenticeship and have been less interested in screening and preparing Negroes to qualify. More attention should be given by these groups to qualitative placement efforts. Thirdly, only a small number of our interviewees had any relationship at all with an AIC. Few had ever heard of them. Only four of the sixty-one Negro apprentices interviewed were referred by an AIC. The placement success of several other sources approaches or equals that of the interviewees who went through the AIC channel with its more accessible information, available counselors, and advanced testing facilities.

Test Experience of Negroes Admitted into Formal Apprenticeship Programs

Testing has been a central issue concerning the admission of Negroes to apprenticeship programs. The experiences of the sixty-one Negro apprentices interviewed during this study are presented in Table A-3. As is clear, the testing requirements of local unions vary widely. Thirty of our interviewees were admitted after passing written tests, which were either given alone or in conjunction with oral examinations; twenty-nine others who were admitted were not required to take any written examinations. In other words, almost half of the Negro apprentices interviewed gained admission without being asked to take written tests. Moreover, in at least two instances where written tests were given, the Negro youths were given copies of the test in advance by a sympathetic JAC official. In another instance, the Negroes taking the written test were given permission to swap papers during the examination. The only one who failed was the one person who sat at a table by himself. Moreover, mention should be made of the experience of the Negro applicants who were given special tutoring through the WDL and the New York printers' programs, and who then successfully passed the written examinations. Those who attended these special classes were unanimous in stating that they felt the preparatory sessions spelled the difference between passing and failing. Indeed, we made the point in our discussion of these programs that the preparatory sessions made significant differences in the success of Negro applicants in passing tests.

Table A-3

Written Tests and Oral Test Experience of Negro Applicants
Who Were Accepted into Apprenticeship Programs

Written test only	11
Oral examination (or interview) only	22
Written and oral examination (or interview)	19
No written or oral examinations given	7
Information not clear from interview	2
Total	61

It is difficult to draw a specific conclusion concerning whether or not tests represent a more formidable barrier to Negroes than to whites taking the same examinations. It is clear, however, that when Negroes are given special preparation to take the tests or when they are not required to take written examinations, entry is greatly facilitated. It is likely, of course, that such would be the case for any group. As discussed in Chapter II, however, without special preparation Negroes generally have not done as well as whites on written tests.

Educational Background of Interviewees

Table A-4 indicates the educational background of the 127 interviewees. The most obvious conclusion to be drawn from these findings is the prevalence of those who attended regular (or academic) high schools. Of course, since regular high schools are more numerous than any other kind, the likelihood is strong that any interviewee would have attended these regular institutions. Moreover, many academic high schools offer a variety of

Table A-4

Educational Background of Negro Interviewees by Classification

	In Apprenticeship Program	Application Pending	Rejected by Union	Failed to Complete Requirements	Dropped Out after Being Accepted
No high school diploma	6	0	1	1	0
High school diploma only	41	10	21	17	8
Regular public high school	(27)	(5)	(13)	(13)	(5)
Parochial high school	(1)				
Vocational high school	(8)	(4)	(7)	(2)	(2)
Indeterminate	(5)	(1)	(1)	(2)	(1)
High school equivalency diploma	5	1	1	1	0
High school diploma plus additional educational experience	9	0	2	1	2
Total	61	11	25	20	10

course curricula to their students. Nonetheless, the number of Negroes attending academic high schools and those who have obtained additional education beyond high school imply that those with such backgrounds find apprenticeship programs more accessible. A vocational education does not increase one's chance for entry into an apprenticeship program; if any pattern prevails from our limited sample, the reverse is the case.

Rejectees

Table A-5 shows that of our twenty-five interviewees who were rejected for apprenticeship programs, fourteen failed written tests and six were rejected after their oral interviews. Thus, 80 per cent of the rejectees interviewed during this study were turned down during the qualification phase of the admission process. It is logical, of course, to expect that failure to pass an examination would be the most common reason for rejection for any program which has more applicants than openings in its program.

Table A-5

Reasons for Negro Applicants' Being Rejected by Apprenticeship Programs to Which They Had Applied

Failed written test (no oral exam given)	14
Within age limits when applied, but when application was processed at later date applicant was too old	2
Failed oral test (after having taken written exam)	6
Told no class was going to be formed that year	1
Forgot to bring medical report on his health to oral exam—not allowed to proceed with interview	1
Not a high school graduate	1
Total	25

Those Who Failed To Complete
Admission Requirements

Table A-6 presents the reasons cited by the interviewees who expressed an initial interest in apprenticeship but who subsequently failed to complete all of the admission requirements. No clear-cut pattern emerges from this table. However, many of these applicants apparently were recruited too hastily and/or were poorly informed of the nature of a vocation in the skilled trades. Other studies of those who failed to complete the requirements taken from our city studies indicate a variety of reasons. However, it was noted in our Cleveland study that the single most important reason given was "decided to go to college."

The Dropouts

Negro participation in apprenticeship programs can be increased in two ways: by increasing the number admitted and by decreasing the number who drop out after having been admitted. (It should be emphasized that very few of our interviewees related any trouble of a racial nature after they got on the job, and none of them dropped out for this reason.)

Table A-6

Reasons for Failing To Complete Application Requirements to Apprenticeship Programs

Time lapse between submission of application and the beginning of the program was too long	2
Union never notified applicant after he had submitted initial forms	1
Arrived late for written examination—denied permission to take test	2
Could not get off from work on the day that written examination was given	4
Did not want to take pay cut	2
Decided to go to college	1
Was not really interested in the trade to which he applied	3
Was poorly informed as to what apprenticeship is (applied to painters program because he wanted to be an artist—was disappointed when found out what it was)	1
Forgot admission letter to written test—denied permission to take test	1
Asked friend to submit application while he was away, but friend forgot	1
Out of town until after deadline for submission of application had passed	1
Could not contact Human Relations staff official in time to submit application before deadline	2
"Had other things to do" instead of turning in application form	1
Thought fees were unreasonably high	1
Total	**23**

Note: The number of reasons exceed the number of interviewees, because some applicants had more than one reason for not completing their application.

Table A-7

Reasons for Dropping Out of an Apprenticeship Class after Having Been Admitted

Decided he wanted something else	2
Lack of steady work	2
Would have to move to location of job	1
Wanted to go to college	1
Did not like outdoor work	1
Did not like manual work (returned to college)	1
Found work not challenging enough (went on to graduate school—had a college degree)	1
Wanted job with more money and more responsibility	1
Total	**10**

Table A-7, therefore, assumes special significance, since it is concerned with reasons that ten interviewees voluntarily left apprenticeship training after having once been admitted. Three of the dropouts did so in order to go to colleges or universities. The other reasons vary but it does seem that several underwent serious disillusionment after becoming apprentices.

It is conceivable that better counseling and prior information about what apprenticeship entails could have avoided some of these problems. It is this type of knowledge that is—for understandable reasons—most difficult for the Negro community in general and civil rights groups in particular to obtain. Since there is only a negligible number of Negroes who have served apprenticeships, it is almost impossible for many Negroes to have an awareness of the actual nature of an apprenticeship program. Frequently, they do not even know the most elementary things—such as that the work is frequently outdoors during winter months, that it is necessary to attend classes (often at night), and that there are many nepotistic traditions in almost all apprenticeship programs. In Cleveland, for example, after extensive efforts by civil rights groups, a Negro applicant became the first of his race to be accepted as an apprentice in a particular trade. Although the young Negro apprentice had possessed the abilities to qualify, he was totally unaware of the traditions surrounding apprenticeship. He began to receive some hazing from the journeymen and was asked to run such menial errands, usually required of apprentices, as getting coffee and putting tools away for the journeymen. He felt he was being discriminated against unjustly and was on the verge of dropping out. It was not until the Urban League investigated that they discovered that *all* apprentices are hazed during their first year. The Negro apprentice was being exposed to one of the many informal traditions that surround the institution of apprenticeship. Informed of this, he returned to his job and, subsequently, has progressed satisfactorily in his training. Yet, for lack of being properly indoctrinated before entering the program, the accumulated hours of effort by many people in recruiting, preparing, and pressing for his admission could all have been for naught. There were a few cases among our interviewees where Negro youngsters would have dropped out—or actually did so—and were deterred from doing so or were persuaded to return by the civil rights groups who helped get them in initially.

Thus, while much of the thrust for increasing Negro participation in these programs has centered upon obtaining and dispensing information about when union programs are accepting applications, where applications can be obtained, and the examination dates, far too little attention has been given to providing the type of information which explains the nature of apprenticeship itself. To help reduce the dropout problem (and therefore contribute to increasing Negro participation), it is imperative that this type of knowledge be given to Negro apprenticeship applicants. Possibly the Industrial Training Advisors of the BAT could be of assistance in this educational chore. If not, then maybe representatives from various JACs could periodically meet with civil rights leaders, school counselors, and AIC officials in order to inform them of these vital basic facts.

II. QUOTATIONS FROM INTERVIEWS

Counseling

New York: Workers Defense League Official

Another problem is that the information that has been fed down to these kids concerning apprenticeship programs has been very bad. This is especially true of the advice given by school counselors.

Cleveland: BAT Official

The counselors in the predominantly Negro schools rarely inform the students about apprenticeship. They usually do not know much about the job market. They usually advise the good students to go to college and follow in their footsteps. They overlook the skilled trades.

Cleveland: BAT Official

The school and industry people continue to damn each other. There is a great need for co-operation on the part of these groups. The school people criticize the union people because they feel that the unions are not doing enough for the less than gifted kids. They were particularly critical of the union standards, nepotism, and tests. On the other hand, however, the counselors are showing partiality to the white-collar and professional occupations. They seem to think that it is disgraceful to work with your hands. Apprenticeship is nothing to be ashamed of!

Cleveland: High School Counselor (Negro High School)

Programs to increase the qualifications of Negroes for apprenticeship programs should go all the way back to the junior high school level. It is that time that it is necessary to make plans for his courses to take proper curricular selection, etc. It is really too late by the time Negroes become seniors and then find out that they have taken all the wrong courses. In Cleveland, the Negro population is concentrated in the East Side. The East Side schools are not equipped to properly prepare students for apprenticeship. They lack, for example, the proper shop equipment, the latest machinery, etc.

Most Negro boys do not ever conceive of an opportunity for vocation in one of the craft trades. It is a new occupational outlook. They are very suspicious all the way when a counselor attempts to suggest that a boy with aptitude toward one of the crafts actually enter one of the crafts.

I invited Bill Webb, regional director of BAT, to come out and speak to the senior class. Following his speech, fifty-five boys lined up in my office expressing an interest in apprenticeship. This does show that there is an interest once the apprenticeships are explained to Negroes. Consequently, it has been suggested that lists should be compiled of students, Negro students especially, interested in apprenticeship and see what happens to them after they apply for apprenticeship programs. That is to follow up on their interest. The Department of Labor officials here in Cleveland have stated that if we could find the bodies, they would get the locals to comply. So far, nothing has been done. The locals here in Cleveland have been cracked, but they need the help of the federal government. So far, we are not getting it. Especially from the Department of Labor.

Detroit: President's Committee on Equal Employment Opportunity Official

The counselors in the schools are so busy handling social problems, they don't do and cannot properly perform their counseling duty. Consequently, even if you do have the best trained counselors possible, they would not have time to do a good job for proper counseling, with respect to the apprenticeship area.

I can get people, but I cannot get them into the apprenticeship program.

In other words, the work is there, the qualified people are there, but currently it is impossible to get them into the apprenticeship classes.

Education and Experience

Detroit: School Official

The education system here in Detroit has lacked a program to orient people toward the building trades. Many that come here interested in apprentice training or something in this line have never had any courses in shop or any drawing courses, and very little math. And these people for some reason feel that they want to become craftsmen . . . but they lack the preparation.

New York: Workers Defense League Official

Vocational school education gives absolutely no background for some building trades—as, for example, bricklaying.

Newark, N.J.: U.S. Government Official

The contractors bid jobs on a basis of competition between each other. Therefore, they need qualified help. On the other hand, civil rights groups claimed that they have been frozen out of apprenticeship programs. But in Essex County, the civil rights groups could find only five Negroes who were interested in being plumbers. Vocational schools simply do not produce students who can be apprentices. All the union apprentice programs require a high school diploma, experience on the job, and passing a written and oral exam. Negroes do not have the education. Also, vocational schools do not provide adequate background. In the past in many of the apprenticeable trades and today in many cases also, the sons of journeymen were used in summers working under work permits. Consequently, they got experience by the time it became time to take the apprenticeship written and oral examination. Through their experiences on the job they were and have been able to perform better than many of the Negroes.

Houston: BAT Official

The biggest problem that faces the Negro is two-fold. First, he needs a vastly improved educational background along with a domestic environment that is conducive to acceptance and encouragement of careers in the skilled crafts. Second is the need for sufficient and proper dissemination of information with respect to the opportunities that exist in the skilled crafts.

Detroit: UAW Skilled Trades Official

Furthermore, any college dropouts—people who have been to college for one or two years or are going to night classes—have tended to do very well on the test for apprenticeship openings, far better, of course, than the people who come directly from high school.

The vocational school backgrounds are very bad as a source of training for apprenticeship. Many apprentices today come from community colleges where they are often taught by academicians rather than by skilled craftsmen themselves.

Cleveland: Community Relations Board Official

Since the schools here in Cleveland have not been preparing adequately Negro students especially to qualify for union apprenticeship programs, it has made it very easy for unions to exclude Negroes. Furthermore, most unions as part of their interviewing processes require that an applicant have some knowledge of the trade. This is a requirement that is impossible for a Negro, especially, if he has not had any chance to be in contact with the union or with the trade. Consequently, he can get no points for having had work experience. Furthermore, many of the union qualifications allow a certain number of points on dress and appearance. This doesn't make any sense to me. Here in Cleveland, there have been efforts made to orient graduates on the possibilities of entering apprenticeable trades. The Negro high school seniors have been quite receptive to the idea. Only to find out then that when they file applications, they meet many serious roadblocks. This ruins their initiative and the initiative of others. Consequently, Negro high school students are very suspicious of trade unions, as are the counselors of these students. This year, seventeen boys who graduated from one high school were taken to a local union, they were escorted. They were all interested. They took time to report for the test. When the day came for the final test, many of them received letters saying that they were not eligible to take the test. No notice, however, was given to the Community Relations officials. Consequently, we were at a loss to understand why many of these Negro boys did not show up to take the test. We could not explain why they didn't show up. As it was, they were tricked. All but two of the seventeen boys got letters. We are currently investigating this particular case right now, for possible prosecution.

Washington, D.C.: President's Committee on Equal Employment Opportunity Official

Vocational training in Washington has been utilized as a source of placing dropouts from the academic curriculum, but there has been an increasing tendency for the apprenticeship tests to emphasize mathematics and English, which are not stressed in a vocational curriculum in vocational schools. Why has this suddenly become necessary? The formal education requisites associated with apprenticeship programs seem to have been raised with the imminence of Negro applicants for apprenticeship programs.

Detroit: AFL-CIO Regional Official

Pre-apprenticeship programs are very good for minority youths. This is essentially because minority youths typically do not get the proper school background to compete with the more advanced white kids. Furthermore, the counselors tend to steer the minority kids into the easiest courses in high school.

Recommendations

Detroit: UAW Skilled Trades Official

Discrimination is one problem, but aptitude is another. Many of the Negro youths have never seen a machine. And, moreover, most underprivileged youths do not stack up on tests. Consequently, pre-apprentice-ship programs are the answer to a social problem. We have high hopes that it will help these underprivileged people in taking tests and actually being able to compete with people with better backgrounds. New technologies are causing the necessity to re-evaluate constantly the apprenticeship pro-gram. Furthermore, technology is causing problems with respect to union standards. There is, in a sense, a need for postjourneyman training.

Cleveland: Federal Government Official

The Labor Department has not used its power in this area. It should use injunctions to get more results. Furthermore, the government itself has become a major factor in the construction field. Not only the GSA but also the Defense Department, the Atomic Energy Commission, etc., do a great deal of building. Not to mention the entire federal road building program. The federal government should get figures on employment on all of its own construction jobs and then use its injunction powers to enforce and dictate the same attempts put forth on private industry.

Detroit: Trade Union Leadership Council Official

What is needed is the ferreting out of interested students in apprentice-ship programs. Moreover, there is need to help motivate Negro youths toward apprenticeship programs. Also, there is need to educate the Negro community, especially the civil rights groups, concerning the apprentice-ship programs themselves. The civil rights groups recently used union prac-tices as a rallying device, but very few of them actually understand apprenticeship themselves.

Motivation

Washington, D.C.: Urban League Official

The Negro youths with high motivation and abilities are motivated toward white-collar jobs. Consequently, qualified Negroes have preferred to go to jobs on the lower-income rungs of white-collar jobs. They would prefer to take lower-paying white-collar jobs than higher-paying blue-collar jobs, as a matter of status, ofttimes in the Negro community. Educa-tion concerning the middle level of opportunities is what is needed in those occupations which have less status but provide more income.

Washington, D.C.: AIC Official

There are plenty of qualified Negroes here in Washington. But the problem is the qualified Negroes do not go into apprenticeship. Those who are qualified don't want to work at the trades, so to speak.

Detroit: School Official

Recently the Superintendent of Schools for Detroit asked me if I could supply him with a list of a hundred names of possible Negro apprentices. I said I could not, that it would be impossible for several reasons. *First,* most Negro kids today who graduate from high school are highly motivated towards college. *Secondly,* there has been discrimination in the past in certain unions; consequently there has been a hesitancy about applying

261

to these unions. *Thirdly,* there has been a very poor job done by unions and by public officials explaining that currently the door is open.

Detroit: Trade Union Leadership Council Official

The entire issue is a very complex one. Negroes of very high achievement level go on to college. They are simply not made aware of opportunities in apprenticeship areas. Many Negroes don't understand the nature of the problem. Trade Union Leadership Council has asked the Board of Education to help locate interested and potential applicants, and to make school counselors aware of the apprenticeship field, and to make the students aware of the subject. TULC has sent applicants to the nonunion Negro electrical association here in Detroit. Not to the electrical union.

Pittsburgh: President's Committee on Equal Employment Opportunity Official

In Pittsburgh the Urban League has been discussing apprenticeships in the Negro high schools. They had 150 Negroes who expressed an interest in apprenticeship. The Urban League disqualified all but nineteen, and they referred them to Westinghouse; of that number, eight were accepted. None of the 150 applicants had any interest at all in building trade apprenticeships. The Urban League claimed that it was due to the exclusion in the past. The students felt that if they were accepted it would only be as a form of tokenism.

Most Negroes seem to want white-collar jobs, those that are capable of applying for apprenticeship.

Pittsburgh: Urban League Official

The problem that the Urban League has faced is that the kids we are asking for are typically college-bound. Secondly, the kids who would be interested in apprenticeship programs don't know anything about them. They lack any visual focus concerning apprenticeship.

Detroit: AFL-CIO Regional Official

Negro kids—the kind of kids that the trades unions and craft unions especially are looking for—are oriented toward college. In part, this is due to the past in which Negro parents realized that there was very little opportunity for their kids in these areas. Consequently, they have tended to turn them whenever possible toward the professions. Consequently, there has been a need for a change in the attitude of the Negro parents to try to motivate their kids to move toward the trades.

Apprenticeship Information Centers

New York: Workers Defense League Official

The AIC has provided no information. In fact, many people in the State Employment Agency don't seem to know that there is a city AIC. The AIC has been nonworkable in New York City, mainly because it is impossible for the city to get information from the unions. Consequently, the AIC alone is not sufficient to create much advancement in this area.

Moreover, these types of centers typically attempt to build up a placement record. Consequently, they discourage the hard placements in order to keep a good record. They shy away from the apprenticeship area. Therefore, state employment security agencies are not typically very effective in filling openings in apprenticeship programs. The amount of work that is required to secure a placement in an apprenticeship is extremely long and extremely costly and the results are a very small numerical return.

Philadelphia: President's Committee on Equal Employment Opportunity Official

There is no AIC in Philadelphia. BAT has consistently resisted efforts to establish such centers in the city.

Philadelphia: BAT Official

AICs were discussed for Philadelphia. It was decided not to introduce them in the city. Instead, state Youth Opportunity Centers (YOCs) were established; consequently, there are three of them in Philadelphia today. It was felt that they would suffice to cover the needs of the city. Also, there was no positive community interest for the establishment of AICs.

Detroit: Trade Union Leadership Council Official

The AIC has still not done too much. It still tends to act too much as a reporting agency. If the AIC idea fails, it is going to be very bad. On the advisory board for the AIC, you have all the people who have the power to correct this matter. The important point is, however, that they haven't done anything about it.

Cleveland: Community Relations Board Official

With respect to the AIC, "it is a job." In other words, it is a waste of money. It has made no contribution at all. It is really only window dressing. As an indication of the inaction of the AIC, the Human Relations Board has recently been attempting to give information to counselors concerning apprenticeship programs. This is something that the AIC should have done, but it has done nothing. In fact, the AIC still has not received the standards from all the locals.

Detroit: President's Committee on Equal Employment Opportunity Official

With respect to apprenticeship information centers, the group has not done anything to beat the bushes to really recruit people, especially minority people, for apprenticeship programs. The Urban League, however, has sent some people to the Apprenticeship Information Center.

Testing

Cleveland: BAT Official

Where the various JACs have been under fire by the civil rights groups and other pressure groups, they have called in a third party to do the testing. They usually get the public employment service to do the aptitude testing. To some people this might seem to be a fair practice. But it's not very significant. Because the unfair practices are usually committed when the union administers the written and oral exams.

New York: Building and Construction Trades Official

The city of New York has various skilled trades on its payroll who do various repairs in the building work. In all these special classifications the city gives tests. As a result there have been very few minority people who have passed the test given by the city. Those that do pass the city test are the same kind of people that can pass the test given by the union for admission in their apprenticeship program. Why don't these minority people apply to the city? They get the same pay rates, they have 250 days guaranteed employment a year, etc. The point is that they cannot pass the test which is given impartially to all applicants.

Pittsburgh: Plumbers Union Official

The oral exam definitely has more weight, it was designed that way.

Cincinnati: Roofers Union Official

The apprenticeship school program has done the Negro more harm than good. Before we had this damn school and all these damn tests things weren't so bad. I would recommend that the apprenticeship program be thrown out of the window. Our standards are unbelievable. I can't pass the test myself. Some of this stuff is too tough. Furthermore, it's not necessary.

Detroit: Ironworkers Union Official

Apprentices are much better qualified since we have set up the standards with BAT. We are getting some pretty smart boys. There was a time when you could describe an ironworker as someone who wore a size 40 shirt and a size 3 hat. This is no longer true. Also there was a time, in the old days, when they were all whiskey heads. They still drink a lot, the old ones, that is, but we are getting a much better quality of apprentices these days.

The oral exam was designed to "weed out undesirable applicants." For example, we had a fellow apply who had worked for five years as a hairdresser. We were kind of suspicious. You know that's quite a jump from a hairdresser to an ironworker. We asked him why he wanted to get into the program, he said he liked the money. We turned him down because we did not think he was really interested in this trade.

Impediments to Progress

New York: Workers Defense League Official

One problem that we have run into with apprenticeship is the fact that a person graduates from his high school in June, but apprenticeship programs may not begin for another year or so. Which means that in the meantime he has gone out and secured a job or been drafted. This is especially true of minority people who have not come from families of craftsmen and who are not familiar with the procedure by which apprenticeship testing is conducted and the time when classes are actually convened.

Houston: School Official

To begin with, there is a lack of openings in organized labor for Negroes. I feel that the situation is much the same as it has been for many years. Even though qualified workers can be licensed, since this is done by the state, nevertheless, they have difficulty finding rewarding work since it is necessary to be a union member to work on many types of jobs or projects—construction.

I am not at all happy with the rate of progress in the area of training in general and apprenticeship specifically. There is a lack of pinpointing of responsibility on any single individual or group for the fact that little if any progress has been made. I feel that some sort of committee or group should be vested with responsibility for gathering *all* the facts and then making sure that they are known by those in a position to do something about the problem. I place great emphasis on involving the citizenry in such efforts to increase the participation of Negroes in a broader spectrum of occupations.

Pittsburgh: Human Relations Commission Official

One of the real problems in Pittsburgh is the lack of motivation by both the civil rights groups and the youths themselves to really push this issue. No one in Pittsburgh is doing anything really about apprenticeship programs, although there is a great deal of talk about it.

Philadelphia: BAT Official

Certain rules such as those of Title 29 and the new state standards here in Pennsylvania are going to make it even more difficult to increase minority participation. Under the written rules, you must have a high school diploma or its equivalency.

New York: Building and Construction Trades Council Official

You find that there are several problems in increasing Negro participation in apprenticeship programs. *First* of all, the apprentice has to have a job. *Secondly,* there is the issue of recruitment, of finding qualified applicants for the apprenticeship program—people who will stay with the program. *Thirdly,* the union will have no part of any type of reverse discrimination, simply to increase the number of any minority groups in the program. Those people who are studying this issue of minority participation should admit that recruitment is the basic problem. It is the most difficult problem of all—recruitment of qualified applicants. I hope that if this report should find that recruitment is the issue, rather than simply discrimination, that it will not hesitate to point out that fact rather than what people want to hear. I hope that you will point out where the true problem lies and will not hesitate to say so if you do find that recruitment is the issue.

Cincinnati: Special Recruitment Program Official

We know that there were several skilled Negroes here in Cincinnati, and that practically all of them were nonunion because they were not allowed to join unions.

We concentrated our effort at the journeyman level because we felt that this was the proper place to start. We felt that the successful placement

THE NEGRO AND APPRENTICESHIP

of Negro journeymen would have a great impact on the aspirations of Negro youths. Most Negro kids don't know what apprenticeship is. Those who know what it is do not have much faith in it. They don't feel that they will be accepted if they apply.

Cincinnati: Special Recruitment Program Official

The contractors were generally co-operative, but they were afraid of the reactions of unions. They were afraid of work stoppages.

We also ran into some reluctance on the part of the Negro craftsmen:

1. The Negro craftsmen who are nonunion argued that they would make more money by remaining out of the unions. They argued that although the nonunion pay scale is lower than the union pay scale, they are able to work longer hours.
2. Several of these men were worried about the physical danger they would be exposed to. One guy put it this way: "It's not very easy to work at dangerous heights and on narrow ledges when you are working next to guys who hate your guts."
3. The one Negro who penetrated the bricklayers union complained that he was given the most difficult assignments, and that pressure was put on him by the white workers. He mentioned that he was often placed in the "corners," and that the white workers who worked at his sides would try to step up the pace so that he could not keep up.
4. The union tests were extremely difficult. The Negro craftsmen felt that the tests were unfair and not relevant to performance in the trade. Two union business agents told me that the tests were designed to keep "undesirables" out. They told me that many of the journeymen in the union cannot pass the exams. They said that they were not opposed to Negro entry into the unions but that the rank-and-file members are opposed to it. They also mentioned that they are restricted from doing anything about it, because they have to depend on the rank and file for votes.
5. Many of the laborers were reluctant to become apprentices because they did not want to take cuts in pay, and because they did not want to go to school after working an eight-hour day.

Detroit: Trade Union Leadership Council Official

BAT has been of very little assistance in this area. They have been doing things a certain way so long that happenings have become habits. Furthermore, most of the officials of BAT are from the craft trades themselves.

If BAT really felt that this issue of Negro participation is a serious problem, that would make a material difference in this area here in Detroit.

Detroit: Trade Union Leadership Council Official

The local unions lack a commitment to the civil rights issue. Apprenticeship programs are typically dominated by the labor unions. They have a leading role with them as far as selection is concerned. Consequently, management is essentially penned in. It can do little actually to increase selection procedures.

Pittsburgh: President's Committee on Equal Employment Opportunity Official

The Urban League did compile a list of skilled Negro workers in Pittsburgh; none of them were sent to the union. Many of them were self-employed, and did not really want to join a union. Others were working as independent contractors and a few were employed by others. These Negro skilled workers tended to fill many small jobs, and they had plenty of work to keep themselves busy. In this line of work, work tends to be continuous in the nonunion sector and there is less risk of layoff.

The real problem is in obtaining Negro applications. Smart Negroes simply will not apply for apprenticeship. They have far bigger ambitions. The top Negroes today want to go to college rather than to work with their hands.

The Negro is just not interested in applying for apprenticeships in the building trades. It is very difficult to get him to even make application today. The Human Relations Commission in Pittsburgh and the Urban League have had a very difficult time. In fact they have not been able to furnish an interested contractor with a single Negro applicant for apprenticeship. The real problem in Pittsburgh is the one of how to get bodies; this is the real issue.

Washington, D.C.: President's Committee on Equal Employment Opportunities Official

With respect to the twenty-eight applicants to the sheet metal workers, the union hall is way out from the center of the Negroes' population; it is in a white neighborhood and all its employees and officials are white. It is a very foreboding place for a single Negro applicant to go on an interview. Once he gets to the union hall, should he go in, there is the problem as to whether the applicant has been informed of all the pre-requisites. There are many ways to circumvent the letter of the law, for example: The applicant may ask the union official, when he fills out his application form, about the prerequisites. The official, at the time he fills out the application form, tells the applicant that he needs to show his high school diploma with his application. The applicant does not have it with him. He then has to go home and get his diploma and return to the union hall, paying the transportation costs involved himself. He is then told that he needs to supply a birth certificate with the application, so he must, in many cases, then go to the Municipal Center in Washington to get a photocopy of the birth certificate, for which there is usually a charge of at least $1.00. He then returns to the union hall only to be told that his application must be accompanied by a transcript of his high school grades. The applicant then must go to the high school and request a transcript. Usually, a high school will not give a transcript directly to the applicant, but will send it directly to the union. This procedure can also lead to several weeks' delay, during which time the transcript is actually processed and sent to the union hall and processed by the union—which can be a lengthy process, if the union desires. Then if all the above con-

267

ditions are met, the applicant again goes to the union hall, only now to be told that he needs to show proof of a physical examination that he is qualified to do the work. Again he must now pay the cost of the exam and the transportation costs back and forth to and from the union hall between each of the above stages. This is an indication of the difficulties involved in getting the Negro to apply for apprenticeship programs. There is no reason why all these requisites for apprenticeship application cannot be stated at one time to an applicant, preferably even by the AIC.

Washington, D.C.: President's Committee on Equal Employment Opportunities Official

The real problem to increasing Negro participation is that we are dealing with people who initially did not want Negroes in their programs.

Then there is the entire issue of test evaluation. Ofttimes the building contractors claim that they do not discriminate, and would have no objections to Negroes working on their jobs. But it is the unions with which they deal that have the strongest prejudices. If the contractor raised the question with the union of increasing Negro participation in the trade, he fears the union will seek reprisals against him in that the next time that the contractor needs workers, the union will send over incompetent workers as a reprisal. The unions seem to keep a certain amount of incompetent workers around for this very purpose of keeping contractors in line. This is a further indication of the stranglehold that unions have on management in the construction industry.

Detroit: AFL-CIO Regional Official

Here in Detroit the carpenters and the trowel trades are no real problem. The real recalcitrant problem is the sheet metal workers and the pipe trades.

There is a real political problem involved in increasing minority participation in the unions—namely, the business agents will want to be re-elected and the unions have traditionally operated in a "club" atmosphere, in which the father-son relationship was dominant. This is the real problem—the social side of the apprenticeship program and the craft union. A business agent who is sympathetic to increasing minority participation is no good to the cause if he is out of office. Title VII will help here, since the business agent can blame it on the Civil Rights Act that he must comply.

Union Attitudes

New York: Workers Defense League Official

With respect to the feelings of the union membership concerning this issue, if enough of these qualified people get into the union, the current composition of the union will be markedly changed. The old members feel very insecure about this. They are scared, not of Negroes per se, but rather of the new and even more qualified workers who are coming into the unions and changing the composition of the unions to very qualified type people.

San Francisco: Carpenters Union Official

We do not discriminate. We have had Negro members in our locals for thirty years. This is partly because San Francisco is a cosmopolitan city and partly because it's easy to get into our union. Our union is very large, and we try to organize everybody. Although it's easy to get into this union, once you get in you're on your own. We accept almost anybody that a contractor agrees to hire. If a contractor wants to hire a journeyman, he simply calls us and we will test the man and let him in if he does O.K. on the exam. The same is true for apprentices. Most of our apprentices are sponsored by contractors. Most of the Negroes who are in the union started out working as laborers, and picked the trade up gradually by watching, and by doing, carpenter work whenever they could. As soon as they could get a contractor to sponsor them, we gave them tests and admitted them. A lot of Negroes transfer into our locals from other locals, primarily from the South. A lot of them were pile drivers who switched. Some were shipwrights or stage riggers who switched.

We have also had many Negro apprentices over the years. However, most of them become journeymen, but they *never* finish the program. They usually complete the on-the-job training but not the related classroom training. We have had only two Negroes complete our program since it was started in 1937, even though we have had a lot of Negroes in these programs. But, because most of these guys do not complete this related training, they cannot get jobs as foremen. We will allow a man to work as a journeyman even though he has not completed his related training, but we will not give him a certificate and he will not be able to work as a foreman.

Houston: BAT Official

There is now concern at the BAT with the "damn you" attitude resulting from attempts to force immediate integration of locals. More is to be said for diplomatic encouragement than coercion—but, of course, one runs the risks of accomplishing nothing with less severe policies.

Houston: IBEW Official

There is little concern with job scarcity or fragmentation. In mid-fifties there was some job scarcity consciousness, but not today; nearly 75 per cent are foremen within two years of completing apprenticeship.

Detroit: BAT Official

There is simply a drastic shortage of qualified Negro applicants. For example, the carpenters have for the entire summer [1965] had a standing order for six Negro carpenter-apprentices; they could only get five and have been scouting the entire summer.

There has been a reversal in attitude. The reversal occurred about two and one-half years ago. There is acceptance today here in Detroit of Negroes in apprenticeship programs. But the problem is that it is quite easy for many of the Negroes who qualify for them to go into the colleges in the South and get a very easy degree.

The employers pay a great deal of money to finance apprenticeship. Therefore, they are getting picky about who they will take into their program. They would rather not take the vocational student, since often he is an outcast. It is true, however, that if the wage rates were lower, then they [the employers] could afford to be more risky in their selection process.

Houston: Cement Mason Official

I am of the opinion that there are great many costs to other locals in the area who have refused to integrate. The cost has been in terms of greater competition from nonunion, nonwhite labor as well as the sacrifice of revenue in terms of initiation fees and dues for these workers. There has never been any serious problem whatsoever with an integrated membership of the cement masons. There is no real fear on the part of whites that the Negroes will "take over the union." Nor is there any corresponding feeling on the part of the Negroes.

Houston: Carpenters Official

There are a remarkedly small number of apprentices who are related in one way or another to other carpenters. I attribute this to a growing feeling on the part of carpenters against their sons' becoming carpenters.

New York: Building and Construction Trades Council Official

The grandfather clauses are now outdated, in that most sons of skilled tradesmen have had more education than their fathers, and consequently have no intention of following their fathers into these skills.

Pittsburgh: Plumbers Union Official

We do not have any Negro journeymen. We have had about four Negro journeymen apply but they flunked when they were tested, and one who applied failed to come for the exam. We went for several years without ever receiving an application from a Negro.

Pittsburgh: Carpenters Union Official

For many years, no Negro boys applied. When they did, they applied and got in because of a relative or friend.

Pittsburgh: Carpenters Union Official

The carpenters have never discriminated against Negroes. Negroes have been in this union for as long as I have been alive.

Many of the boys who have made application had no desire to be carpenters. The HRC and the other organizations went around to the high schools and took the "cream of the crop" and then sent them to us. Most of these boys did not want to be carpenters.

Cincinnati: IBEW Official

We have about seventy-five apprentices, and close to seven hundred journeymen. None of them is a Negro. Eighty or ninety journeymen have made application and are waiting to get in. I don't know if any of these guys on this list are Negro. We have *never* had a Negro member. We tested about five Negroes about three or four years ago but none of them passed.

270

We don't have any Negro members because none of the Negroes who apply are qualified.

We don't have any waiting lists for apprentices. We just started a class. We take about twenty-five apprentices in per year; this allows us to replace the men who die or retire. We are looking forward to a very good year.

Our tests are fair: the Negroes just aren't qualified. Our tests are administered by a professor at Xavier University. You can get our qualifications from BAT.

Cincinnati: Glaziers Union Official

We have never had a Negro boy apply to our program. If one applied and if we had work it would make no damn difference to us.

There are two Negro glaziers here in town. We would love to have them but we can't organize them. Our initiation fee is $300.

Cincinnati: Roofers Union Official

We don't discriminate, because we don't really give a damn. One of our Negro apprentices is a dope addict. We know it, and we still don't give a damn.

Cleveland: Skilled Trades Committeemen (UAW)

We have twenty-two apprentices at the present. We have about six Negro apprentices. We have always insisted on integration, but we have had a problem getting the applicants. We called Urban League, NAACP, etc., and told them we wanted some apprentices. They were not able to find many.

Cleveland: Ironworkers Union Official

Supply and demand is what determines whether or not we expand our program. If demand is high we expand; if demand is low we do not. For example: in 1956–57, we had two hundred apprentices, because there was a lot of work then. In 1958 we had fifteen apprentices because there was not enough work to go around. In 1956–57 we had 1,800 men working; in 1958 only 300 of our men had jobs. The apprentices won't stay in the program if there is no work, even if you give them all "A's."

If you want to have some more Negro apprentices you have to first see to it that more of them are qualified for apprenticeship.

Cleveland: IBEW Union Official

Friendship and association play an important part, too. When apprenticeship openings are announced, the journeymen try to get their friends, relatives, and associates in. They don't have Negro friends, relatives, and associates. Because they associate with their own kind, mostly. This is not discrimination, this is human nature. All or a lot of apprentices are sons of journeymen in the trade. My dad was a journeyman in this union before I got in.

I don't know exactly what to suggest to increase Negro participation. I guess the key is education. More Negroes need to be qualified. Education is the key to the whole racial problem. And this is true on both sides of the color line. Because there are a lot of dumb whites.

Cleveland: IBEW Official

Our union is open to anybody. We don't take any special measures to attract anyone who is not interested in us. As far as the Negro youngsters are concerned, I don't think the interest is there. A lot of them come to take the test but they don't follow through.

Detroit: Ironworkers Union Official

I have been in this business for eighteen years. To the best of my knowledge, no Negroes have ever applied to this program. We have not found it necessary to do much business with the AIC. We do not solicit people from any place. We don't have time. Our applicants usually know someone who is already working for us or in the union. We do not advertise or publicize our programs.

There are about a hundred ironworker apprentices in the Detroit apprenticeship school. The programs usually begin in September. About thirty-two boys have taken the written exam and are waiting to take the oral examination. A lot of them don't show up for the oral. No Negroes are in this group which is waiting to be tested.

Cleveland: IBEW Union Official

We just started a program about six weeks ago. We did not have one single Negro applicant. Our next program will start in September. We will test in August or July. We always allow one week for the acceptance of applications.

The father-son situation was prevalent in this local for some time. But this is no longer the case since the standards have been established. This is good because a lot of guys who got in because their fathers were journeymen turned out to be poor or mediocre mechanics:

1. Sometimes the guys became electrical workers because their fathers forced them into it.
2. Sometimes sons got in who had the desire but didn't have the "smarts." They cannot get in now if they don't meet the standards and pass the exams.

These standards take the pressure off us. Now a member can't blame us, the agents, if his son does not get in. Because if he does not pass the test he will not be accepted.

Cleveland: IBEW Union Official

We would be better off if we had more Negroes, but the integration is slow. We got two boys in, in 1963 and 1964. But we have not found a qualified Negro applicant since then. It would be better if we could have a steady flow of them, like a few each year. This way the men would get used to it better.

The Negroes who apply to us usually come from the bottom of the ladder. I guess all the smart ones go on to college, since there are a lot of opportunities opening up for Negroes with education. The AIC hasn't been of much help either. We informed them about our program, and they did not send one single Negro. I haven't seen anything come out of the AIC. We have notified them each time we started a class.

Cleveland: Plumbers Union Official

Negroes have applied. Most of them failed the test. Some don't even show up for the exam after they apply. Some of the ones who do come, come late. We give a written and an oral examination. Yes, our oral exam is designed so that we can turn a boy down if we don't want him. If we get an applicant who is one of these beatniks, or something like that, we can flunk him. But this is not done very often.

Management Attitudes

San Francisco: Management Industrial Relations Official (Machinists)

Most of our Negro apprentices come in through normal hiring procedures. However, some do come from the AIC. One of the big problems is that Negroes don't seem to know much about apprenticeship. The youngsters are not familiar with it so they don't apply. The civil rights groups view it as some kind of mass employment process.

Many Negroes cannot get in because the standards are too tough. But the standards cannot be lowered. These are highly skilled jobs, the machines are complex, and there is steady upgrading. Once we train a man to be a machinist, we give an additional year for tool-and-die training. In addition, if a man gets two years of college he can qualify for a management position. At one time all of our people have worked in the shop.

Another problem is that management is not doing enough training. Some feel that it's too costly, they like to "pirate." We have found that if a boy stays with us for four years he does not cost us a cent.

New York: Workers Defense League Official

Management today is increasingly speaking out on the issue of qualified apprentices. Traditionally, labor has dominated the JACs. Employers were complacent; management now wants to upgrade the skilled workers. So now management is speaking out on discrimination issues in an attempt to get more qualified people trained in the new technologies.

Cleveland: Management Official (Carpenters)

As of late, we have not been able to get any apprentices. We haven't received any applications. In addition, we have a hard time persuading the contractors to take on apprentices. The contractors are becoming aggravated because they don't want the kids to go to school during the day. The contractor has to pay the apprentice a full day's salary when he is in school. We require them to attend school once a week.

Attitudes of Apprenticeship Officials

Cleveland: BAT Official

Some of the civil rights organizations around town have taken about seventeen Negro boys from committee to committee to committee. But you know damn well that these boys were not interested in five different trades. Then when they fall on their face, they yell discrimination.

Then too, the Negro youngsters who can pass the tests can go much higher today; so, they overlook apprenticeship.

Detroit: BAT Official

Any Negro who wants apprenticeship in Detroit can get it. Maybe not immediately, but this is the way it is in apprenticeship. You can't simply walk in and get a job immediately. The Negro, however, must be at the same level, not at a lower level, as a white applicant because all the unions give tests. Currently, the UAW pays apprentices $2.60 an hour plus $1.00 in fringe benefits. Consequently, tests must be given in order to get only qualified people rather than just taking anyone. Apprenticeship is very costly to the employer, as he pays all the cost of training in the city of Detroit, so we must have tests.

Legal Action

New York: State Human Relations Commission Official

The State Commission has direct regulatory powers over unions and JACs. This power has been used in only three cases so far. The first case was that against the plumbers in Rockland County; secondly, against the sheet metal workers; thirdly, against the ironworkers in Albany.

Cleveland: BAT Official

We have developed standards which must be adopted if Ohio apprenticeship programs are to be recognized by the Department of Labor. To a large extent most programs are in compliance with our standards and the state standards. But this is simply a matter of going on record as being in compliance. There hasn't been any change in actual number.

With reference to apprenticeship, as the standards for equal employment have been established, there has been a tendency for JACs to raise standards for admission to the programs. This raising of standards has resulted in the exclusion of Negroes.

Attitudes of Apprentices

Cleveland: Pending—Plumbers

My high school counselor never discussed apprenticeship with me. I was never counselled by anyone during the four years I spent at East Tech. E. Tech is a typical ghetto school. Most of the boys end up walking the streets even though they have graduated from there. Even though they know a trade they can't get into apprenticeship because they are Negroes. Most of the boys would make good mechanics, but they get bad grades in English and stuff like that, even though they get A's in Shop.

Cleveland: Rejected—Pipefitters

When I got to the Urban League the counselor there asked me if I was interested in apprenticeship training. I told him yes even though I was not really interested. He asked me if I was interested in pipefitting. I told him yes, but to be frank, I didn't even know what pipefitting was at that time. I wanted a job, it didn't matter what kind of job I got, I just wanted a job.

Pittsburgh: Apprentice—Carpenters

Before I took the oral exam, I met with my high school counselor. He instructed me to be sure and convince the JAC that my lifelong ambition was to be a carpenter, and not to tell them that I would like to go to college.

Pittsburgh: Rejected—Operating Engineers

The only thing that will convince Negro boys that it makes sense to apply is for them to see some Negroes operating those machines.

Brooklyn, N.Y.: Apprentice—Typographers No. 6

I haven't seen any resentment, to tell you the truth. I have maintained ever since I have been working where I am now an attitude of being aloof, because I don't play no kind of card game . . . we kid; I don't play cards. Lunch time they have a little poker game, small stakes, and I've never even kibbitzed once. Yet, down through the years, anything that I have asked them to show me, everybody has helped. So I've learned a lot from them, from all three shifts. We don't socialize, we're not overly friendly, I don't see them because most of them live in other areas of the city, or out in the suburbs. Maybe there is somebody that doesn't like me but this I don't know. Anyone who I have approached and asked to show me something, they have all co-operated. And when I was taken off the presses and given a desk, everybody came around kidding about who you know, so I don't say that there isn't prejudice, but I haven't seen it.

New York City: Dropout—Ironworkers Local 40

Some difficulties I ran into with one of the senior foremen. We had a disagreement and I think he didn't like or we couldn't get along together or something like that. In fact I know we couldn't get along. He wanted me to do the impossible. [What do you mean impossible?] Like—say walk out on a beam when I feel I should be given a little more time getting familiar with how to walk out on something without just going out there. You know. [How many feet were you working up?] This was about twenty stories high. [And he wanted you to immediately . . .] Yes, without trying to work my way out on a beam. He figures that after a week I should know how to walk on a beam. But it takes balance and self-confidence, you know, you've got to get your nerves.

New York: Apprentice—IBEW

Father-son relationship is very prevalent during the summer. Sons and close relatives of journeymen are brought in on jobs during summer vacation from college.

San Francisco: Apprentice—Machinists

I have not had any trouble of a racial nature since I have been in the program, but there is discrimination in the shop. For example, the white boys always get to work on the new and big machines. As soon as there is an opening on a new machine, they put a white boy on it. It's a subtle kind of discrimination, and I think it is more of a discrimination for than

275

discrimination against. For example, our foreman is an Italian, he favors Italian apprentices. The foreman in the assembly department is a German, and his entire department is German. But I still think this is a good company.

Cleveland: Apprentice—Ironworkers

I haven't experienced much discrimination. I get along O.K. with most of my co-workers, except those damn *Indians*. They come from other locals in New York and Canada—I got into a hussle with one of them. He was a journeyman. He sent me down from the twenty-fifth floor to get six cans of pop and he didn't want to tip me. When I brought the pop back up to him I stood around waiting for my tip. You know, like bellhops do if you don't want to tip them. He just ignored me. So I asked him for a tip. He got real mad with me. Then a few days later when I was going around asking the journeymen in my group if they wanted coffee, I came to him and I asked him. He said, "Get the hell away from me, 'NIGGER,'" and he spat in my face. I wanted to fight him right then and there, but I knew I would get the worst end of it so I didn't say anything. This was when I was working for Bethlehem Steel on the first job. He and some other Indians were the only ones that I had any trouble with.

Cleveland: Rejected—IBEW

Most of my friends think apprenticeship is good, but you have to go through too much crap to get it because you are colored. Several of my friends applied and were turned down, because the union said they flunked the quiz. Some did not even apply because of the $10 fee; the ones who did pay it felt real bad because they had spent $10 for nothing.

Washington, D.C.: Apprentice—IBEW Local 26

I would encourage other Negro high school graduates to seek apprenticeship training in this and other unions, especially if they did not want to go to college or to hang on the corners and if they want to earn a profitable living like $10,000 a year.

Washington, D.C.: Rejected—Plumbers, Pittsburgh

I wanted to enter apprenticeship because I wanted to get into the union. That's where the money is.

Most of my friends know about it, but don't know how to get into the programs. They feel that going to trade school is just a waste of time. Because if you study to be an auto mechanic, you will end up getting a job washing cars; if you take up bricklaying, you will end up as a hod-carrier. You don't have a chance to really practice what you learn in school like the white boys do.

Detroit: Apprentice—Sheet Metal Workers

I think that they [the union] are doing everything they can to get Negroes into the program. But Negroes don't seem to want apprenticeship. When they get out of school they want to jump in the factory, make money, and buy a car.

Cleveland: Dropout—Sheet Metal Workers

I dropped out of the program because I wanted to go to college. I like sheet metal, but I think that I will be exposed to greater opportunities if I go to college. I am majoring in industrial engineering. I wrote a letter to the company and the union and explained my decision. The company president called me in and discussed my decision with me. He tried to persuade me to go into mechanical engineering. He told me that if I ever needed a job I could come back when I want to. The union gave me a leave of absence. They told me that I could come back to the program if I didn't make it in college.

A white boy who quit the program to go to college was refused re-admittance when he dropped out of school. This happened before I dropped out.

Cleveland: Rejected—IBEW

I had no special preparation. If I had had training and more math, I believe I could have succeeded. I had a good chance but simply didn't score high enough. I knew I didn't do well.

New York City: Rejected—Sheet Metal Workers No. 28

I went to an all-white school and their classroom work was much more advanced. I went to junior high school and then I moved from there and went to a colored school in the Bedford-Stuyvesant section and the work they had was to me like a breeze, because the school in the white neighborhood was more advanced, much harder.

277

INDEX

Advisory Committee on Equal Opportunity in Apprenticeship and Training 204–5

AFL-CIO, 225, 243: Civil Rights Committee, 102, 153, 225; Department of Building and Construction Trades, 225; Human Rights Committee, 92, 93, 94. *See also* Urban League

Agency Coordinating Group, 210

Alameda County (Calif.) Manpower Development and Training Act Advisory Committee, 163

Antidiscrimination policies, 236

Apprentice School, Detroit, 137, 139, 141, 144

Apprenticeship: advantages of, 24; attitudes of apprentices, 274; characteristics of programs, 18; guidance counselors' bias against, 240; employer's views on, 13, 14; information and counseling, 239; registering of programs, 14; significance of programs, 232; standards, qualifications, and procedures, 15; unregistered programs, 21. *See also* Unions

Apprenticeship Information Centers, 18, 94, 120, 130, 133, 143, 144, 164, 167, 186, 208, 210, 247, 252, 262: Advisory Committee, 107, 210, 211; evaluation of, 212; most successful, 213

Apprenticeship officials: attitudes of, 273

Apprenticeship Training Information Center, N.Y., 69, 72

Archbishop's Committee on Human Relations for the Catholic Church in Detroit, 148

Area Coordinator, PCEEO, 157

Area Redevelopment Administration, 147

Asbestos Workers: Local 2, 116; Local 24, 153

Associated Electricians of Detroit, 145

Atlanta, Ga., 183ff.

Barr, Mayor Joseph M., 113

Barrett, Harold, Jr., 204, 206

Bay Area Rapid Transit, 162: and Urban League, 167, 208; job opportunities, 162, 163, 178

Booth, William H., 59

Bradford, Arthur, 167

Brennan, Peter J., 47, 55

Bricklayers, 185: Local 2, 141; Local 4, 157; Local 64, 92

Brooklyn, Central, Coordinating Council, 73

Brooklyn, Committee for Job Opportunities, 54

Brown, Gov. Edmund G., 163, 165

Building and Construction Trades Council, 51, 53, 95

Building Material and Construction Teamsters Local 216, 161

Bureau of Apprenticeship and Training, 7, 11, 18, 94, 107, 124, 145, 220, 238: nondiscrimination regulations of, 186

Bureau of Employment Security, 7, 18, 153, 210

California: AICs, 216; Apprenticeship Council, 161, 163, 165, 166, 168; Conference on Apprenticeship, 164, 165; Division of Apprenticeship Standards, 25. 161; Plan for Equal Opportunity, 164; State Advisory Committee to the U.S. Committee on Civil Rights, 168; State-wide Committee for Equal Opportunity in Apprenticeship and Training, 209

Carlino, Joseph F., 70

Carman, Dr. Harry J., 60

Carpenters, 185

Celebrezze, Mayor Anthony, 102

Cement Masons, Atlanta, 185

Central Brooklyn Coordinating Council, 73

29 CFR 30, 16, 71, 84

Chapple, George, 110

Chicago Apprenticeship Information Center, 223

Chicago Plan, The, 222, 223

Childers, J. L., 163

Chrysler Motor Company, 142, 147

Cincinnati, O., 121ff.: Board of Education, 131; Building Trades Council,

121, 124; City Council, 125; Human Relations Commission, 126; Municipal Youth Commission, 129; Roofers Union, 264; Special Recruitment Program, 265; Vocational Foundation, Greater, 130

City Commissions on Human Rights, N.Y., 53, 59, 64, 65, 81

City governments: role of, 235

City of Pittsburgh vs. *Plumbers Local Union No. 27,* 117

Civil Rights Act: Title VI, 197; Title VII, 131, 195, 196

Civil Rights movement, 244

Civil Service Commission, 194

Clark, Dr. Kenneth B., 42, 75

Cleveland, O., 99ff.: AIC, 107; Board of Education, 105; Community Relations Board, 104, 260; NAACP, 108; Urban League, 108

Commission on Human Relations, Philadelphia, 84, 89, 90–93, 96, 97, 117–20

"Committee of Twenty-eight," Cincinnati, 126

Committee on Exploitation, N.Y., 29

Community Relations Board, Cleveland, 102, 105, 106, 110–11

Composition Roofers Local 30, Philadelphia, 88

Congress of Industrial Unions, 196

Connecticut Commission on Civil Rights, 27

Construction Industry Joint Conference, 219, 226, 237

Construction projects, city: closing of, 97

Corbett, Raymond, 47, 70

CORE, 65, 128

Counseling, 38, 257

Counselors, 208, 240, 258

Crutcher, Paul, 144

Dandridge, Paul, 93

Davis-Bacon Act of 1931, 15

Demonstrations, 1963, N.Y., 51, 95, 128: Downstate Medical Center, 52; Harlem Hospital, 52; Madison Houses, 53; Rochdale Village housing project, 53; Rutgers housing project, 52

Derryck, Dennis, 73

Detroit, Mich., 137ff., 259, 260: AIC, 137; BAT, 269; Ironworkers Union, 264; public school system, 137; Tooling Association, 147

Discrimination, Law Against, 63

District of Columbia Apprenticeship Council, 209: Commissioners, 209

Division of Apprenticeship Standards, Calif., 165, 167, 168, 169, 171, 172

Downstate Medical Center, N.Y., 53, 54

Dresher, Dr. Richard, 145, 146

Dropouts, 23

Economic Development Administration, 162

Economic Opportunity Act, 95

Economic Opportunity Commission, 95

Education, 42: and experience, 259; background of interviewees, 253; educators, 241; improving level of, 259

Electrical Joint Apprenticeship and Training Committee, 16

Electricians, 185

Elevator Constructors: Local 6, 116; Local 17, 105

Emergency Task Force, Cincinnati, 129

Emorich, Richard T., 148

Employers, 242

Equal Employment Opportunity Commission, 195

Fair employment practices: city agencies, 191, 192

"Father-son" relationships: and apprenticeship, 18, 36, 96, 252

Federal apprenticeship regulations, 197ff.

Federal Committee on Apprenticeship, 11, 15

Federal policies, 236

Fitzgerald Act, 11

Florida Advisory Committee, U.S. Commission on Civil Rights, 27

Foltman, Felician F., 13

Ford Motor Company, 142

Foster, William, 92

Gateway Arch construction project, St. Louis, 196

General Motors Co., 142

George-Barden Vocational Education Act (1946), 12

Georgia: Apprenticeship Council, 186; Employment Service, 186

Glaziers: Local 252, 92; Local 718, 161; Local 963, 153

"Grandfather clauses": in apprenticeship, 270

Graphic Arts Employment Committee, Philadelphia, 93
Green, Ernest, 73
Green, Scott, 76, 77

Haggerty, Neil, 219
Hanna, Charles F., 25, 165, 166
Harlan, Robert, 157
Harpole, Ellsworth H., 105
Henning, John F., 204, 209
Hirsch, William, 110
Houston, Tex., 175ff., 259, 265: BAT, 269; Cement Masons, 270; Carpenters, 270; IBEW, 269; Negro participation in selected building trades in, 178
Howard University, 205
Hughes Tool Co. case, 181, 193
Human Relations Commissions, 94, 130, 133, 134, 161
Human Relations Committee, Building Trades Council, Pittsburgh, 116

Industrial Training Advisors (ITAs), 207, 208, 238
Information: dissemination of, 259
Ingram, Theodore, 180
Injunctions against discrimination: in construction, 261
Interim Committee, San Francisco-Oakland, 161
International Association of Machinists, 186
International Brotherhood of Electrical Workers, 16: Local 3, 50, 58, 60, 72, 81, 110; Local 5, 116, 118, 119; Local 6, 161, 172; Local 26, 151; Local 38, 102, 104, 105, 110; Local 58, 141, 144; Local 98, 88, 89, 90, 91, 92, 96; Local 126, 88, 90; testing program, 144
Ironworkers, 185: Local 3, 116; Local 17, 105; Local 40, 47; Local 401, 92; Local 790, 161

Job Availability Committee, Cincinnati, 129
Jobbing shops, Detroit, 142
Job Opportunities Bay Area Rapid Transit, San Francisco-Oakland, 162, 163, 173
Johnson, Pres. Lyndon B., 64
Joint Apprenticeship Committees, 13
Joint Committee for Equal Employment Opportunity, N.Y., 51, 52, 72

Joint Construction Activities Committee, Detroit, 140
Jones, Jimmie, 92, 93, 94
Journeyman-apprentice ratios, 15, 19

Kuhn, Alfred, 125

Lathers, 185: Local 9, 153
Lattimer, Lewis Howard, 62
Law Against Discrimination, N.Y., 63
Leadership Committee, Cincinnati, 126, 128, 132
Lockheed Corp., 186, 187

Management attitudes on apprenticeship, 273
Manpower Administrator, 209
Manpower Advancement Program, Cleveland, 108, 109, 110
Manpower Development and Training Act, 11, 95, 108, 147, 163, 219, 221ff.
Manpower policies, 234
Manpower Report of the President, 1963, 23
Master Builders' Association, Pittsburgh, 116, 117, 118
Max Hayes school, Cleveland, 99
Mayor's Friendly Relations Committee, Cincinnati, 125
Mays, Edward, 60, 61
McComb County, Mich., Community College, 141
McCormick, Robert, 60
McDaniel, J. C., 179
Meany, George, 47, 65, 151
Medical Committee for Human Rights, 75
Mengerink, William, 107
Michigan Employment Service, 143
Military deferment for apprentices, 15
Miranda Case, 193
Motorola Case, 44
Mulveany, Warren, 94
Murphy, Ray, 72, 77

NAACP, 59, 66, 107, 110, 125, 128
National Aeronautics and Space Administration, 175, 180
National Apprenticeship (Fitzgerald) Act of 1937, 11
National Electrical Contractors Association, 16
National Industrial Conference Board, 242
National Institute of Labor Education, 219, 220
National Labor Relations Act, 192

National Labor Relations Board, 65, 66, 131, 181, 192, 193
National Training Advisor, 207
Negroes: in Atlanta apprenticeship programs, 185; participation in union apprenticeship programs, 49, 84, 183; policies to increase the number of Negro apprentices, 191; supply of qualified Negro applicants, 231; unqualified, 41; for apprenticeship programs, 41
Negro Trade Union Leadership Conference, 93, 94, 95
Newark, N.J., 259
New York City, 47ff.: Building and Construction Trades Council, 55; Commission on Human Rights, 50; Department of Labor, 54; School of Printing, 66, 67
New York State, 47ff., 259: Advisory Committee to the U.S. Commission on Civil Rights, 50; Appellate Division of the State Supreme Court, 59; Apprenticeship Law, 70; Building and Construction Trades, 264, 265; Commission Against Discrimination, 49, 62, 66; Commission for Human Rights, 62, 71, 77; Employment Service, 54, 66, 67, 72, 75; Federation of Labor, 47; Law Against Discrimination, 50; Plumbers Case, 193. See also Workers Defense League

Oakland, Calif., 159ff.: AIC, 215; Adult Minority Project, 163; Building Trades Council, 163
Objective standards: for apprenticeship programs, 200
Office of Manpower, Automation and Training, 5, 219: Division of Special Programs, 101
Office of Manpower Policy, Evaluation and Research, 5
Ohio Civil Rights Commission, 128, 130, 132
Ohio Plan, 124
Operating Engineers, 185: Local 3, 161; Local 542, 90
Opportunities Industrialization Centers, Inc. (Philadelphia), 93, 95
Oral interview, 23
Otis Quick Scoring Test of Mental Ability, 74

Painters, Atlanta, 185: Local 751, 116
Painters' Council, 51, 153

Pennsylvania: Bureau of Employment Security, 93, 94, 97; Human Relations Commission, 116
Philadelphia, Penn., 83ff.: BAT, 265; AFL-CIO Human Relations Committee, 91; Board of Education, 91; Chamber of Commerce, 95; Commission on Human Relations, 87; Council on Community Advancement, 94; Municipal Services Building, 87
Pinkston, Theodore, 102
Pipefitters Local 120, 105
Pittsburgh, Penn., 113ff.: Human Relations Commission, 265; Plumbers Union, 264; Public Housing Authority, 118
"Plans for Progress," 187, 194, 225
Plasterers, Atlanta, 185
Plumbers: and pipefitting, 185; Local 1, 53, 59, 77, 78; Local 2, 47, 59, 64, 66, 71; Local 27, 116, 117, 118; Local 55, 102, 103, 105; Local 98, 141; Local 690, 88, 91, 92; and Pipefitters Local 38, 161
Pope, William, 105
Prairie View A. & M. College, Tex., 179
Pre-apprenticeship programs, 147, 218, 260, 261
Preferential treatment of Negroes, 201ff.: legality of, 202
President's Committee on Equal Employment Opportunity, 28, 83, 157, 181, 193, 194, 260
President's Committee on Government Contracts, 153
Printers, Atlanta, 185
Printing Industries for Philadelphia, 92, 93
Printing industry: developments in, 66, 92
Progress: impediments, 264ff.
Public policy, 11, 235
Public schools, Philadelphia: apprenticeship classes denied use of, 91, 92, 97
Punitive legal measures, 231

Qualifications, apprenticeship: lack of, 41. See also Tests

Railway Labor Act, 192
Recommendations: general policy, 233ff.; specific, 235ff.
Reedy, William, 166
Registration of apprenticeship programs: importance of, 14

Resolution No. 51, California Conference on Apprenticeship, 166
Rockefeller, Nelson, 54
Rodgers Committee, 54, 55, 58
Roofers, 185: Local 30, 91, 92

St. Louis Building and Construction Trades Council, 196
San Francisco-Oakland, Calif., 159ff.: AIC, 215, 216; San Francisco Archdiocesan Catholic Interracial Council, 161; Carpenters Union, 269
San Jacinto, Calif., High School, 175
Schnitzler, William F., 220
Schoemann, Peter T., 64
Schools. See Public schools; Vocational schools
Scranton, Governor William, 94
Screvane, Paul R., 52
Sheet Metal Workers, 76, 185: Local 19, 88, 90, 91, 92; Local 28, 58, 62, 70, 75; Local 65, 105; Local 102, 151, 153, 157; Local 355, 161
Sheffield, Horace, 143, 144
Shelley, Mayor John F., 159, 161
Sher, William, 137
Smith, Edward E., 118
Smith-Hughes (1917) Act, 12, 137, 187
Soffieto, Dominic, 166
Southern Christian Leadership Conference, 205
Southern Regional Council, 176, 178, 184
State Apprenticeship Councils, 11, 199
Statewide Committee for Equal Opportunity in Apprenticeship and Training for Minority Groups, Calif., 164, 168
Steamfitters: Local 420, 88, 91, 92; Local 449, 116; Local 638, 59
Stone and Marble Masons Local 2, Washington, D.C., 153
Strauss, George, 35
Sullivan, Reverend Leon, 93, 95

Taconic Foundation, 72
Taft-Hartley Act, 65
Talent Search Committee, Cincinnati, 129, 133
Tarshis, Morris, 54
Tate, Mayor James H. J., 87
Testing, problem of, 43
Tests, 200, 252: "culture-free" or "culture-fair" tests, 44; and qualifications, 240

Texas Southern University, 176
Thompson, Albert, 68
Tile and Terrazzo Workers Local 3, Washington, D.C., 153
Tilesetter Helpers Local 17, Cleveland, 105
"Tower Amendment," 44
Trade Union Leadership Council, 143, 144, 148, 252, 262, 263
Training for Apprenticeship, 219
Tucker, Sterling, 156
Turner, Dr. B. A., 39, 176
Typographers Local 6, 66, 67

Unions, 243: attitudes of, 13, 268ff.; interest in apprenticeship programs, 13
United Auto Workers: Skilled Trades Dept., 142, 147
United Federation of Teachers, 78
United Freedom Movement, Cleveland, 103, 104
U.S. Civil Rights Commission, 207
U.S. Department of Labor, 130, 194: regulations (29 CFR 30), 16
U.S. Employment Service, 153
U.S. Office of Education, 42, 79
U.S. Supreme Court, 192
University of California, 171
Unregistered apprenticeship programs, 21
Urban League, 94, 102, 107, 110, 118, 119, 205, 227, 262
Urban League–AFL-CIO Agreement, 227

Van Arsdale, Harry, 60, 61
Vocational schools, 259
Vocational students, 270
Voluntary programs of compliance, 255ff.

Wagner, Mayor Robert, 54, 65
Washington, D.C., 151ff.: AIC, 153, 204, 213; Trade School, 137; Urban League, 156
Western Electric Co., 77, 242
Westinghouse Co., 262
Wirtz, Sec. W. Willard, 65, 204
Workers Defense League, N.Y., 45, 61, 67, 72, 80, 81, 109, 242, 252, 262

Youth Employment Program, 219
Youth Opportunity Centers, Penn., 263

Designed by Gerard A. Valerio

Composed in Baskerville by Monotype Composition Company, Inc.

Printed offset by Universal Lithographers, Inc., on Perkins & Squier, R

Bound by Maple Press, Inc., in Columbia Riverside Linen, RL–1651